Only since you proved it —

do I know that I was right.

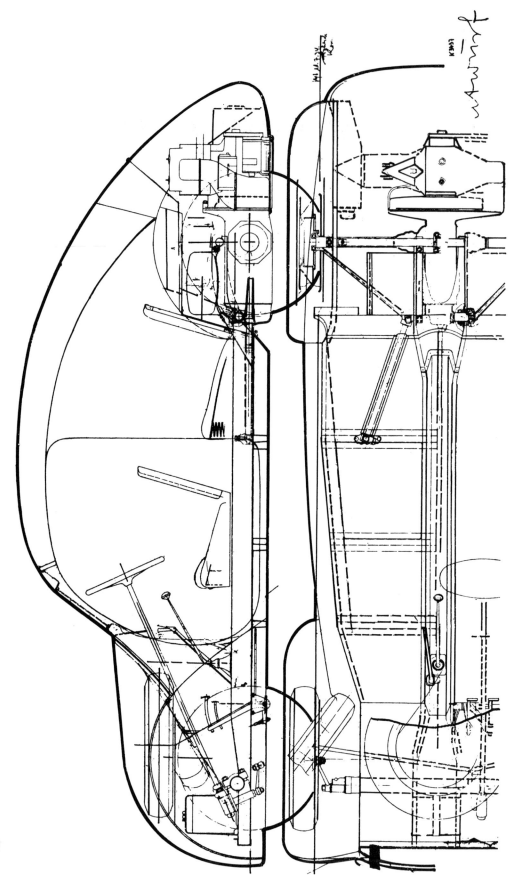

No other model in the world has met with the pre-production seasoning period credited to this automobile. Chassis layout and body form were pretty well resolved more than 30 years ago—as this drawing dated July, 1934, will confirm. Ahead, even then lay several collapsed efforts at manufacture. Ahead, for fourteen years yet to come, every repeated trial to reach production would also wither and die. Nine lives later Volkswagen was dead, and literally buried, when Heinz Nordhoff condescended to take a drive in the car . . . .

VOLKSWAGEN
NINE LIVES LATER

The Lengthened Shadow
of a Good Idea

DAN R. POST

with more than 500 illustrations

HORIZON HOUSE

1966

ARCADIA, CALIFORNIA

Copyright

1966

DAN R. POST

Printed in the United States of America

INTRODUCTION

Look into the years of development behind most any make of modern automobile and you will likely come up with a progression of committee-forced changes based on the premise that *bigger is better* — a commercial success by reason of more-car-per-car engendering more-sale-per-sale.

Some admire such a story of colorless odds imposed artificially to stimulate sales (though rarely owner satisfaction). To others, and I must count myself in this latter group, it would prove quite unexciting.

In contrast for its honesty, venture into the background of the now ubiquitous Volkswagen, presently being produced at the rate of one every 11 seconds, and soon to tick off its ten millionth unit. You stumble upon a drama more absorbing, and stranger, than fiction. VW's "unchanging" design policy has violated the tenets set forth by most automaking experts, yet this constant *less*-car-per-car policy has proven an unqualified success. It has given one accustomed to being owned by his cars the opportunity to reclaim his status as master. The odds against all this were staggering, and never lacking in color.

When I bought my first VW in Southern California in 1954 the car's generation-long, oft-arrested gestation period lay behind. Already VW was a byword in many countries on the Continent, but it was still a novelty all but unknown in the United States — where only 8,894 other non-conforming motorists bought a new VW that year.

VW was troubled finding a home among American agents in those days, unbelievable as it appears today. Most seasoned auto dealers, when approached by VW representatives, rejected the proposal of a VW franchise with a belly laugh. Recalling that laugh today must aggravate an ulcer for those still in the business, for they turned thumbs down to the dealership that a few short years later would become the most productive franchise in the industry.

Even though the product enjoyed no national advertising at this time — and for some years to follow — it was hard to keep the virtue of true value a secret. As the car began to outmanuever and outlast others on the streets of America, on its own recognizance, its resale value touched a highwater mark yet unseen in the industry. Eventually VW would come to be regarded in the U.S. less as an imported car, than as a synonym for transportation. Giants in Detroit would bend their products best to buck the inroads this David would be making.

Acceptance of the venerable Volkswagen today in 130 countries, with abruptly unlike roads and needs, has everybody trying to diagnose what makes the "unchanging" beetle so much more wanted than any other small car . . . Some say it's the cleanly engineered product . . . Others claim its well-trained dealer organization (with emphasis on *Service first/ Sales later*) could sell two million tricycles if the factory asked them to . . . Still others point to a concentration on unembroidered fact — first in product, then in every related avenue from promotion to service relations.

Only rarely may the business historian point to the working of simple cause and effect with the assurance that is possible here. The *why* of success is clear. Acceptance by the public followed naturally the rendering of a greater value. Volkswagen's value translated to people in countries everywhere without language barrier, for there was nothing "foreign," nothing hard to comprehend, about exemplary efficiency.

While the persistence of Ferdinand Porsche as he forged out his People's Car against repeated defeats and the triumphs of Heinz Nordhoff in engineering refinement and production have been clinically recorded by the British and German biographers K. B. Hopfinger and Richard von Frankenberg, it remained for Dan Post to document these struggles with hundreds of illustrations and highlight the remarkable story in a once-over tale for the American reader-in-a-hurry.

Chronicled for the first time is Volkswagen's shattering record on the world's toughest proving ground — the American scene — from rejection by nearly all, to native acceptance like apple pie.

The author has developed a pictorial biography in which the car itself is the central figure. Random reading to enlighten odd moments may begin wherever the book opens. If your admiration for the car transcends its essential utility you are going to enjoy the account that gave this book its title.

R. H. Gurr, Chief Engineer
WED Enterprises, Inc.

Glendale California
October 15th 1965

CONTENTS

ACKNOWLEDGEMENTS

A book of this sort, by its very nature, cannot be produced successfully without access to facts, records, photographs, and special assistance from many sources and individuals. Although it stands by itself as a finished product, it must necessarily reflect a pooling of helpful efforts.

Fortunately, in the preparation of VOLKSWAGEN, NINE LIVES LATER such cooperation was forthcoming in generous quantities whenever it was sought. In some cases, this meant a sacrifice of personal time and effort which is sincerely appreciated. Grateful and lasting thanks to:

Richard Genzen at the inception of the book idea for valuable assistance in obtaining documentary reference material. Günther Molter, the distinguished German motoring journalist, for professional assistance in obtaining background material and photographs. Kurt Worner for many excellent photographs taken by him during a career as motor racing photographer on the Continent. James M. Sitz for cooperation in securing much additional factual data, including original photographs of Dr. Nordhoff.

K. B. Hopfinger, the able British biographer, for repeated reference to his excellent book *Beyond Expectation: the Volkswagen story*, on which some incidents of the early lives have been based.

Motor Revue and Siegfried Werner for the construction sequence of the Karmann-Ghia. Gertrude Dick and Julie Barner for translation. Derek Rickard for the B.I.O.S. reports. Strother MacMinn for review of the rough work. Arthur R. Railton for long hours devoted to reviewing the manuscript and the captions, and for many valuable suggestions and corrections as to technical accuracy. William T. Barker and Chad Champlin for background information on the *Schwimmwagen*. Dr. Fred D. Rice for photographs from Heinrich Hoffmann (Hitler's personal photographer). Alfonso de Hohenlohe for his moving report of the classic *Pan-Americana*. Jack Garrison for specially drawn line cartoons.

John W. Chandler, Henry Elfrink, Arthur A. Miller and Einar W. Anderson for professional assistance in developing material. James J. Scott for comparative analysis of technical points in manuscript and captions. Volkswagen AG, Volkswagen of America, Inc., and Porsche AG (and *Christophorus*) for technical and historical material and nearly countless illustrations. *Gute Fahrt* and *Road & Track* magazines for many excellent photographs and additional material.

The anonymity of individual photographs in many instances does not permit this credit for every photograph used, but acknowledgement of sources of the illustrations appears below.

Aberdeen Proving Grounds, U. S. Army: 72-75 above, 78 above. Alken Corp.: 266-268. American Motors Corp.: 178. Anthony Pools: 192 above. *Australian Motor Sport*: 145 below. Australian News & Information Service: 171 right, 173 above. The *Autocar*: 171 left, 264 above. *VW Autoist*: 183-185, 203 below, 233 above. *Automotive News*: 142, 190, 199, 207, 211, 304. *Besser fahren mit dem Volkswagen*: 118. *Better Motoring*: 186. Beutler: 262, 263. Robert Bosch: 100. *British Intelligence Objectives Sub-Committee* Final Report No. 998, Item No. 19: 70, 75 below, 89 below, 90, 93, 94 above, 96, 113 below, 114, 115. Chevrolet Division, G. M. Corp.: 226 below. Daimler-Benz AG: 28 above, 29 above, 56. Devin Enterprises: 265. *Flug Sport*: 120. Ford Motor Co.: 191, 226 center. *Foreign Car Guide*: 145 above, 146 above, 264 below center. *Fortune*: 316 (Erich Lessing-Magnum). Jack Garrison: 137, 141. *Gute Fahrt*: 19 below, 42 center, 77 below, 103, 104, 127, 182, 233 center, 261 above, center, 264 above center, below. Hebmüller: 258. Heinrich Hoffmann: 43, 44, 46, 50, 52, 60. Alfonso de Hohenlohe: 133, 135, 138-140, 143, 144. Wilhelm Karmann GmbH: 242, 243, 250, 251 above, 252, 253. Los Angeles *Times*: 205. Günther Molter: 80, 174 above. The *Motor*: 55 below, 124 below. *Motor Revue*: 241, 244-249. *Popular Science*: 76 above, 83 above. Porsche AG, and *Christophorus*: 5, 17-28 below, 29 below, 30-32, 34, 35, 37-42 above, below, 45 above, 47 above, 48 above, 51, 53-55 above, 57-59, 62, 64, 66, 71 above, 83 below, 108, 116, 213 above, 269, 272-274 below, 275-293 above, 294-303, 305-308. *Road & Track*: 13, 146 below, 179, 180 below (Jack Campbell), 293 center, below. Friedrich Rometsch: 257, 259-261. James M. Sitz: 3, 175. Studebaker-Packard Corp.: 204. *Time*: 91, 206 below, 309. U. S. Army: 92, 94 below, 95, 97, 102. Volkswagenwerk pre-1948: *Kdf* promotional literature: 65, 99. *Schwimmwagen* operator's manual: 68, 69, 79 above, 81, 82, 84-87. *Type 11* operator's manual: 123, 128, 129. Volkswagen AG: 15, 61, 67, 71 below, 76 below, 78, 79 below, 88, 89 above, 117, 119, 121, 124 above, 125, 126, 130-132, 147-170, 172, 173 below, 174 below, 176, 177, 180 above, 181, 187-189, 192 below, 193-198, 200-203 above, 206 above, 208-210, 212, 214-222, 224-226 above, 227-233 below, 234-240, 251 below, 253-256, 310, 315. Kurt Worner: 14, 16, 45 below, 47 below, 48 below, 49, 101, 105-107, 109, 110, 271, 274 above.

THE BEETLE'S HOUR

"... a true value, rather than something the people in reality do not want."

While Volkswagen was introduced with a chassis then unique among passenger cars, its backbone already had been proven in the crucible of racing. Typical of this test-studded lineage was a torsion bar and trailing arm suspension which Dr. Porsche had perfected through world record-breaking runs in his Auto-Union Formula I racing cars.

One summer day in 1950 an aging little Austrian with a *fliege* moustache was being toured through the Volkswagenwerk by Dr. Ing. Heinz Nordhoff, then a comparative newcomer, just two years on the Volkswagen scene. But the latter's presence as General Director already was being marked as a miracle.

Like sparrows perched on the topmost joist of a soaring hayloft, the two men on a catwalk high over the busy factory floor were dwarfed by the cavernous expanse below. As their eyes met there was a smile of understanding.

To Dr. Ing. Ferdinand Porsche the many sounds from Volkswagen assembly below dissolved into a rendition of the Grand Finale to a single musical number on which he had spent an adult lifetime in the composition. Though his eyes were moist they twinkled as he looked to the younger man.

To the host, a trim figure of a man, recently turned fifty, the same sounds rising from the production activity below came through as an unfinished symphony, to be bettered, tomorrow, and tomorrow, with many arias yet to be composed.

Both men had put their hearts into the same basic work — in reality not a piece of music at all, but an unorthodox little automobile whose distinctive shape, in days to come, would be as universally known and accepted as that of a bottle of *Coca Cola*.

Production at the time of this meeting, scaled against assembly today, could barely be considered serious manufacture at all. Today a new Volkswagen rolls off the assembly line every 11 seconds every working day. In all the world only Chevrolets and Fords move away from their factories at faster clips.

When Volkswagen's present prominence among world automotive manufacturers is framed against its obscure origin, and oft-arrested development, the contrast is one of intense human interest with more than full measure of sweat, blood, tears — and more sweat. It is the dramatic achievement of two determined men, the *father of the concept,* and his successor, the *father of production reality*.

Automobile history has confirmed that the world was waiting for the Volkswagen. In the USA the little car demonstrated a maturity among motor car goliaths; it eventually instrumented a thorough regrouping of values in the American car concept. Motoring budgets were so reduced by VW's true economy that new money was freed for other purchases; literally, the car stimulated the whole economy in the United States, just as it had in more than 130 other countries in the Free World.

"It appeals more to me to offer the buyer a true value, a product of highest quality with a low purchase price and an incomparable resale value," Dr. Heinz Nordhoff reflected in 1958, "than to allow myself to be hounded by a group of hysterical stylists, who want to try to sell something to the people which in reality they do not want."

Every effort of the Volkswagen organization today reflects the same dominantly apparent *first quality* which has become a hall mark of the name. For the world-known Frankfurt Automobile Show recently VW's mammoth exhibit was a show in itself. Ships and railroad cars used to carry VWs to all parts of the globe were lavishly portrayed in token full scale . . . It was a far cry from the days when Volkswagen was present at the show only in spirit, as Adolf Hitler made a traditional rite of reporting each year's "progress" on his People's Car project at the opening celebration of the gala international affair (then held in Berlin) during the mid-1930's.

Possessed of a personal warmth of character, peculiar to itself in the realm of inanimate objects, Volkswagen fast became a companion wherever it ventured. Sometimes men waxed such fervor over it that the car wavered on the borderline of the world of the animate. Usefulness for play was no less than worthiness for work. For ski racing on a frozen lake in Bavaria it was quite natural for VW to appear as part of the team.

Not only the Product is unique. So is its Company. Volkswagen AG is the only automobile manufacturer to accumulate its capital from the sale of its product, rather than from stockholders. Recently when stock was sold for the first time, and Volkswagen *GmbH* (a limited liability company) became Volkswagen *AG* (a publicly held company) its stock went into more hands — with the sole exception of International Telephone & Telegraph — than any other corporation in the world.

To say that Volkswagen AG is the largest industry in Western Germany, that it employs more than 92,000 workers in six vast plants, creating over 6700 vehicles each day is simple fact. But it is oversimplification. It omits the most colorful automobile saga of our time.

While Volkswagen already is taken very much for granted in the United States, the stranger-than-fiction success story of the world's littlest giant is not generally known in the America of the 1960's. Yet, the American owner who becomes apprised of some details from his Volkswagen's fantastic past is more than likely to handle his car with a new depth of appreciation.

Volkswagen truly lived and died the *nine lives* of the fairy tale cat before the incarnation that earned world acclaim. Once it was Hitler's pet. Later it provided a diversion from reality for war-weary members of a collapsed Third Reich. Even political assassination before a firing squad of adverse technical opinion from British Intelligence experts of the Occupation failed to sound final Taps for the People's Car.

For the hearty Volkswagen these actions only set the stage for a *tenth* life, under Heinz Nordhoff, which proved to be the most fruitful of all.

TEMPERING AN IDEA

Testing the unorthodox, whenever it promised a better solution, brought a succession of conservative employers to odds with the imaginative young practical engineer.

When Gottlieb Daimler's first successful lightweight internal combustion engine falteringly drove a motorized coach in 1883, Ferdinand Porsche was just an eight-year-old boy in the small Bohemian town of Maffersdorf, in what is now western Czechoslovakia. But he already showed mechanical aptitude and interest which would later make him one of the world's great contributors to the development of the automobile.

Ferdinand's father was the town's master metalsmith, and young Porsche inherited his father's technical mind. After spending a time as an apprentice in his father's shop, Porsche gained formal training at the *Technische Hochschule* in nearby Reichenberg.

PORSCHE AS YOUTH

Two fields of technical development seem to have captivated Porsche early in life: electricity, and the motor car. Porsche built an electric light plant in his father's workshop when he was seventeen years old. He could not afford an engine for his first home-made generator, so instead he fitted the machine out with a hand-driven flywheel. Porsche's mother reports in a later letter that various members of the Porsche family had to go down to the basement periodically and give the wheel a few hefty turns — so that Porsche's hand-built accumulator batteries would not run down. Porsche earned his spending money by installing electric bells and telephones, which he had designed and made himself, in the homes of friends. He already had plans while in his teens to build two motor vehicles, one of which was electrically powered; but he had to give them up because his studies took up too much of his time. Porsche was later to combine these two youthful interests in his early automobile design in Vienna.

A proud inventor stands before a home electric plant of his own construction in this photograph from the Porsche family album, inscribed "taken April, 1894, before leaving for Vienna." A critical study of the generator reveals the objectivity in design and classic simplicity in curcuitry that would mark much of Ferdinand Porsche's work to come.

In April, 1894, Porsche made his move to the glamorous, lively city of Vienna, at that time center of the Austro-Hungarian empire and of all the new Austrian technical industry. Although his limited schooling did not permit him to meet formal entrance requirements, nevertheless he attended classes at the Vienna *Technische Hochschule* and at the University for a time. Porsche's first position in Vienna was with an electrical engineering company; but his career really started when he joined the Jacob Lohner company as chief automotive designer in 1898. The twenty-four-year-old Porsche had found enough opportunity to observe and study the few automobiles then in Vienna to hit upon his main concern in automotive design: the transmission of power from the engine to the wheels. Porsche quite naturally applied his knowledge of electricity to this problem; the result was the battery-powered "Lohner-Porsche Chaise," which featured electric motors mounted directly on the hubs of the front wheels.

THE LOHNER-PORSCHE CHAISE

The Lohner-Porsche Chaise, now on exhibit in the Vienna Technical Museum, was originally a very successful, highly praised exhibit in the Paris 1900 World Exposition. It looked very much like a horseless carriage, had a maximum speed of 9 mph, and a maximum travelling range of thirty-two miles between battery charges. The two electric motors delivered a peak of 7 hp. This unusual car established Porsche as a designer with original ideas; its success gave him courage to continue with his own personal development.

The first Lohner-Porsche was as novel at the Paris Exposition in 1900 as it is quaint today on display in Vienna. Visitors to the fair were surprised that the compact front wheels actually contained electric motors, in Austria's sole entry at the Exhibition.

Improvements began immediately; a lower operating position was achieved in the succeeding model by relocating the storage batteries from underfoot to underseat.

Protocoll

über die

RECORD-FAHRT der Firma JACOB LOHNER & C⁰.
mit deren Electromobil am 23. September 1900.

Anwesend beim Start in Schottwien Km.-Stein 79: Prof. Georg Göbel, Gen.-Secretär Fasbender.

Beim Ziele: E. v. Ritschl, V. Kadlczik als officieller Zeitnehmer.

Gattung des Wagens: Electromobil System Lohner-Porsche, ohne Carrosserie.

Gewicht: Complet 1120 kg.

Fahrer: Porsche, ohne weitere Besatzung.

Strecke: Schottwien, Km.-Stein 79 bis zum Hotel Erzherzog Johann am Semmering Km.-Stein 89.

Distanz: 10 Kilometer.

Abfahrt: 6 Uhr Früh mitteleurop. Zeit.

Ankunft: 6 Uhr 14 Min. 52¹/₅ Sec. mitteleurop. Zeit.

Benöthigte Zeit für 10 Kilometer bei 400 Meter Steigung:
14 Minuten 52¹/₅ Secunden.

Diese Zeit gilt als bisheriger Record für sämmtliche Gattungen Electromobile und erscheint hiedurch vom Oesterr. Automobil-Club als anerkannt.

Wien, 24. September 1900.

V. KADLCZIK m. p.   G. GÖBEL m. p.   E. v. RITSCHL m. p.
officieller Zeitnehmer.   Capitän.

Z. HARMSEN m. p.   K. FASBENDER m. p.

Für die Richtigkeit der Abschrift verantwortlich
Der General-Secretär:
KARL FASBENDER.

RECORDS VOM 8. SEPTEMBER 1900
Semmering-Rennen

Categorie der **Motocycles**	14.38¹/₅	Categorie der **Electromobile**	22.27¹/₅
Tourenwagen	16.57	**Voiturettes**	22.49²/₅

Porsche's racing career, which was to pace most of his automotive developments to come, began in the Fall of 1900 when he pushed the "streamlined" nose of a special lightweight, battery-powered Lohner-Porsche to a new record in a speed run over the famous Semmering highway in Austria.

← In this official document of the Austrian Automobile Club Porsche's record run was duly certified. Porsche charged up the winding steeply climbing Semmering 10 km. test road at 41 km/h (about 25 mph), chopping the standing electric automobile record of 22½ minutes down to just under 15 minutes for the run.

In the next year Porsche substituted a gasoline engine and generator combination for the batteries, and the firm began to produce the faster "Lohner-Porsche Mixed."

Special appeals of the Lohner-Porsche "Mixed," which used Daimler engines producing up to 70 hp, were described within this brochure presenting the 1902-04 series. The hub motors provided literal front-wheel-drive, which also counteracted to provide electric brakes, with "completely noise-free driving" and "none of the disadvantages of other designs using clutch, chains or gears."

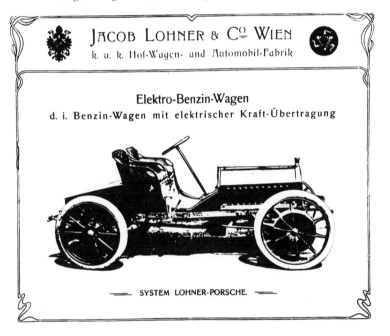

JACOB LOHNER & Cº WIEN
k. u. k. Hof-Wagen- und Automobil-Fabrik

Elektro-Benzin-Wagen
d. i. Benzin-Wagen mit elektrischer Kraft-Übertragung

SYSTEM LOHNER-PORSCHE.

Porsche continued to drive in speed trials, establishing a new hill climb record in a "Mixed" racing version in 1902 at Exelberg. All official runs were made with a second man riding as passenger and ballast.

Soon Porsche's designs at Jacob Lohner were recognized and respected abroad for their practicality, as well as their novelty. No one had found a way to make batteries lightweight. Their range for powering a straight electric car severely limited driving range, yet electric drive was quiet and smooth. By means of a dynamo, Porsche used the power from a gasoline engine to drive electric motors at the wheels, eliminating the extreme weight of the batteries, and extending driving range to the capacity of the fuel tank. It was a reasonable combination, and Porsche applied it through a progression of models.

The "Mixed" system proved ideal to motorize fire fighting equipment since a horse-drawn steam pumper could be coupled to the Lohner-Porsche power section with less modification than would be necessary with a rear drive. Vienna and London were early users of this self-propelled rig.

Thus early in his career Porsche showed no hesitation to use the unusual in his solution of engineering problems. Soon the conservative and financially somewhat limited Lohner firm began to handicap Porsche in his attempts to develop a new form of power transmission. This feeling of limitation led Porsche to resign from the firm — the first of many instances wherein Porsche felt his creative spirit stifled by a conventional, limited automobile company.

He made very successful use of the hub-mounted electric motors for a number of years; even his series of military tractors and trucks for the Austrian Army in the first World War were powered by the combination of gasoline engine, generator, and electric motors. Porsche later returned to the idea of hub-mounted electric motors in his design of military vehicles for the German armed forces in the Second World War.

Porsche's use of electric hub motors illustrates how he never hesitated to use whatever design seemed best to him for any particular problem—be the solution old or new, established or unorthodox.

Nr. 30　　　　　　**Allgemeine Automobil-Zeitung.**　　　　　　Seite 9

Automobile Dampfspritze der Wiener Feuerwehr.

In 1906 Porsche became technical director of Austro-Daimler, the parent company of the Steyr-Daimler-Puch concern. He was to remain with the company for seventeen fruitful years, during which Porsche-designed cars won wide recognition, particularly in racing circles.

PORSCHE'S METHOD OF WORKING

Early in his career Porsche developed the method of working which he retained for his entire life. He would conceive an idea in privacy, covering many pages of his notebook with rough sketches. Then in a few days he would bring his work to a meeting of his staff; they would discuss the idea and begin to work on its finer details. Then certain members of the staff would begin work refining various parts of the design. Porsche would go around in the office from desk to desk, arguing about various solutions proposed by the men on his staff. He was always eager to listen to new and different ideas, but he was equally ready to criticize whatever he believed was incorrect, unoriginal, or not good enough. In this way the staff worked as a team to bring the drawings to their final form.

PRINCE HENRY " MAJA" CARS

One of the most famous Porsche cars for Austro-Daimler was the 28-30 hp "Maja," named after the second daughter of its financial backer, Herr Emil Jellinek. (His first daughter also provided the name for a famous series of automobiles: Mercedes.) The Maja achieved great popularity among European royalty, and it took honors in the 1910 Prince Henry Trial from Berlin to Munich. The car had such advanced design features for its time as a four-speed transmission and a solid driveshaft. Porsche, still interested in improving the car's performance, added the unusual *"Tulpenform"* (tulip-shaped) body pictured here, and drove the car to further racing success in the next year's Prince Henry Trial. This car, housed in a light alloy body of unusually aerodynamic design, had a maximum speed of 87 mph, far beyond that of any competitors in 1910.

By 1910 the power transmission for gasoline engines had been refined and Porsche developed a straight gasoline car of unexcelled grace. Reflecting advanced aerodynamics for its time, Porsche's four-passenger Maja for Austro-Daimler (named at the direction of a financial backer) proved to be as lithe as it appeared. In one of the most important sports events of the time—the Prince Henry trial— Ferdinand Porsche, at the wheel of the lead car himself, led the Maja team to the first three places for speed and endurance, giving the car a reputation as "unbeatable" among touring cars in the 1910-1911 period.

Experience in aircraft engine design for A-D led Porsche to an increasing preference for air-cooled engines, as did his work in designing vehicles for the Kaiser's war effort.

To Porsche, efficient design had to look efficient, as well as function in tempo. An advanced aero motor design for Austro-Daimler in 1912-15 featured aircooling and opposed cylinders and valves—features that one day far in the future would be incorporated in a People's Car.

While Porsche's gas-electro designs gave way to straight gasoline cars, his "Mixed" system was yet to be proved again in special purpose vehicles. As war approached, he developed a truck-tractor unit for Austro-Daimler to pull the 305 howitzer. An 80 hp Skoda engine generated power for the usual individual hub motors. While a monster in itself, this creation would soon be dwarfed by Porsche's next development.

The tremendous range of Porsche's imagination came into play in developing an even heavier tractor-trailer unit, which by means of a relatively light engine could be operated with as many as ten lightweight stake cargo wagons. Electric power was transmitted to motors in each of the four powered wheels of each trailer, by cable, as well as to the traction wheels of the power unit itself. Steering was unique; each trailer followed in the path of the front unit, like a serpent; and thus the wagon could enter any pathway no wider than its lead unit required. Mountain passes could be negotiated with ease.

Another version of this tractor-trailer design was adapted to haul the heaviest gun ever motorized—the 420 mm. "Big Bertha," a piece of artillery that fired a shell weighing close to a ton. Its barrel weighed 17 tons stripped—26 tons set up for operation. To carry this behemoth six independent tractor-trailer units were necessary. Each power unit used a 150 hp. Skoda engine to power a generator, which in turn supplied each of the eight hub motors of the trailer. Each axle of the trailer could steer independently. The "C-Train" could negotiate Alpine passes and was also adaptable to running on standard rails.

Formal recognition for his pioneering design work was first conferred upon Ferdinand Porsche, at the age of 41, principally as a result of his outstanding work at Austro-Daimler, when the Vienna Imperial *Technische Hochschule* awarded him his first honorary Doctorate, in 1917.

DIE KAIS. KÖN. TECHNISCHE HOCHSCHULE IN WIEN WILL, DIE SCHWELLE DES ZWEITEN JAHRHUNDERTS IHRES BESTANDES ÜBERSCHREITEND, DIESEN ABSCHNITT IN IHRER GESCHICHTLICHEN ENT- WICKLUNG FEIERLICH BEZEICHNEN, INDEM SIE EINE REIHE VON MÄNNERN EHRT, DIE SICH UM DIE WISSENSCHAFTLICHE ODER PRAKTISCHE AUSBILDUNG DER TECHNIK VERDIENT GEMACHT HABEN; DIESER AKADEMISCHE AKT SOLL AUCH DIE ERINNERUNG AN DIE GROSZE ZEIT FEST- HALTEN, DIE DER TECHNIK SO GEWALTIGE AUFGABEN GESTELLT HAT WIE KEINE ZUVOR IM SINNE DER DIESE ABSICHT VERWIRK- LICHENDEN BESCHLÜSSE DES PROFESSOREN- KOLLEGIUMS VOM 6. JULI 1916 VERLEIHT SIE DEM DIREKTOR DER ÖST. DAIMLER-MOTOREN- AKTIENGESELLSCHAFT

FERDINAND PORSCHE

ALS DEM GEISTIGEN FÜHRER EINES HEIMISCHEN GROSZUNTERNEHMENS, DAS SICH UM DIE AUS- BILDUNG DES AUTOMOBILWESENS UND DER FLUGTECHNIK HOHE VERDIENSTE ERWORBEN HAT, DIE WÜRDE EINES DOKTORS DER TECHNISCHEN WISSENSCHAFTEN EHRENHALBER

ALS ÄUSZERES ZEICHEN DIESER VON SEINER MAJESTÄT DEM KAISER ALLERGNÄDIGST GE- STATTETEN EHRENBEZEIGUNG IST GEGEN- WÄRTIGE URKUNDE AUSGEFERTIGT WORDEN

WIEN, DEN 20. JUNI 1917

The First Great War had far-reaching effects on the geography and economy of Europe. The defeated nations were stripped of much of their territory, and they found it difficult to regain the economic position which they held before the war. The economic conditions in impoverished post-war Austria were not at all conducive to the production and sales of the large touring-cars then in vogue; and lighter, smaller cars, such as the small Citroen 5CV, the Austin 7, and the small Renaults, became popular throughout all of Europe.

Porsche became intrigued by the problems of small-car design. His interest in the small car grew in the course of several long conversations and visits with his friend, Dr. Hans Ledwinka, noted designer for the Tatra firm in Czechoslovakia. The two designers shared small-car ideas, such as the rear-mounted, air-cooled engine, independent suspension by coil springs or torsion bars, the central tube chassis, and the swing axle. These features were later to appear in the Volkswagen.

As a sports car the little car was full-fendered and carried a spare at the tail. For racing it was stripped of lamps and all but the right front mudguard, and dual spares were mounted midships. An inspired string of driving successes, foreshadowing the Porsche car records of a world yet to come, brought the car renown in its day.

Count Sascha Kolowrat, an Austrian film magnate, gave Porsche his only opportunity (besides the Maja) while with Austro-Daimler to build a small car. With Austro-Daimler's support and Kolowrat's financial backing Porsche designed a high-performance, 1100cc, four-cylinder, overhead valve racing and sports car, which he named the "Sascha."

SASCHA

The "Sascha" was A-D's most famous post-WWI racing car. It had a 4 cylinder, 1100cc, inline engine, producing from 40 to 50 horsepower, with an overhead, gear-driven camshaft. It reached 89 mph in a flying kilometer in 1922—quite an accomplishment for a small engine so long ago.

The first trial of the Sascha came in the rugged 268 mile 1922 Targa Florio road race in Sicily. Sascha took first and second in its class, the 1100cc division, and, competing against other cars of much greater displacement, finished seventh. Various motoring journals considered the Sascha to be the outstanding car in the grueling race. Significantly, the Sascha cars drove back to Vienna the next day under their own power. Porsche had designed the car for normal road driving as well as racing, especially since Austro-Daimler did not have the money to ship the cars from Vienna to Sicily and back by truck!

In triumph three Sascha cars returned from victory in their class in the 1922 Targa Florio. Alfred Neubauer, who drove the best time, shown here in the lead car, was later to join racing's all-time-greats as the brilliant head of the racing department at Daimler-Benz.

3308

Porsche returned to designs for the grueling Sicilian Targa Florio shortly after his arrival at Stuttgart. Behind the wheel of a supercharged Mercedes, in the Spring of 1924, Christian Werner pushed his Porsche-designed team car over the four 56-mile-laps of quick rises and sudden corners in this primeval gravel road course to attain a new track record —an average speed above 41 mph.

Victory in the battering Targa Florio contest brought new prominence to the winning car's designer. Porsche was formally heralded later the same year when the *Wuerttembergische Technische Hochschule* in Stuttgart conferred upon him another honorary Doctorate of Engineering.

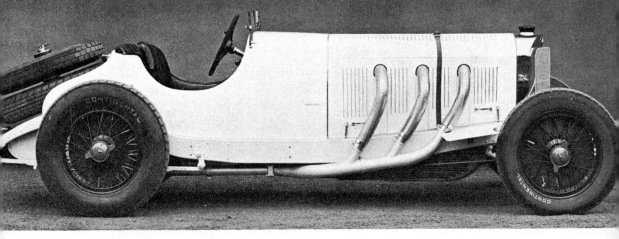

One of the classic sports cars of all time was Porsche's Super Sports *mit Kompressor,* designated the Mercedes-Benz *SSK,* in which the supercharger was distinguished from previous blown Mercedes models by being constantly engaged.

After a severe racing accident involving one of their drivers, Austro-Daimler decided to abandon almost all racing car development; they decided to stress production of large touring cars. Porsche felt himself held back more and more by A-D. Finally the differences of opinion between Porsche and the Austro-Daimler board became intolerable, and Porsche resigned in April, 1923. On April 30, 1923, Porsche became technical director of Daimler-Motoren, A. G., which from 1926 onwards was known as Daimler-Benz. During his years in Stuttgart Porsche developed the world-famous large sports cars bearing the designations S, SS, and SSK. But he still believed in the small car; and Daimler-Benz gave him the chance to design a medium-sized two liter, six-cylinder car, the Type "200 Stuttgart," introduced in 1926. Porsche then began to work on an even lighter one liter car, but some members of the board of directors remained opposed to all small car plans, especially since the "200 Stuttgart" had not been a complete success mechanically: numerous owners complained of difficult starting in cold weather. The unwillingness of an established auto manufacturer to produce a smaller car once again led to Porsche's resignation from an important technical position. Porsche left Daimler-Benz, and on January 2, 1929, he became technical director and chief engineer of the Steyr-Werke, A. G., firm, located in Steyr, Austria.

Porsche completed two important and widely recognized designs for Steyr—a large car, named the Steyr "Austria," and a smaller two liter car, which bore the designation "Steyr 30."

But financial and in part personal considerations led Porsche to leave Steyr and establish his now world-famous engineering consulting firm in Stuttgart.

During Porsche's brief tenure at Steyr the line was to include two models refined by his hand—the "30" and the big "Austria", here shown with a previously designed smaller 1½ liter model. He came to leave Steyr when the firm was absorbed by financial interests which would bring it together with Daimler-Benz.

OFFICE, STAFF, LOCATION

Porsche was faced with many problems in 1929. His current employer at the time, Steyr, was being taken over by Austro-Daimler. He did not wish to stay with a firm whose activities would be so limited as Steyr; in the new combined firm, his "Austria" design would be taken out of production, and the company planned to build only A-D large cars. His freedom in the firm would be curtailed by the same board of directors who had opposed him at Austro-Daimler seven years earlier.

Porsche long had wanted the independence of his own firm, but he knew also that his office would require a shrewd financial manager and a live staff of engineers if it were to be successful. Porsche had a series of discussions with his old collaborator at Austro-Daimler, Karl Rabe, in the autumn of 1929. Rabe agreed without hesitation to join the new office as head designer. He and Porsche then found just the man to manage the financial activities of the new venture in Adolf Rosenberger from Pforzheim, a former auto racing enthusiast and shrewd, experienced businessman.

Porsche's next problem was one of location. He had purchased a villa in Stuttgart during his stay with Daimler-Benz; the house was at the time rented out, but Porsche had always longed to return to his hillside home. He wanted to locate his office in an environment which would be stimulating and where business would be good. Thus the natural location would be Stuttgart, which already housed a University, an excellent *Technische Hochschule,* an auto research institute, and numerous important auto component manufacturers — among them Bosch, Mahle, and Hirth.

Porsche found little difficulty in securing a good staff for his new office. Nine designers joined the original Porsche team. Among them were the expert on air-cooled engines, Joseph Kales, who had formerly worked for the Tatra and Skoda firms, and Erwin Kommenda, the body designer who supplied the styling for the NSU cars and would later draw up the Porsche 356. Rounding out the staff were designers whom Porsche brought from Steyr and Austro-Daimler; Porsche's personal driver, Goldinger; and his son Ferdinand "Ferry" Porsche.

From the time when he completed formal apprenticeship training at the Robert Bosch factory in Stuttgart, at the age of 20, Ferry Porsche was at his father's side in the family's consulting firm. It was to be his life work, and one day the young engineer would guide the tradition established by the elder Porsche to new laurels.

The Porsche engineering firm opened for business on December 1, 1930. Porsche at last had a measure of independence and could pursue some of his own more original ideas. He gave numbers to the various ideas on which he worked, though reportedly he started with number 7, so that prospective clients would think the new company was already swamped with work. The most important of these ideas was Project 12, the "Small Car."

3

THE IMAGE ENDURES

"The car must be simple in design to be low in price — yet long-lasting
and reliable for *genuine* economy."

Late in November, 1930, a small notice in the *Stuttgarter Zeitung* announced the formation of a new engineering development company; its name was "Dr.-Ing. h. c. Ferdinand Porsche, G.m.b.H." The public took comparatively little notice of Porsche's new firm in its modest quarters at Kronenstr. 14; but in the next months Porsche created there the basic small car design which was to affect the daily life of every German *Bürger*.

The Porsche workshop soon became a well-integrated, productive team. The group worked together harmoniously, displaying the greatest respect and loyalty to its even then famous director. Although the various engineers earned smaller salaries at Porsche than might have been obtained elsewhere, the work was stimulating and more than made up for the difference in pay.

The firm achieved note for its disregard of the accepted method, of the already proven. Every design problem was for Porsche a new and unique challenge. He tested and criticized each suggested solution from every conceivable approach. Sometimes he discovered a more efficient, practical, or beautiful solution than had ever been achieved before.

Porsche felt that contemporary small cars did not live up to the potential inherent in their small size. He considered their conventional chassis arrangement, front engine, rigid axles, and high, square body structure to be outmoded and impractical. He vowed to create a fresh, new small car which would be free from the shortcomings of existing models.

Porsche had long been intrigued by the problems of small-car design; and by the time the Porsche engineering firm began work extensively on Project 12, he had already established the basic pattern for his design. Much of today's Volkswagen can be seen in the early Project 12.

Often Dr. Porsche would mull over design details with his staff until a solution would suddenly come to him. Here a point is pondered with Joseph Kales, head of his engineering technicians.

PORSCHE'S SMALL CAR CRITERIA

Early in his career Porsche set up standards which his ideal small car must meet, based on the motoring conditions prevailing on the European continent at the time. In 1931 an automobile was still largely a luxury and a diversion for the upper classes in Europe, long after it had become more of a necessity in the U.S. If many people were to afford a small car at all, it had to be low in original price and economical in operation. The average income in Europe has always been low compared to that of the U.S.A., and in 1931 the entire Continent was struggling to get out of the Great Depression. All gasoline had to be imported into Europe and always has been heavily taxed by the various European governments. Rubber for tires must also be imported. Operating an automobile in Europe was and is expensive for the average working man.

Porsche's Project 12 had to be durable and roadable, too. Europe's road system then even more than now reflected the days of equestrian travel. Roads were narrow and winding; pavement surfaces were generally uneven, old, and full of chuckholes; and in 1931 Hitler had not yet built any of the now famous German *Autobahnen*. An automobile buyer with a limited income would want his car to be a lasting, durable machine which would retain its value.

The small car had to be of such a simple design that it would be easy to produce in great quantity; and if the car were to be widely sold, replacement parts would also have to be cheaply and easily obtainable.

And naturally the small car should embody those virtues which any owner expects from any price automobile — easy starting, reliability, good handling, comfort, and so forth.

That Porsche succeeded in meeting these standards is now apparent to millions of VW drivers all over the world, but in 1931 Porsche could only rely on his own reason to support his unorthodox design.

Porsche decided to use a rear engine in order to avoid a long driveshaft, save weight, give passengers all the room between the axles, and to allow easy quantity production. But if he were to achieve a good weight distribution, his engine had to be short and light; thus he selected a "Boxermotor" — an air-cooled, flat, opposed cylinder engine — with an integrated transmission and differential.

But there were more problems to solve. The use of a box frame was out of the question; it would require a separate heavy frame for the body. Porsche wanted something lighter, more rigid. He therefore decided on the platform type frame with a central backbone and outriggers, utilizing a swing axle in the rear and his special trailing arm torsion bar suspension up front. The Volkswagen was shaping up.

A small, moderately powered, four or five passenger car built along the conventional boxy lines of the era could not attain a top speed of 60 mph — which Porsche considered a minimum for his car. In order to reach an adequate peak, Project 12 should be built as light as possible and should have an aerodynamically streamlined body form, offering a minimum of wind resistance.

With these features Porsche hoped to have a car marketable to the average income group and operable in any part of the world. Confident of finding financial support when the time for final development came, Dr. Porsche went ahead on his design. Little did he suspect that seven years later a dictator, whom history would brand a madman, would build a huge factory just to produce his little car.

Porsche made inquiries among German auto manufacturers about the possibility of producing his small car, and word circulated in the industry that he had an interesting new design. Business was very poor in the industry in 1931, and all auto producers were searching for some means to help them ride out the slump.

Dr. Fritz Neumeyer, head of the Zundapp Motorcycle Company in Nuremberg, felt that his company should diversify its production, so that the company as a whole might last out the depression in better shape; and he agreed to finance the production of three small-car prototypes, with the stipulation that Porsche use a five-cylinder, water-cooled radial engine. Neumeyer thought that the public would not trust Porsche's radical, air-cooled layout. It was unusual for Porsche to yield on such a design point; but inasmuch as Neumeyer was footing the bill for his pet project, Porsche felt compelled to concede.

The cars were built after hours in absolute secrecy. Zundapp supplied most of the mechanical parts, while Reutter, a Stuttgart coach builder, constructed the wood and aluminum bodies. They were ready for testing in April, 1932.

WHEN A PROTOTYPE BECAME A PROTOTYPE

First of the large designing contracts to come to the independent Porsche designing office, designated as number 7, was from the Wanderer automobile firm at Chemnitz, later one of the four firms to form the Auto-Union. Models in 1.7 and 2 liter sizes were developed, accepted, and put into production. Porsche also designed a streamlined 3.25 liter 2-door model. Only one of this type actually was built, however, and this prototype became Porsche's private automobile.

The contribution Porsche's big 3.25 liter prototype made in the development of Project 12 body design may be seen graphically in the accompanying photos of the Wanderer car and the Zundapp *Volksauto* prototypes which followed. The windshield pillar, roof line, and windows reveal molding and some other details that are clearly common to both designs if not identical; Porsche's exclusive Wanderer, a prototype itself, had in turn served him as a basis for the development of the little rear-engine Zundapp body.

Porsche adapted the Wanderer body design to the short-wheelbase, light car chassis by reducing some dimensions and cutting the body off immediately forward of the windshield and front doors, rather than by scaling down the whole Wanderer design. The door openings were narrowed at the front to set up a whole new shortened forward section. Porsche reduced height by cutting away several inches of sill area from the original blueprints. Rear engine ventilation was provided in the Zundapp by the addition of louvred side panel insets which resembled sweeping rear quarter windows.

Body design of the big, supercharged 3.25 liter Wanderer prototype, which Porsche long used as his personal transportation, very strangely anticipated the lines of the Zundapp *Volksauto*.

Project 12, which became known as the Zundapp *Type 12,* adapted the general lines of Porsche's personal Wanderer neatly to small car specifications, while an unmistakable resemblance to its progenitor was retained. It was tested first in April, 1932.

ZUNDAPP *VOLKSAUTOS*

All three Zundapp prototypes had water-cooled five-cylinder radial engines, which were tilted slightly forward from the vertical to fit better into the aerodynamic rear deck. The Stuttgart body firm, Reutter, built two timber and aluminum bodies in the beetle-like sedan shape, later supplied a boxy cabriolet body for the third of the prototypes. The eventual *Volksauto* design called for an all-steel body, but Reutter used wood and aluminum for simplicity and to speed the secret, after-hours body construction. The details of the Zundapp *Volksautos* reportedly corresponded quite closely to Porsche's earlier Project 12 specifications.

Initial testing results were not good. The engine overheated, and it was not accessible for repairs. Faults were noted in the transmission, and even the torsion bars broke on several occasions. At the time that the prototype tests revealed to Herr Neumeyer that the little Zundapp car required extensive re-development to be acceptable for production, the Great Depression was causing a wave of new interest in minimum-upkeep, two-wheeled motor vehicles. As Zundapp's motorcycle sales rose sharply late in 1932, Neumeyer lost all interest in diversification into the small car field. In order to terminate his agreement with Porsche ahead of time, he released all rights to the *Volksauto* to its creator. So Porsche was free to continue development from this point on.

THE RED CARPET

Porsche's Austro-Daimler racing successes and his famous SS and SSK cars for Daimler-Benz had received wide publicity; they had made the Porsche name known around the world. Porsche designs and innovations were being used by auto manufacturers all over the continent. But it still was with some surprise that Dr. Porsche received a series of letters early in 1932 bearing the stamps and postmarks of the USSR. Porsche, as did most Europeans at that time, considered Russia to be an undeveloped wilderness, a land of primitive peasants.

The Russian correspondence to Porsche indicated that he would soon receive a visit from a group of Russian engineers, who wished to speak with him and possibly place contracts for designs. Porsche, who only three weeks before had borrowed on his life insurance policy to pay the salaries of his office staff, was only too willing to meet the Russians at their convenience. His office assumed that they would be most interested in tractors or other motorized agricultural tools. But the Russian engineers, after politely leafing over a number of old Porsche tractor designs, remained distant.

Finally, after gravely reciting a number of political slogans about the latest communist plans of technical development, the Russians revealed their true purpose in coming to Germany: they invited Porsche to take an industrial tour of Russia. The official government invitation read: "We would like to show you that the period of reconstruction has begun in Russia. Technical progress, the motorizing and electrification of town and country, is being advanced by our new country's impetus. We would like you to judge for yourself the possibilities which exist in a country that has unlimited space and inexhaustible natural resources of wealth."

Porsche accepted the invitation. Three weeks later began one of the strangest trips ever made by a German citizen through the vast Soviet empire. The Russians may never after have permitted a foreign engineer to see their technical achievements, working methods, and potential of development in such an open-faced manner. Porsche was escorted in the finest accommodations through Kiev, Kursk, Nijni-Novgorod, Odessa, the Caucasus, Crimea, and even beyond the Urals. He saw every conceivable kind of factory, from the most primitive to Russia's newest secret plants in Siberia, as well as the Model A Ford plant which Henry Ford in good faith had helped set up two years before. Evenings he was a guest of honor at countless dinners and receptions. One evening Porsche jestingly remarked that he still preferred Pilsner beer to Russian vodka; the next evening he found a bottle of Pilsner, flown in by the Russians that day from Bohemia, beside his plate at dinner.

Gradually the Russian plan revealed itself to Porsche. The Bolsheviks were not inviting the Porsche engineering firm to bid for a contract. *They* were doing the bidding, and they wanted to buy Porsche, the master engineer. When his touring party returned to Moscow, the Russian government submitted a contract to Porsche. His proposed title was to be "State Designer and Engineer of the USSR." Here at last he would have complete freedom to develop his ideas; the resources of an entire nation would be at his command; and he would receive the unlimited financial support which he previously had so seldom found. Porsche was greatly tempted.

Then he looked at the fine print, and certain clauses in the contract disturbed him. He would be compelled not only to move his family to Russia, but also to give up all contact with the West, except on order of the Russian government.

Still holding fast to his dream of developing a "People's Car," he reflected that the bleak economic climate in Russia made prospects for such an automobile far distant. He would also have to give up his second hope of building a new, revolutionary racing car. Dr. Porsche had always been attached to his homeland and its traditions. Even while the Russians were feeding him caviar he became aware of how much he appreciated the security and warmth of his established home and, moreover, how greatly he depended upon this culture to develop his ideas.

Porsche turned down the Russian offer, and a short time later he was back in his train compartment, heading westward, gazing out the window at the vast Russian and Polish fields. As soon as he arrived in Stuttgart, Porsche knew how far away he had really been. He returned immediately to his design office and picked up his work just where he had left off. Russia was not for Ferdinand Porsche.

The fact has been little circulated that Henry Ford assisted the USSR in setting up a factory to produce the Model A in the Soviet Union. Terms of the agreement called for repayment of vast investments in dies and machine tools, and even in U. S. made parts, which Henry Ford obligingly furnished this "peace-loving" backward nation to get the project under way. While Russia turned out the Model A in substantial quantity, as her sole volume car for many years, she never obliged Ford by repaying a single dollar as originally agreed. The Ford Motor Company eventually was compelled to write off the entire affair. One source reports the chassis was still being built in the USSR in the early 1950's—as a light truck with a more contemporized body.

After Porsche had lost Zundapp's backing for the small car, he turned to NSU, a motorcycle firm located in Neckarsulm, north of Stuttgart, and attempted to interest them in his project. Porsche suggested using his Zundapp designs as a basis, but he wanted to return to his four-cylinder opposed, air-cooled engine. Herr Fritz von Falkenhayn, NSU's managing director, liked Porsche's suggestions, agreed to finance and test three new experimental models. Porsche revised his design extensively, and prototype construction got under way in January, 1934.

On the drawing boards since 1932, the NSU *Volksauto* came to be known as Type 32, even though actual construction of prototypes did not come about till the Winter of 1933-34. An opposed, four-cylinder, aircooled engine layout was now applied to the design for the first time, as were a turbine cooling fan and an integral engine-transmission.

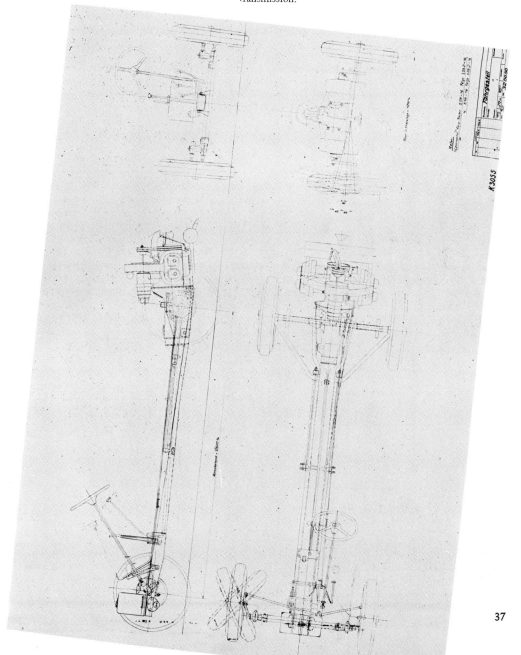

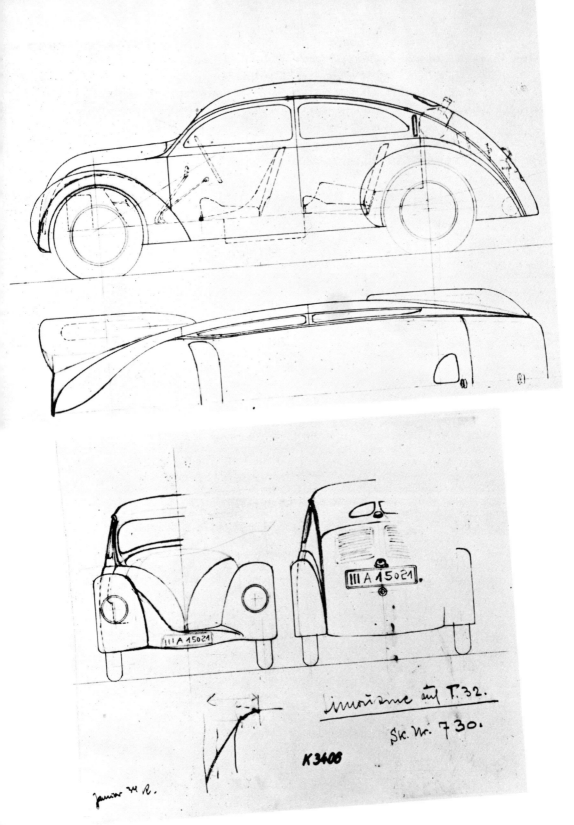

Configuration for the body design of the Type 32 was established through a series of rough, preliminary sketches in January, 1934.

THE NSU *VOLKSAUTOS*

Construction and testing of the NSU *Volksauto* prototypes marked an important step forward in the development of the Volkswagen, for it proved the worthiness of the flat opposed- cylinder motor and in many other ways foreshadowed the layout and component details of the ultimate VW model.

Body design, however, had yet a long way to travel to its present form. The three NSU prototypes were larger and roomier than the "junior Wanderer" design of the Zundapp. The floor in the NSU *Volksauto* lay somewhat higher off the ground, as these prototypes used a central chassis of box members, rather than the present VW's platform chassis. Compared with the later production series, the NSU chassis was also longer and wider; but even then the weight of 1760 pounds was, as in today's VW, noticeably light for its size — an advantage of great favor in mass production.

Porsche's now-famous suspension system was used in essentially the same form as now on the NSU cars: four-wheel independent trailing-arm torsion bar suspension, using a swing axle in the rear and Porsche's newly-developed hydraulic shock absorbers.

The designer Erwin Kommenda reputedly was responsible for the body styling of these cars. The first two were bodied by Drauz of Heilbronn, using the widespread Weymann technique — artificial leather over wood superstructure. The third prototype was fitted with an all-steel body by Reutter. Practical minimum overhang fore and aft of the wheels was evident in Project 12 from the first; but at the NSU stage the wheelbase was longer than would be ideal for a light car. Later, as other makes stretched out their overhang, the VW was to retain its "wheels at the corners" concept and at the same time shorten its wheelbase; the result was a healthy contrast with other often cumbersome cars of the 1950's.

The Drauz-bodied Type 32 prototype was tested in open, cross-country runs, once as far as Paris. Inquisitive viewers were informed only that it was "an experimental model."

Between two familiar Wanderers stands the Type 32 with body by Reutter. While sketches placed the headlamps neatly within the front fenders, in actual construction of this prototype standard lamps were mounted in slight depressions in the front fenders in a conventional manner.

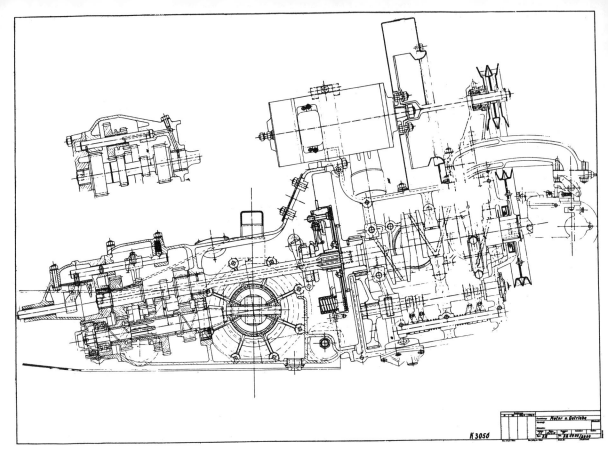

K 3056

Designed along the now familiar opposed four-cylinder, air-cooled ohv layout, with integrated transmission and differential, the engine was tilted slightly forward to fit a more streamlined rear deck. Engine size in the NSU was somewhat greater than in either the earlier Zundapp or later VW designs; the 20 hp engine displaced some 1470 cc. In the NSU cars the battery was located under the spare tire in the hood compartment, while the gas tank perched over the air impeller shroud in the rear. Fine access for service, such a strong point in today's VW, was not a feature of the *Volksautos;* the distributor was located behind the engine in an all but inaccessible spot.

Study of an engineering drawing of the integral engine-transmission-differential of Type 32 reveals Porsche's thinking in canting the engine upward toward the rear: at this stage of development the inclined position appeared to simplify the drive lines. It was only coincidental that this configuration permitted a tighter bobtail in body design.

Metal covered wooden frame construction is revealed under the open motor door. For any service beyond the cursory the Type 32 engine required removal for access. Early aircooling tiptoed a borderline between satisfactory cooling and overheating in this prototype; dual fan belts were employed as a safety measure.

Testing of these prototype cars went on quite successfully; the only complaint was one of excessive engine noise. Herr von Falkenhayn remarked: "It sounds like a worn-out stone-crusher." But the car had good performance, and it held the road very well, even at its top speed of 73 mph. The NSU *Volksauto* also held the promise of inexpensive quantity production.

But once again manufacture of Porsche's small car was blocked — this time by a trade agreement between NSU and the Italian Fiat company. In 1930 NSU had agreed to sell its automotive department to Fiat and produce only motorcycles. Fiat, in turn, was to build a factory in Heilbronn and there manufacture cars under the name "NSU-Fiat." Under the terms of this agreement von Falkenhayn was forced to give up the small-car idea and settle financially with Porsche.

Project 12 plans had been thwarted again by unfavorable circumstances in the German automobile industry. But Porsche was patient; the merit of his design had been proven. He was confident his car eventually would become the car of the People; but in 1933 he had no idea of the strange circumstances under which the VW actually would be developed.

One Reutter bodied car was stored in 1940 in a remote and overgrown shed in the Hohenlohe area of Southern Germany. It survived the war. One day in 1945 an NSU employee located the car, obtained legal ownership, replaced the broken headlights, battery, and tires, and started using it as his personal vehicle. Though the odometer has registered over 200,000 miles, the car is reputedly still capable of 70 mph.

After the war the surviving NSU Type 32, with body by Reutter, suffered minor body modifications that disturbed its historic authenticity. The separate headlamps, which originally nestled in the fenders, were discarded, the depressions in the fenders where they were mounted were filled, and new lamps were inset low in the fenders. The bumper was also arbitrarily replaced with a later bumper. While these alterations tended perhaps to update the elderly car for its private owner, they were unfortunate in light of the car's historic significance.

On this page, by
reaching into the
future for a moment
for comparison with
an early model pro-
duction VW, the
reader may evaluate
how successfully the
little Austrian had
endured financial
drought and engineer-
ing condemnation, in
persisting with his
unorthodox concept
toward his eventual
goal. The Type 32
represented only the
car's Third incarna-
tion. How far Por-
sche had come! Yet,
how far he had yet
to go! After NSU a
progression of
lethal setbacks lay
waiting for the Volks-
wagen before *The
Idea* would culminate
in the omnipresent
VW of today.

4

ANGEL WITH HORNS

"The problem of a people's car will be attacked with courage, boldness and determination. What cannot be accomplished in one year, will, perhaps, be taken for granted in ten years."

Porsche began construction of his NSU prototypes in January, 1933. Germany was at that time sunk deep in depression, and politicians on another continent were promising their people "A chicken in every pot." An even more important event in the Volkswagen's life story occurred on January 30, 1933 — the day Adolph Hitler became Chancellor of Germany. Soon after he was to voice the chant, "A car in every family."

Hitler's love of automobiles could be traced back to his youth; but he was a shrewd politician first and foremost, and an auto enthusiast second. Hitler both envied and despised the American capitalist who drove to work. But after he read a biography of Henry Ford, it was a product of capitalism, the mass-produced automobile, that he wanted most for the German working man. What better means could he have found to consolidate his power and gain greater public support than to give the people a dependable yet inexpensive car?

A few days after his election Hitler gave the first of many bombastic political speeches at the opening of the annual Berlin Automobile Show. His oratory began to portray the pleasures of car ownership. He stressed the importance of small, economical cars, and he stated that the living standard of a nation was judged by the total length of its good highways.

Der Fuehrer also asserted that the prestige of a nation was upheld by its successes in international auto racing competition. Shortly after this auto show speech, Hitler called Porsche to Berlin. From this meeting came the Government-backed Auto-Union racing cars, which were soon to become world famous.

With his ascendancy to the Chancellory Adolph Hitler was able to expand his long-latent craze for cars. Oftentimes he would ride beside his driver when traveling around Germany on political excursions, sometimes pausing to chart the countryside with a view to the vast *Autobahnen* he proposed.

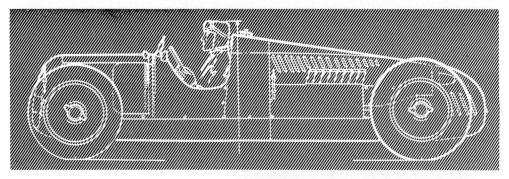

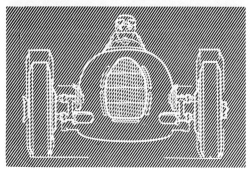

Hitler's motive in showing a keenness to re-establish Germany's eminence in the world of automobile engineering was to draw international prestige, which he hoped might distract attention from the country's still slippery economic status. His approach to Auto-Union led directly to a call for Dr. Porsche's attention to the project.

AUTO UNION RACING CARS

Porsche had always been interested in automobile racing, and perhaps his greatest accomplishments in racing design came during his work in the 1930's for the Auto-Union company. The international racing formula from 1934 to 1937 allowed an engine of any power and design as long as the total weight of the car did not exceed 1600 lbs.

Porsche designed such a car on his own initiative in 1933. It had a 45 degree, V-16 engine, maximum speed of 182 mph, maximum rpm of 4500, a displacement of 4358 cc, and a 7:1 compression ratio. The engine was mounted in the rear, and the suspension was by torsion bars, similar to VW. When representatives from Auto-Union came to Porsche in 1933 and asked him to design a racing car for their new factory racing team, Porsche simply sold them this design. Auto-Union took over the building and racing of the car. The car was continuously improved in design and performance from 1934 until 1937, when the international formula was changed.

It happened that Porsche already had just such a car on the drawing boards, unsponsored since its beginning in November 1932. A supercharged, sixteen-cylinder power package had evolved in a chassis of novel suspension, as Porsche had transplanted the Grand Prix formula rules of the time into his own original concept. But this largely unique suspension, which introduced trailing arms, torsion bars and the swing axle, proved precursor to that VW one day would make universal.

Once the Auto-Union cars were on their way to world fame Hitler's promotion—much of it by telephone from his suite in the Berlin Kaiserhof Hotel—took a new direction, to generate a scheme that only was to reach full flower long years after its financial angel with horns had been buried beneath the rubble of even bigger schemes gone awry.

One of Hitler's closest confidants, Jacob Werlin, who previously had been associated with Daimler-Benz, visited Porsche's office in Stuttgart in the autumn of 1933. Through Werlin's influence Hitler called Porsche to Berlin again for a secret meeting. Hitler instructed Porsche at this meeting to prepare a memorandum for the government, describing his ideas of small car design.

HITLER'S SMALL CAR CONCEPT

In this conference with Porsche at the Kaiserhof Hotel in Berlin Hitler set forth his own five-point conception of what a People's car should be:

1. Speed	For the great new *Autobahnen* (then under construction), the car had to be capable of a sustained speed of 100 km/h (slightly over 60 mph). Previous small cars had never approached this performance.
2. Economy	Gasoline consumption could be no more than 7 liters per 100 km, or approximately 33 mpg; the car also had to be economical to repair.
3. Family size	Seating must accommodate four or five persons. "We cannot separate the children from the parents," said Hitler.
4. Air cooling	The vast majority of owners had no garages. They would have to leave their cars outside all year round, and the hazard of a frozen radiator must be eliminated. The engine must be air-cooled.
5. Low purchase price	The car had to sell for less than RM 1000 ($250).

During his tenure at various motor car makers Dr. Porsche had enjoyed a faithful association with Karl Rabe, all but continuously since 1913. While Porsche personally directed all projects, he relied on Rabe for formal engineering details. It was Rabe who held the title of Chief Engineer for Porsche's engineering office. The two were great friends; Rabe enjoyed the challenges in Porsche's system of stimulating advanced design by insisting on a variety of solutions to every problem, in turn resolved by group discussion and criticism.

In a discussion with Rabe and Kales, Porsche decided to take the NSU *Volksauto* as a basis and refine its design. Porsche's memo to the Government on January 17, 1934, was simply acknowledged by the Ministry of Transport. Then for eight long weeks of waiting Porsche received no word from the government. In the interval he continued his work on racing cars.

Auto-Union's racing fame began in 1934 when the official factory team—led by Hans Stuck, the old mountain-climbing champion from Austro-Daimler days in the Twenties—pressed on to victory in the German Grand Prix. Success in the Swiss Grand Prix followed soon after.

Attributes of the then unique swing axle, trailing arm suspension and rear engine placement features were proven in a crucible of racing as the 650 horsepower V-16 Auto-
Union car followed Hans Stuck's first victory with a string of major victories in speed
events all across Europe.

The first major victory by the Auto-Union car came in the Grand Prix of Germany
in 1934; and the Auto-Union racing team shared with that of Daimler-Benz nearly every
major auto racing honor in the next three years. Auto-Union even brought the car to
America for the 1937 Vanderbilt Cup race, in which Bernd Rosemeyer drove the car to
victory.

At the beginning of the Freiburg hill-climb dash in 1937, Germany's ace driver Bernd
Rosemeyer awaits the green flag. Visible across the starting line is a string used to assure
uniform starting. Later in the year Rosemeyer drove his Auto-Union to prestige for
Germany on a new continent when he captured the Vanderbilt Cup at Long Island, N. Y.

Hans Stuck, who has remained prominent as a driver to recent times, behind the wheel of the Auto-Union during the *Bergpreis* at the Grossglockner hill-climb in the Austrian Alps. The cars had undergone continuous changes through the years, and by this event in 1939 a more streamlined nose form was in service.

Auto-Union also developed various streamlined versions of the car for speed record attempts in 1937 and 1938. Rosemeyer was the first man to travel over 250 mph on a normal road — in a flying three miles on the *Autobahn* between Frankfurt and Darmstadt. Rosemeyer was later killed in the last of these speed record attempts near Leipzig when his streamlined car was swept off the *Autobahn* by a gust of wind early in 1938; it was believed he was traveling close to 275 mph at the time of his accident.

Bernd Rosemeyer confers with the Auto-Union's designer before record runs on the *Autobahn* with the full streamlined version of the car, at a site near Frankfurt in 1937. Hitler's government support of Auto-Union's endeavors, the whole impetus behind the world-known racing team, coincidentally, afforded Dr. Porsche a proving ground for engineering features that was to bring a robust heart to his concurrent project—the People's Car.

Germany's new Chancellor, a convincing speechmaker, mustered support for much that he proposed. One of his early "promises"—at first only a light reference by a professional politician carried away by the smoothness of his own tongue—stirred such rapport from the German people that Hitler recognized it as an issue worthy of development to advance his own stead.

The next Berlin Auto Show came in March, 1934, and Hitler made there another of his now typical political speeches. This time he irrevocably committed himself and the motor industry to a wild and wonderful dream, when he said:

".... It is a bitter feeling to know that millions of good, industrious, and able people are excluded from the use of a means of transportation that could become for them a source of unknown joy — especially on Sundays and Holidays. The problem is one that will be attacked with courage, boldness, and determination. What cannot be accomplished in one year, will, perhaps, be taken for granted in ten years."

Der Fuehrer had spoken, and his words resounded among the working classes as the promise of a brighter future — a change in outlook from defeat and depression to hope and prosperity.

But to the *Reichsverband der deutschen Automobilindustrie,* an organization of all producers in the German motor industry, Hitler's words foreshadowed only confusion. The German auto makers did not see how a car could be produced cheaply enough for the middle classes, much less for the great mass of German workers. They regarded Hitler's words merely as political propaganda, and no one suspected development of a small car soon would be included in the official Nazi Government budget.

With imagination afire from Hitler's national pledge, various independent firms, some comparatively obscure, undertook to draft their own *deutschen Volkswagen** models, then gave token publicity—as with this published ad—in hopes of encouragement from *der Fuehrer*. This motorcycle maker's proposal, like others of the period, failed to secure official recognition and quietly advanced from bid to oblivion.

Volkswagen* appears with capital **V not as a trademark name here, but by German language rule capitalizing every noun. Reference is simply to a German people's car.

Porsche too was beginning to have doubts whether the *Volksauto* would ever become a reality. The Minister of Transport advised him after the show that there would be a delay in the small-car project. Porsche's suggested price of RM 1500 was considered too high, and the Ministry recommended in the meantime he give thought to the problem of reducing costs.

Werlin reestablished contact with Porsche in June, 1934, relaying a definite order to continue development of the VW. Hitler sought to solve the cost problem in an "administrative" way: various car producers were to supply components for a common design by Porsche, and the official sponsor of the project was to be the Society of German Automobile Manufacturers.

Porsche's immediate task was to build three prototypes. The Auto Makers' Society authorized an inadequate budget of RM 200,000 and, adding insult to injury, imposed the unreasonably short deadline of ten months for prototype construction. To conserve time and money, Porsche installed a workshop in his garage in Stuttgart; there the work on "VW Series 3" was started. Porsche simply had to carry through the small-car designs which he had used in the ill-fated *Zundapp* and *NSU Volksautos*.

Perhaps the first photograph of a Volkswagen "prototype" was this shot which appears to be a small scale model of the Series 3, deceptively ensconced before a full-scale hedgerow as an outdoor backdrop, to lead the casual viewer to "see" the car in full size.

Each Winter the motor makers marked the opening of their auto show by personally touring Adolph Hitler and his military aides through the hall for the first look and touch. As the years passed and *der Fuhrer* managed to further his prematurely celebrated People's Car project to their private dismay, the automobile executives adopted a stringently two-faced role, as they graciously conducted their leader through a showing of their competitive wares.

By the time Hitler spoke at the 1935 Berlin Automobile Show his dream had taken on a semblance of form. Dr. Porsche was readying prototypes of his aircooled rear-engined small car and the annual talk now detailed his development. While the usual cheers came from Nazi Party stalwarts and the general public showed great enthusiasm, those within the German auto industry privately were antagonized anew by this progress report.

As he droned on about his favorite project the word "Volkswagen" was heard again and again. In English language terms it would have appeared that Hitler had coined a trade name, whereas in truth it was only generic reference to a yet nameless people's car, for in German *every* noun receives capitalization. Only years after the Third Reich had become but a sorrowful memory, with the advent of postwar production, was VW to become a trademark title.

HITLER COMPLIMENTS AMERICA

Contrary to his usual attitude, Hitler paid America a great compliment at the opening of the Berlin Auto Show of 1936. His opening remarks were: "I do not doubt that the outstanding ability of the designer and at a later date the economic acumen of the manufacturers, will make it possible to make available to the German People a car which is low priced and cheap in operation, similar to what the American people have enjoyed for a long time . . . ."

Herr Schickelgruber had failed to mention that an American in 1936 had to work only 300 hours to own his car, while at the estimated price for the Volkswagen, the German worker would require 800 hours.

Porsche and his small staff of engineers — including Rabe, Kales, and Porsche's son, Ferry — concentrated only on the technical aspects of the enterprise, without concerning themselves with the politics of the VW. Design and construction of the prototypes dragged well past the arbitrary ten month deadline, as a number of power plant problems were met and licked. Refinements were also made to the unorthodox chassis and suspension. Porsche, fully aware of the hostility his small-car project created in the established German auto industry, was more than ever concerned that the VW Series 3 pilot cars would prove their worth when they were handed over to the Society of Manufacturers for testing.

Twenty-eight months after Porsche received the initial authority from the Nazi Government, the gestation of the beetle in Porsche's Stuttgart garage was completed. Three prototypes — which motor industry critics immediately dubbed "ugly ducklings"— were turned over to the Society for study on October 12, 1936.

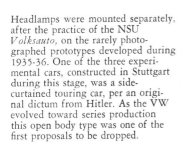

Headlamps were mounted separately, after the practice of the NSU *Volksauto,* on the rarely photographed prototypes developed during 1935-36. One of the three experimental cars, constructed in Stuttgart during this stage, was a side-curtained touring car, per an original dictum from Hitler. As the VW evolved toward series production this open body type was one of the first proposals to be dropped.

While the German people had been kept apprised of progress toward the People's Car, early test running on public roads was not scheduled for public relations value, and secrecy was the watchword. Even an inquisitive police officer was lightly dissuaded when he approached the test drivers with the question they were trained not to hear: *"Was ist das?"*

Testing began at once. Strenuous around-the-clock runs were conducted over a distance of 30,000 miles. Herr Emil Vorwig, the technical director of the Society, interpreted the test results:

> On the whole the test cars proved themselves on the 50,000 km trip. The structure proved itself suitable, the faults and shortcomings discovered are not of a basic nature and can presumably be corrected without great difficulty. Certain components, such as the front axle and brakes, require more testing for their further development. The gas and oil consumption falls within acceptable limits. The driving capabilities and characteristics of the car are good. The Volkswagen shows attributes which recommend further development.

After performance of the three hand-built cars confirmed the design's general worthiness thirty additional units, incorporating improvements from the original test data, were built in series for further testing, in 1937. This run retained the familiar front-opening doors and small, forward hatch opening from the prototypes, while its headlamps, following a trend among several makes of the time, were filleted into the fenders.

One of Porsche's staff road tests a
Series 3 prototype chassis during the
winter of 1935-36 on the premises
at Stuttgart.

The appearance of no other automobile could have brought the *Käfer* (beetle) sooner to mind; the
nickname attached itself to the shape of the VW from the first. A high, louvered section at the back
had been emphasized in the design of the Series 3 by the absence of a conventional rear window.

One burdening point of concern, however, was the car's weight. In order to
conform with Hitler's weight specifications, inexpensive cast iron would have
to give way to more costly light metal alloys. It was difficult to believe the car
could be sold anywhere near the proposed price of RM 1000. The People's Car
was yet far from production.

Quite reasonably the Society of German Automobile Manufacturers wanted
no further part of the Volkswagen project, which conceivably could put them
out of business or at least damage their market to a great extent. Their reluctance to participate in the development of the VW became apparent **even to**
Hitler. In December, 1936, the Ministry of Transport requested and received
the complete set of VW test and prototype records.

Daimler-Benz had readied its own small, rear-engine, two-door sedan, the Type 130 for 1935,
concurrent with its reluctant cooperation with Porsche in the development of the competition. It
was a product of free enterprise and was necessarily priced at many times Hitler's boasted price
for the *KdF*. Among the other car makers there was only utter contempt for Dr. Porsche's
People's Car.

OPEL'S "VOLKSWAGEN"

Hitler was being guided with his usual entourage of Nazi bigwigs through the exhibits of the 1937 Berlin Motor Show. When he stopped at the exhibit of Opel products, he was greeted warmly by Herr von Opel, who directed Hitler's attention to a small, nice-looking car standing on an Opel display stand. A sign on the car read, "RM 1400 — Opel's latest — The economical car for the small man." Opel said proudly, *"This* is our 'Volkswagen,' Opel's obtuse remark bittingly reconfirmed to Hitler the tongue-in-cheek support the whole German auto industry was lending to his state-sponsored design.

Opel soon learned the consequences of acting independently, contrary to Hitler's wishes. A few days after the show the *Reichstag* enacted laws restricting the supply and distribution of iron and steel. Although no specific reference was ever made to any personal disagreement between Opel and Hitler by the government ration offices, every subsequent application by Opel executives for steel to build the small car was refused; the light Opel never was produced.

At this stage *der Fuehrer* realized that a separate company had to be established by him if his People's Car project was to be carried through to production. He and Robert Ley, head of the *Deutsche Arbeitsfront* and Minister of Labor, discussed all the VW data; action was soon forthcoming. A Government-owned company was chartered to perfect the VW design and build production facilities. The project was financed from the treasury of the *Deutsche Arbeitsfront*, the Nazi Party Labor organization. Porsche was installed at the helm of the new VW development company in February, 1937, with Werlin and Dr. Bodo Lafferentz as members of the board. Now encouraged for the first time to develop his car with secure financial backing, Porsche set out to perfect the Volkswagen with fresh vigor.

Thirty prototypes of the ugly duckling were finished later that year with assistance from the shops of Daimler-Benz. This improved design was called the "VW Series 30." A crew of 200 Stormtroopers, chosen at random from the ranks, carried out an extensive and punishing series of secret tests on the Series 30 in order to discover the bugs in this potential production model as quickly as possible.

The first series production, constructed with the assistance of Daimler-Benz by Nazi Government order, were finished to showroom standards, and road tested extensively. Performance records compiled by Ferry Porsche from this pilot run made it clear to the builders that the Volkswagen idea was emerging at last as a basically sound light car design.

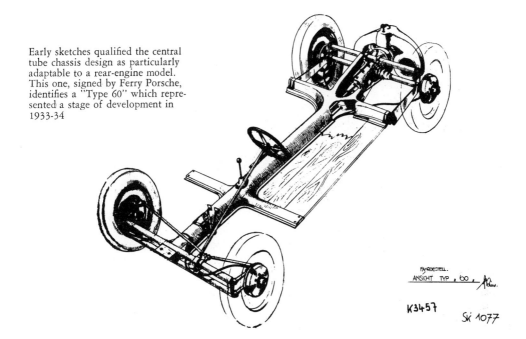

Early sketches qualified the central tube chassis design as particularly adaptable to a rear-engine model. This one, signed by Ferry Porsche, identifies a "Type 60" which represented a stage of development in 1933-34

FAHRGESTELL.
ANSICHT TYP . 60 .
K3457   Sk 1077

The cars were produced without a budget ceiling such as would have been imposed in a private enterprise, and expenditures ran into the millions of Reichsmarks. The test cars traversed a total distance of 18 million miles, under all driving conditions, over the *Autobahnen* of Germany and backroads in the Alps. But the car which emerged from the ordeal was sensational.

As consultant on many other government projects during the Thirties, Porsche once tested a series of tractor prototypes toward the end of a "People's Tractor". One model explored his time-proven electric hub motors with power from a gas generator. Several license numbers reappear on various Porsche-built vehicles in this period. These were assigned to the engineering office and transferred loosely among the test vehicles.

Formal pomp and ceremony characterized the laying of the cornerstone at Wolfsburg. Somehow, construction material was allocated almost on schedule and the vast, mile-long plant took form according to plan.

THE WOLFSBURG FACTORY

Selecting Wolfsburg as the factory site was the work of Dr. Bodo Lafferentz, an economics expert and lecturer as well as assistant to Robert Ley in the *DAF*. Looking for an area accessible by both railroads and canals, Lafferentz studied maps until he decided on Lower Saxony as the general locale. He then surveyed the countryside from a low-flying airplane to select the exact location. His choice was a twenty square mile parcel of land taking up two-thirds of the estate of Count von Schulenberg (which surrounded the 14th century Wolfsburg castle) and one-fourth of the adjoining estate belonging to Herr von Wense. The desired land was quickly confiscated by the government — the owners receiving "compensation on Government appraisal terms" — and ground was broken for the huge plant on the bank of the Mittelland canal. The foundation stone was laid in a ceremony attended by Adolf Hitler on May 26, 1938.

The task of designing the plant that would produce a car for the People had at first been assigned to the architectural department of Braunschweig University; but later, through the efforts of Werlin, the job was reassigned to Herr Peter Koller, a relatively unknown engineer for the small town of Augsburg. Hitler's favorite architect and Koller's former teacher, Inspector-General of Building Herr Speer, acted as consultant.

The factory was to be built on a scale unheard of in all Europe. All the energy and resources at the command of the Third *Reich* were devoted to construction. Proposed production in the primary stage called for a first shift of 10,000 men and a second shift of 7,500 men, producing an annual total of 400,000 cars. In the second stage an expansion to 30,000 workers was planned with a quota of 800,000 to 1,000,000 units yearly.

Koller's plans were officially approved by Hitler early in 1938; and construction of the mammoth plant began as soon as material reached the site. Koller at the same time drew up the plans for the city of Wolfsburg, which at that time of course did not exist, including apartments and community facilities for 15,000 families. By the beginning of the war only 2500 units had been completed; and the foreign prisoners who worked in the factory during the war were housed in semi-permanent barracks. Hitler did make one change in Koller's plans; he forbade construction of the two churches which Koller had designed for the city of Wolfsburg. After the war Koller was invited back to construct one of the two churches, and it now stands as a universally admired monument of modern architecture.

Oblivious to geopolitics, Porsche continued his activities strictly on a technical basis. Porsche made visits to the U.S.A. with close associates to recruit key American-trained German engineers to return to their homeland and operate the new VW factory. Hitler had boasted earlier that the VW plant "will be the most modern in the world . . . ."; but Germany lacked enough trained engineers to set up such a gargantuan factory. Porsche's trip met with some success, and American engineering skill helped set up the great plant in 1938 and 1939. Many of the heavy tools to equip the VW plant also were purchased in the United States.

PORSCHE IN DEARBORN

On Porsche's second visit to the United States his party was hosted by the Ford Motor Company at the Dearborn Inn. A tour of the vast Ford industries climaxed for Dr. Porsche in a meeting with Henry and Edsel Ford. While interpreters bridged their language handicap, the intense common interest in light motor car design and manufacture brought a warmth to the exchange between Ford and Porsche. Ford had heard of Hitler's plans to build a practical everyday car for the working man in Germany and of the great plant that was under construction to produce the people's car. He indicated interest; but Ford was hardly concerned about any effect the VW might have on the U.S. automaker's market in Germany. When Porsche described the proposed VW Ford is said to have replied. "If you can build better and cheaper cars than I can, then it serves me right." There was no basis for either man to conject that a generation later VW was to become the most universally known car of all.

Bound for home after the voyage to America to recruit German-born technicians, Dr. Porsche is seen on shipboard with his son-in-law, the late Dr. Anton Piëch, then a partner in the engineering office, and the appointed administrative head of the Wolfsburg plant.

Hermann Goering, seen here with his cohort in an early Thirties pose at the Kaiserhof Hotel in Berlin, bowed to an insatiable penchant for gadgets. When he had become No. 2 Madman in the Nazi regime, and was "liberating" the classic art works from museums all across Europe for his own personal collection, his powder-blue Mercedes-Benz carried every conceivable device down to facilities for heating water

GOERING'S FASCINATION FOR MODELS

Although German manufacturers could build some of the machines for the new VW factory, many of the larger machine tools could only be obtained from the U.S.A. The Nazis were not overwhelmingly enthusiastic about spending dollars for American equipment; so Werlin undertook to persuade Hermann Goering, the man who authorized government dollar expenditures, that these tools were necessary and that much would be saved if the machines were bought from America.

Werlin, a born salesman, knew that Goering was a passionate collector of mechanical whatnots. His rooms were filled with guns, tools, and models of machines. Thus, whenever Porsche wanted a specific tool, Werlin would make up chrome-plated show samples of the machine's product, present them to Goering, explain the machine's use in the factory, and then request that the dollar expenditure be made. In a short time Goering's approval for purchase of the American machines would come through.

Goering enjoyed letting the models and parts accumulate in his office, and he spent his spare moments sorting through them. The shiny VW parts also impressed Hitler with his sidekick's intense interest in the Volkswagen project. Goering's collection drew much comment among associates; and even Hitler needled him occasionally about assembling a complete car from the pile of parts in his office.

Porsche and his staff continued to modify and improve the VW design. From the Series 30 cars shortcomings and recommended modifications evolved the production design designated by Porsche and his staff as the Volkswagen "Series 38." Hitler approved this model as essentially suitable for production. At last he had something concrete to back up his flag-waving and drumbeating before the German people.

THE ORIGINAL TYPE 38

Adequate air-cooling was one of the problems that plagued development through the various VW prototypes. In exposed-cylinder motorcycle design the rush of air past the open cylinders traditionally provided sufficient cooling. But a strong assist from an additional force of air was required to do the job in an enclosed rear-engine automobile layout.

The Zundapp prototypes were water-cooled, but they also drew air from the windstream along the side of the car at the rear quarter. Later, in the NSU *Volksauto* prototype, it appeared that adequate air might be taken from the topstream through a louvred area at the rear. Prototypes of this style ran hotter than desired.

Porsche and his staff then developed an impressive high-output blower in the NSU *Volksauto* models to kick the air at an accelerated rate through passageways surrounding the cylinders.

Changing the air intake from the side to the rear had allowed more latitude in styling; but at the same time the blowing fan required an unreasonable volume of outside air. The Series 30 was designed with louvred sections and ducting along the backbone, but the louvred area was so large that it precluded a rear window.

Out of the extensive testing given these cars grew evidence that the blower system could be boosted to greater internal efficiency; and Porsche's crew was successful in achieving this result. The need for a blast of outside air was diminished; less area was required for air intake on the back. Porsche made the louvred area correspondingly minimal, rearranged the ducting, relocated the fuel tank up front, and once again put in a rear window.

The pronounced beetle-like styling, which had been developed somewhat around the high louvring at the rear, now could be softened and refined. Body changes at this time included adoption of front-hinged doors, replacing the prototypes' rear-hinged doors. Front hinging allowed better rear-seat access in a two-door sedan package and afforded the added safety from doors that would tend to close when in motion, rather than to spread open. The rear side window also assumed its present larger form.

From these changes in the Series 30 came the final design known as the Model 38, designated by the year of its development and destined to remain virtually intact for more than a generation to come.

With a showing of the first series-built Model 38 cars, the design breakthrough from the primitive peculiarities of the 30 was clear cut. The old oversize, canted doors of the predecessor had been replaced by doors with vertical pillars; the plateau top had yielded to a restrained rib design in the molding on either side of the top, which joined in a loop on the deck lid. The VW had assumed a balanced appearance that would stand through many hard times to come.

Upon finalizing the production design and completion of the factory, a pilot assembly line handmade a few Type 38's, which found their way into the hands of high-ranking Nazis. The car was publicized to the Germans as the *KdF*, after the Labor Front slogan *"Kraft durch Freude"* (Strength through Joy).

Heavy propaganda overtones in the State sponsorship of the VW development program had always been overlooked at the engineering company. Dr. Porsche and all about him ignored politics both officially and unofficially, and lived only to bring about fruition of their engineering designs— prominent among which was the Volkswagen. Dr. Porsche's immediate perception of the effective was amazing. He could stand at the design board of his son or one of his engineers and say, "This isn't practical. Change it . . . like this." With a few lines he would then show what he meant.

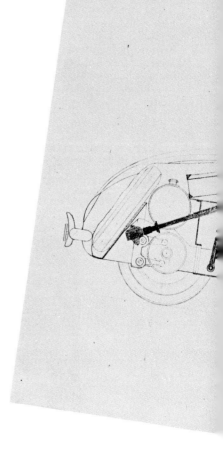

For a time it appeared that the *Kraft durch Freude* organization, through which the car was to be merchandised, would succeed in burying the original designation for the car in favor of its own initials, and nameplates and hub caps were prepared bearing the *KdF*. But the old name, a "natural" to begin with, had been publicly associated with Porsche's project for a long time, and it proved too widespread to kill. Not long after, the car came to be known permanently as the *Volkswagen*.

As the program reached the state where orders were to be solicited, promotion of the car was applied through every avenue at the State's command. The "plum" depicted on a postage issue advertising the 1939 International Automobile Show was a *KdF* car speeding a happy family along the *Autobahn*.

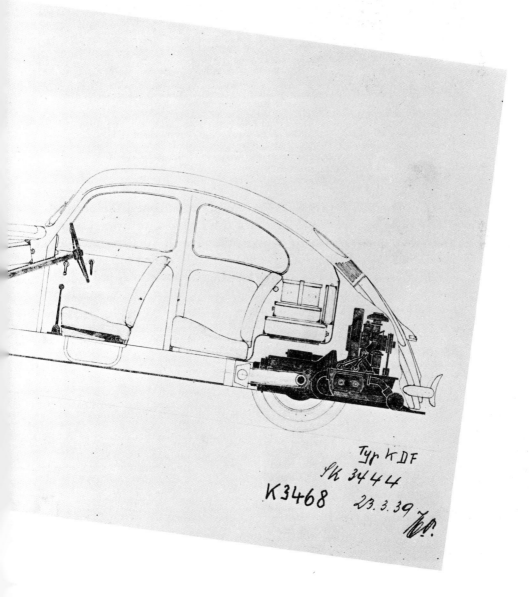

If the factory cornerstone ceremony had been staged grandly the year before, it was dwarfed by the fanfare surrounding Hitler's dedication exercises at the completion of construction. Flanked by actual *KdF* sedan samples, he spoke rather convincingly as he described a rosy future for all The elusive People's Car , so long in coming, stood before the very eyes of the assemblage at last.

A sales drive, launched with full Nazi Party fanfare, outlined the purchasing procedure. The only financial requirements for a buyer were weekly five-mark subscription payments. The little Rhineland jeweler in Burscheid and the baker in the *Schwaebisch* village of Beutelsbach, licking their first *KdF* savings stamps, felt securely on their way to becoming car owners at last.

Early handbuilt units were immediately employed in a closely scheduled display at Nazi political meetings geographically spread over principal cities in Germany. As more cars came off the line some few even were used privately by Nazi bigwigs. Wherever they appeared in traffic for the first time the People, who had heard so much and seen so little, swarmed over them like bees.

Der KdF Wagen

Wie der Wagen beantragt
erspart
versichert
und geliefert wird.

Ausschaltung aller Unklarheiten

Seit die DAF. begonnen hat, Aufträge für den KdF.=Wagen entgegenzunehmen, ist in verschiedenen Veröffentlichungen der Weg geschildert worden, der zum Erwerb des Volkswagens führt. Wie aber der Fragensturm bei allen Dienststellen von „Kraft durch Freude" beweist, besteht noch eine ganze Reihe von Unklarheiten, falschen Auffassungen und unzutreffenden Vermutungen. Aus diesem Grunde beantworten wir nachstehend klar und gültig in einer großen Zusammenfassung alle Fragen, die über Erwerb und Einzelheiten des KdF.=Wagens gestellt werden können.

1 *Wer kann einen KdF.-Wagen erwerben?* Jeder deutsche Volksgenosse.

2 *Was kostet der KdF.-Wagen?* Es sind zu unterscheiden Innenlenker (Limousine), Innenlenker mit Faltdach (Kabrio=limousine), und offener Wagen. Der Preis für den Innenlenker beträgt 990.- RM., der Innenlenker mit Faltdach hat wegen der höheren Produktionskosten einen Aufschlag in der Höhe von 60.- RM. Der offene Wagen wird in den ersten Produktionsjahren noch nicht gebaut; Bestellungen können daher bis auf weiteres nicht abgegeben werden.

3 *Wie wird der Antrag gestellt?* Die Interessenten müssen sich ein Antragsformular, das bei jeder DAF.= und KdF.=Dienststelle ausliegt, beschaffen, es ausfüllen und persönlich unterschreiben. Bei Ehefrauen, bezw. Minderjährigen ist außerdem die Unterschrift des Ehemannes bezw. des gesetzlichen Vertreters erforderlich. Das ausgefüllte Antragsformular wird bei dem zuständigen KdF.=Wart des Betriebes, bezw. der KdF.=Ortsdienststelle abgegeben. Nach Prüfung der Angaben des Antragstellers erhält dieser gegen eine Gebühr von 1.- RM. die erste KdF.=Wagen=Sparkarte.

4 *In welchen Raten kann gespart werden?* Mit der Entgegennahme der Sparkarte und der Bezahlung der Gebühr verpflichtet sich der Sparer, für den Erwerb des KdF.=Wagens wöchentlich mindestens RM. 5.- in Sparmarken zu entrichten. Die Sparmarken sind in allen DAF.= und KdF.=Dienststellen zu haben. Es ist aber auch möglich, in höheren Beträgen, die durch fünf teilbar sind, zu sparen, so daß entsprechende Mengen von Sparmarken gekauft werden können. Notwendig ist es jedoch, daß wöchentlich gespart wird. Die Sparbeträge sind nicht begrenzt, auch eine größere Anzahlung kann geleistet werden. Die Erlegung des Gesamtpreises durch den Erwerb einer entsprechenden Anzahl von Sparmarken ist gestattet. Ein Kauf des Wagens gegen Barzahlung, d. h. ohne Eintritt in das Sparsystem, ist jedoch ausgeschlossen.

5 *Wie kommt man zu Sonderausführungen?* Wählt ein Sparer eine Sonderausführung, z. B. die Kabriolimousine, so kann er den Mehrbetrag von 60.- RM. durch Erwerb von besonderen Sparmarken im Werte von je 4.- RM. entrichten. Hierfür sind auf der 2. bis 4. Karte eigene Felder vorgesehen. Das gleiche gilt für die Transportkosten, sofern der Wagen nicht vom Werk selbst abgeholt, sondern in der zuständigen Gaustadt in Empfang genommen wird.

6 *Wie wird versichert?* Mit dem Erwerb jeder Sparmarke in Höhe von 5.- RM. ist die eigentliche Kaufpreisrate, sowie auch ein entsprechender Anteil der Versicherungsprämie gedeckt. Der KdF.=Wagen ist für die Dauer von zwei Jahren ab Verlassen des Werkes gegen Haftpflicht und beschränkt gegen Kasko versichert, um dadurch den Sparer bei eventuellen Unfällen usw. zu schützen, und um den gesetzlichen Anforderungen zu genügen. Die Zweijahresprämie konnte auf den Gesamtbetrag von 200.- RM. beschränkt werden.

KdF PURCHASE PLAN

The Nazi Labor organization, under the directorship of Robert Ley, established a savings system leading to the purchase of a VW. This plan was to enable the average worker to buy a VW by purchasing a weekly minimum of RM 5 worth of savings stamps. The *KdF* car was not for sale through conventional dealers, but only through the local *DAF* Labor offices; nor could the car be purchased for cash — only through the government savings stamp plan. The money raised by this plan was not diverted to armament production, nor was it used to build the VW factory, which was financed directly through the *DAF* treasury. The money was put in a special fund and kept intact, although no interest was paid on this savings to the stamp holders.

The brochure reproduced here describes the method of savings and purchase. The three models which were to be produced — a closed sedan, a Cabriolet-sedan, and an open car — were available only in blue-grey. Special arrangements were included in the plan for the RM 60 higher cost of the Cabriolet and for two years liability and collision insurance after purchase. The normal method of distribution required the worker to travel to the Wolfsburg factory to pick up his car.

KdF

Even before the Wolfsburg plant was ready to roll, the Nazi government had committed its principal national raw product to support politica! aggression. Assemblies of the civilian sedan became only token, starved for material from the beginning. Agencies with higher priority for steel and aluminum siphoned off the very makings of the *KdF* wagen before it reached Wolfsburg.

CRITICS AND SUBSCRIBERS

While a national enthusiasm for the *KdF* program appeared to support the People's Car without reservation, critics of the car both within and outside of Germany were many. Their criticism ranged all the way to portraits of the whole car plan as a nationwide confidence game in which the VW car itself would never be distributed. Much Nazi publicity surrounded initial deliveries of the VW to officials of the Party in order to convey the idea that the car was actually in production for delivery.

More than RM 280 Million, an average saving of RM 400 per *Kdf* card holder, were raised through the subscription plan.

Ironically, Hitler's wild dream to motorize his people might soon have become a reality had he not forgotten it in a nightmare of world aggression. He ordered the German army first into Austria, then Sudeten Germany, and finally Czechoslovakia and Poland — plunging the world into a war that shattered the hopes of little men everywhere.

It was for another Germany in a new generation to take the dream of the People's Car and turn it into the reality of a fantastic universal acceptance surpassing even *der Fuehrer's* original concept of a motorized *Volk*.

KdF CARD HOLDERS VS. A NEW GERMANY

A decade later, in the new country which would emerge from the ashes of the eventually defeated Third Reich, those who had faithfully filled in their coupon books would organize to press claim for credit toward purchase of the Volkswagen which by then, under new direction, had genuinely come to be. Their hopes would rise and fall repeatedly as low and high courts would toss the claim around for twelve years more, generally summarizing dismissal with an opinion, in effect, that the demise of the *Reichmark* after the war terminated as well claims by individuals against the Nazi government.

But KdF book holders eventually were to fair well for their persistence. In far off 1961 their claim would be recognized by Heinz Nordhoff. Settlements would begin in October, with complete book holders receiving 600 DM credit toward purchase, or a generous 100 DM in cash — for at ten to one, the original 990 RM exchanged to only 99 DM.

5

LEFT OBLIQUE...MARCH!

In the military version's lightness lay its charm. Unfailing performance in both arid desert and freezing arctic spoke eloquently for the air-cooled engine.

It was summer, 1943. The German armies stood deep in Russia. In the past weeks their enemy had retreated beyond the Don River. Where the retreat had been rapid, Russian units often fell behind, losing themselves between the two armies in the vast Russian steppes.

Near Kalatch, where the east bank of the Don drops steeply to the water, infantry captain Grusenko halted his company. They dug in some hundred yards back from the river bank in a heavy thicket, where they could keep the river and the desolate plains lying beyond under observation. There they waited.

For a few days nothing happened. Grusenko was worried. He could make no contact with his superiors and was uninformed about the local battle situation. But the *Politcommissar* was still with the unit, so Grusenko had no choice but fidelity to the Russian cause.

Then, on a clear, dew-fresh morning, as the sun rose dramatically over the horizon, Comrade Private Stofanov heard a noise from the river. He woke the captain, who woke the *Politcommissar*. Together they waited and watched. Suddenly a little vehicle, looking rather like an old-fashioned kneading trough, rolled from the bank onto the level ground and approached the thicket. "Germanski!" snarled the *Commissar* between his teeth, and motioned Stofanov to make ready his gun. Grusenko deployed his company for a capture. His strategy was to capture the Germans alive and possibly find out from them how the war was going.

The Germans were riding along with all the caution of a family on a weekend outing. When they had advanced to a point from which the *Commissar* felt they could not retreat, he ordered Stofanov to fire. At the first shot the company stormed forth with a shout, fully expecting the Germans to surrender.

Germany's total effort for war reached Dr. Porsche's design office when a Nazi governmental order came to adapt the Volkswagen chassis for use in the *Wehrmacht* (German Army). Porsche, anticipating such a request, already had made some notes on the subject, and soon the plant was retooling for models which certainly the *KdF* card holders had never dreamed of.

Two versions of the German People's Car were designed for the *Wehrmacht*. Soon the cars were being built and supplied to the Nazi regime in some quantity. A box-like, four-door, four-passenger touring car appeared early, followed three years later by the amphibious model shown here.

But, to the Russians' surprise, their quarry whipped the motorized kneading trough around and with devilish speed headed back for the riverbank.

"Ah, the Germanskis," screamed Stofanov, "they'll drown like rats!" Stupefied, he watched the little wagon drive down the slope, roll into the water, and swim away like a duck. "Holy Mother of Kasan," Stofanov exclaimed, "now the Germanskis build cars that drive on water!"

What soldier Stofanov had seen was nothing more than an amphibious military version of the Volkswagen. That this machine belonged to the enemy did not surprise him, for those Germanskis were known to build all kinds of fiendish things which were strange to Stofanov's simple peasant mind.

Hitler's totalitarian regime had diverted the German technical genius from wagons of the People to machines of destruction. Shortly after the first pilot production of a few civilian VW Series 38 Sedans for promotional and personal use by Nazi Party bigwigs, Hitler marched his troops into Poland. He knew then that the Second World War was under way, and a total effort to produce the tools of war followed. Hitler transformed the VW dream of the German *Volk* into a nightmare of grotesque military machines, as Germany's vast civilian industrial potential was converted to wartime production.

Dr. Porsche and his staff were pressed into sidetracking the VW sedan project in favor of a lightweight military vehicle, and Porsche went ahead with plans for a machine based on the already developed *KdF* engine and chassis. Porsche always stayed aloof from politics; he designed military vehicles and weapons for the Nazi regime simply because the various designing problems posed a challenge to him. He finished the wartime vehicle in record time, then later continued to modify and improve it.

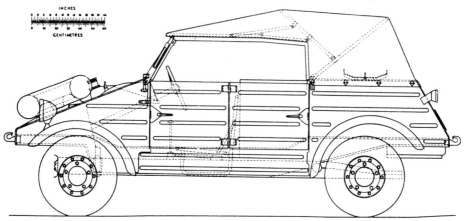

Fig. 1.—Body, side elevation

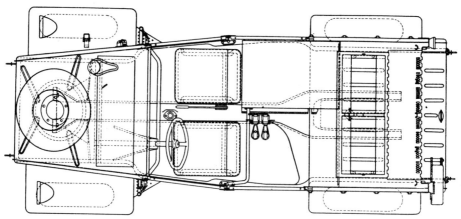

Fig. 2.—Body, plan

Allied studies of the VW actually began as early as 1941 when British Intelligence fell upon a *Kuebelwagen* and spirited it to London for examination by motor industrialists.

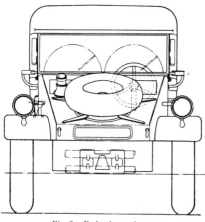

Fig. 3.—Body, front view

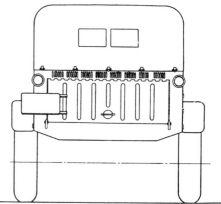

Fig. 4.—Body, rear view

The VW factory, which had stood virtually idle ever since the first few Series 38 cars had been assembled, was converted hastily to various types of weapon production. The VW factory served as an emergency plant, making whatever the armies needed most at the time. When the VW military vehicle was ready for production, the German War department discovered that there were no adequate welding tools in the Wolfsburg area for the production of the military VW body, so bodies had to be built in Berlin and shipped by rail, completely assembled, to Wolfsburg. The first VW military vehicle, a square-lined open touring car using the *KdF* engine and a modified *KdF* chassis, was ready for use in December, 1939.

In this rare photograph a prototype *Wehrmacht* model is being tested for traction. Certain design changes may be noted between first thoughts and the production model below: The rocker panel (body edge below doors) was raised for greater ground-clearance. The spare tire, at first recessed neatly in the nose, was mounted top side for production, to act in greater measure as a protective shield. Except for the body, fabricated by the Ambi Budd Pressworks in Berlin, principal sub-assemblies all were made under the big roof at Wolfsburg. Troops were quick to christen the car after its appearance, calling it the *Kuebelwagen,* or "bucket car".

FROM *KdF* TO *KUEBELWAGEN*

The order to design a military version of the *KdF* car came directly from Hitler himself. Porsche was not entirely unprepared for such an order; he had given the matter some preliminary thought and had even done a few sketchy drawings.

Although many components of the *KdF* car were usable in the military VW, the two vehicles were built on broadly different basic assumptions. While the *KdF* car was supposed to be a cheaply running family car, the *Wehrmacht* VW was to be the simplest, barest form of military transportation, designed without regard for comfort or economy. As a first step Porsche increased the engine displacement from 995 cc to 1,134 cc, then followed with detail alterations to the engine and transmission, beefing them up for heavy use and mistreatment.

Though Porsche's efforts had been for the military, to whom time was more of the essence than funds expended, his hastily executed design made no compromises with its essential premise of lightness, nor with quality of detail. Extensive use was made of aluminum and magnesium base alloys, and a very good finish was imparted to the die castings. In its lightness lay its charm.

One area of knowledge each force disseminated among its troops to the limit of its resources was a thorough working knowledge of the opposing army's arms and vehicles. It could never be predicted just when operable ordnance or rolling stock might fall into the other's hands, with its immediate use *against* its makers a decisive factor. America, like the British, soon possessed samples of the *Wehrmacht* VW for examination.

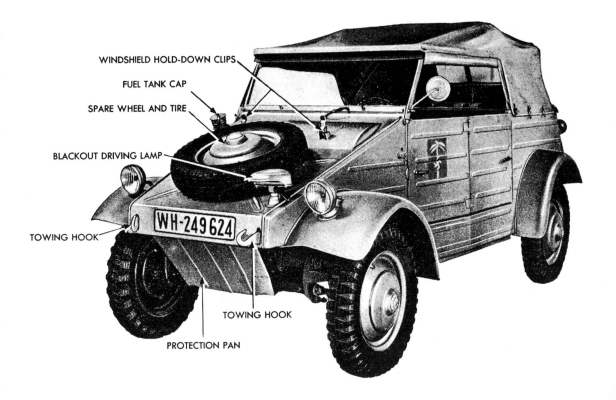

WINDSHIELD HOLD-DOWN CLIPS

FUEL TANK CAP

SPARE WHEEL AND TIRE

BLACKOUT DRIVING LAMP

TOWING HOOK

WH-249 624

TOWING HOOK

PROTECTION PAN

The military vehicle had to be capable of negotiating the most rugged terrain, whether any road existed or not, carrying a load of four soldiers and all their equipment. Hence Porsche also strengthened the *KdF* car suspension and reinforced its chassis, increasing resistance to torsional forces and jolts. He designed a unique hydraulic steering damper — so that the harassed driver, barreling through a plowed field in the middle of the night, would be able to hang onto the wheel, which would simply rise and fall with the undulations of the wheels. In order to obtain greater ground clearance, Porsche modified the stub-axle assembly in the front and superimposed a spur reduction gear on the rear axle ends. He also provided the military VW with a limited-slip differential to help it move through areas of poor traction.

The body of the military vehicle was an open, almost box-shaped four-seater with four quickly detachable doors. Its lightweight steel panels were stiffened by corrugations.

Capable of carrying four fully-equipped troops, the durable little car proved an able-footed wonder of simplicity. By means of a ZF cam-type, self-locking differential — more recently standard in racing practice — it possessed a keen ability to scramble through mud and sand. Even when actually stuck, with an unladen weight of only 1510 lbs. (600-700 lbs. less than the U.S. built jeep), its crew could rescue it in a twinkling.

After disassembly, testing, photographing, and tabulation of the data, the U.S. Army issued results of its study in a technical manual distributed to all units in 1944. Titled "The German Volkswagen" it carried the identifying symbol TM E9-803. (Now long out of print.) These photographs, and the nomenclatured illustrations, next overleaf, are from this official handbook. The stenciled emblem of General Rommel's fabled *Afrika Korps.* may still be seen on doors and deck of this captive specimen.

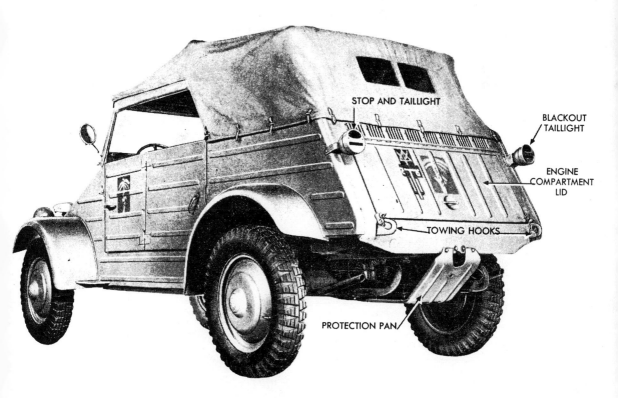

STOP AND TAILLIGHT

BLACKOUT TAILLIGHT

ENGINE COMPARTMENT LID

TOWING HOOKS

PROTECTION PAN

A—HORN BUTTON
B—WINDSHIELD WIPER
C—FUSE BOX
D—AMMETER
E—OIL PRESSURE GAGE
F—SPEEDOMETER
G—BRIGHT LIGHT INDICATOR
H—DIRECTION SIGNAL INDICATOR
J—FUSE BOX
K—DIRECTION SIGNAL SWITCH
L—SPOTLIGHT
M—FUEL COCK
N—MULTIPLE SWITCH
P—LIGHT SWITCH
Q—GEARSHIFT LEVER
R—IGNITION KEY
S—DASHBOARD LIGHT SWITCH
T—TROUBLE LAMP SOCKET
U—CRANKING MOTOR BUTTON
V—CHOKE
W—EMERGENCY BRAKE
X—ACCELERATOR
Y—BRAKE PEDAL
Z—CLUTCH PEDAL
AA—FRONT LIGHT SWITCH

AIR INTAKE HOSE

IGNITION PRIMARY WIRE

IGNITION COIL

OIL BATH AIR CLEANER

SECONDARY WIRE

Looking down into the engine compartment of the *Kuebelwagen,* the owner of a model one whole generation removed will still recognize the ancestry at once, even though every part has been changed in the evolution toward long-life construction, improved efficiency, and quieter operation.

REAR COWLING

FUEL PUMP

A notable part carryover from the Type 38 to the Type 82 (war model) was the instrument panel cluster, probably the only stylized element incorporated in the latter. Supply of this unit already had been laid in from an electrical instrument supplier. *Wehrmacht* construction was simply designed to accommodate the surplus assemblies. (For the record, earliest U. S. production of the jeep also used up existing instrument panels—from Bantam, Ford and Willys, as well as steering wheels, transmissions, and even engines!)

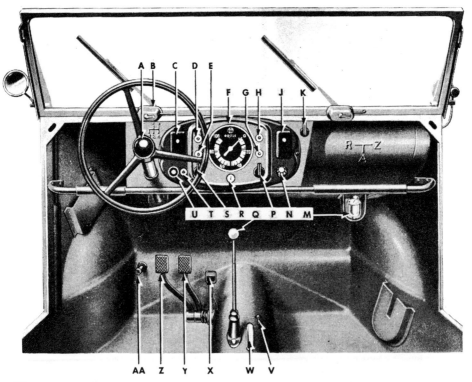

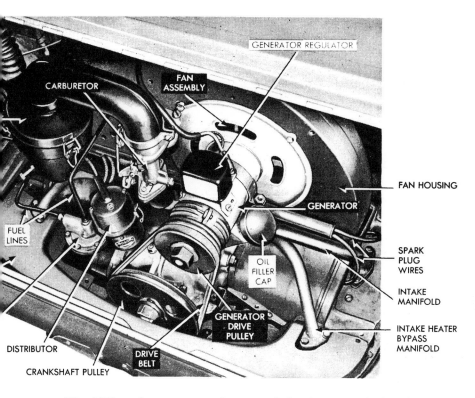

GENERATOR REGULATOR

FAN ASSEMBLY

CARBURETOR

FAN HOUSING

GENERATOR

FUEL LINES

SPARK PLUG WIRES

OIL FILLER CAP

INTAKE MANIFOLD

GENERATOR DRIVE PULLEY

INTAKE HEATER BYPASS MANIFOLD

DISTRIBUTOR

DRIVE BELT

CRANKSHAFT PULLEY

The VW underwent several stages of development during its wartime production. The preface to a revealing report by the British Intelligence Objectives Sub-Committee, entitled "Investigation into the design and performance of the Volkswagen or German People's Car," lists the various models of the *Wehrmacht* VW:

"The car, designed chiefly by Dr. Porsche, was about to go into production as a civilian car in 1939 [type 38], but as a wartime measure a modified vehicle (type 82) was produced for the German army. A similar vehicle (type 21) with an enlarged engine of 1131 cc [*sic*] and 5.25-16 tyres was in production in 1945, and as a temporary measure a few vehicles were produced having a saloon [sedan] body on the military chassis, and were known as type 51. In 1946 the civilian saloon (type 11) was again in production having the 1131 cc engine and 5.00-16 tyres."

Produced only in limited series to run out parts surpluses this model might be identified as a *Kuebelwagen* chassis with sedan body. Called the Type 51 it was utilized by the Germans behind the front, where its lesser utility would not be as sorely felt. Shown is a captured car with English identification.

A waterproof ignition system and a snorkel-like extension on the carburetor air intake, extending upwards to about shoulder height, enabled the military VW to ford streams without the fatal embarrassment of a dead engine.

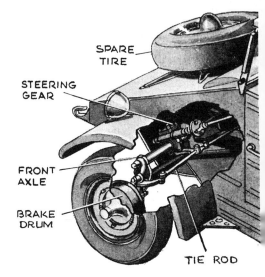

SPARE TIRE

STEERING GEAR

FRONT AXLE

BRAKE DRUM

TIE ROD

In America the existence of the VW was all but unknown among civilians. To those few who had some knowledge of it, technical details were revolutionary and strange. Several U. S. consumer publications carried features about the car, one artist producing this interesting cutaway drawing for *Popular Science*. In another publication a technical writer's experience did not relate the Volkswagen to the world-famous Auto-Union of a few years before, and while he credited the *Kuebelwagen* with being "ingenious in design and economical to run," he proved less enlightening when he attempted to describe the torsion bar suspension by reporting that "springing is accomplished by means of coil springs located within transverse, pipe-like housings."

The initial reaction of most German military men to the war model VW was negative; the conservative Prussian generals wanted no part of such an unorthodox vehicle. But despite initial adverse opinion, the car proved itself worthy, particularly during the Russian and North African offensives. Its unfailing performance in the face of both arid desert and freezing arctic conditions eloquently spoke the case for the air-cooled engine; Hitler issued an

In North Africa the spider from Wolfsburg outperformed many heavier *Wehrmacht* pieces, and was admired even by the local camel drivers. Dr. Porsche had used a hub reduction gearing to obtain a lower over-all ratio by a simple conversion of the original design of the Volkswagen. (Years later the Transporter VW chassis would utilize the same principle.) This arrangement also automatically increased ground clearance—all-important for traversing the rough.

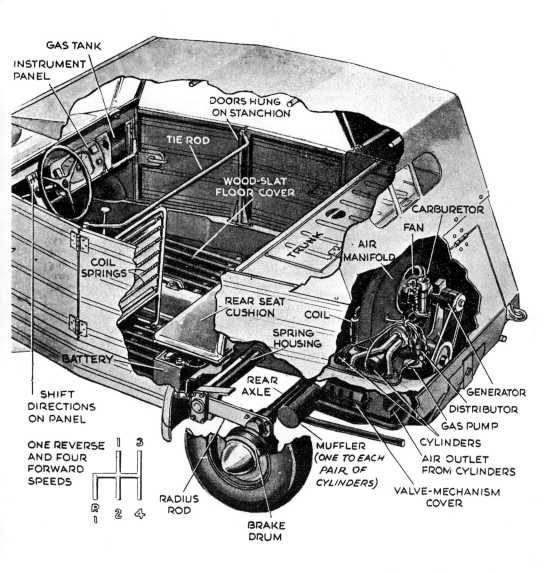

GAS TANK

INSTRUMENT PANEL

DOORS HUNG ON STANCHION

TIE ROD

WOOD-SLAT FLOOR COVER

CARBURETOR

FAN

AIR MANIFOLD

TRUNK

COIL SPRINGS

REAR SEAT CUSHION

COIL

SPRING HOUSING

BATTERY

SHIFT DIRECTIONS ON PANEL

REAR AXLE

GENERATOR

DISTRIBUTOR

GAS PUMP

ONE REVERSE AND FOUR FORWARD SPEEDS

CYLINDERS

AIR OUTLET FROM CYLINDERS

VALVE-MECHANISM COVER

RADIUS ROD

MUFFLER (ONE TO EACH PAIR OF CYLINDERS)

BRAKE DRUM

order that all German military vehicles use standardized air-cooling. The Germans dubbed the *Wehrmacht* VW the *Kuebelwagen,* or "bucket car"; and the distinctively unpretty little car soon became as dear to the hearts of German troops as the Jeep later would become to the Allies.

Hitler was so satisfied with the stamina the tough little car had demonstrated in combat that he ordered the line extended to include a four-wheel-drive model, as well as a halftrack. Under development late in the war, these projected models never were to advance beyond prototype construction.

Anyone for anti-freeze? At the U.S. Army Proving Grounds a prisoner-of-war stands alongside a pre-universal model of its allied counterpart in light reconnaissance. The American jeep was developed and standardized from experiments conducted at this Aberdeen, Maryland, test center during 1940-41. Vehicle number identifies this VW as the one photographed for the U.S. Army tech manual.

KUEBELWAGEN vs. JEEP

Certainly the American (Bantam, Willys, Ford) jeep and the German VW *Kuebelwagen* reflected no imitation one for the other. However, certain attributes were common to both, as they were derived from civilian models for a common purpose. Compact size, minimum overhang, and liberal ground clearance lent each an advantage over regular civilian models — a life and death superiority when traversing uncertain terrain.

While the jeep appeared from the beginning as a four-wheel-drive unit, the *Kuebelwagen* VW, not having the added weight and the duplications inherent in conventional body and frame construction, was 650 pounds lighter than its American counterpart, used a third of the fuel, and in most instances was equally roadable with its 2-wheel drive. Biting into rough terrain was the all-wheel-drive jeep's special forte; while the *Kuebelwagen* possessed a keener ability to scramble through mud and sand; its smooth underbelly sometimes acted almost as a sled. Now and then when the *Kuebelwagen* did run aground, light weight enabled even a crew of two to lift or slide the VW free with comparative ease, whereas the heavy jeep might have been abandoned.

Design of the differential was ingenious for the time, having only a partial slip it obviated wheelspin and particularly adapted itself to rough terrain and muddy conditions. A generation later the limited slip rear end was to be acclaimed as a great new feature among certain U. S. makes.

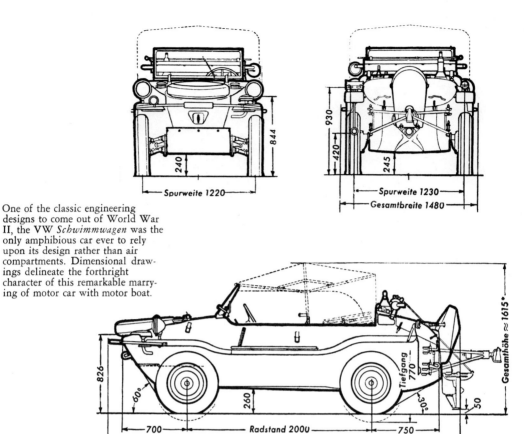

One of the classic engineering designs to come out of World War II, the VW *Schwimmwagen* was the only amphibious car ever to rely upon its design rather than air compartments. Dimensional drawings delineate the forthright character of this remarkable marrying of motor car with motor boat.

Porsche received orders early in 1942 to design an amphibious military car, and by the end of the year an amphibious Volkswagen went into production.

The *Schwimmwagen,* which Grusenko had seen on the steppes, had a personality all its own, and it drew wide acclaim as an exceedingly versatile and durable vehicle.

At a park lake in Hamburg, company officials demonstrate pilot model *Schwimmwagens* on the occasion of presenting the new model to the *Wehrmacht.* Production design (in the line drawings) when examined beside the prototype design (photograph) reveals that the straight-line gunwale (cockpit edge) gave way to a dropped gunwale in order to facilitate entry and exit, allow more able handling of hand weapons, and increase arm room for the driver.

But for side doors, which lent the older *Kuebelwagen* a living room ease of entry and exit compared with the *Schwimmwagen*, the cars had much in common, with their lightness, high clearance and sled-like bottoms all distinct assets in rough terrain. The *Schwimmwagen*, designed nearly three years after the *Kuebelwagen*, represented advanced thinking and knowledge along the same lines, besides being amphibious. With the advantage of four-wheel-drive it was hands down winner in traction contests between the two models. Where the *Kuebelwagen* would ford a stream by driving across on the bottom, the *Schwimmwagen* would nussle in and glide across the surface of the water with nearly the grace and aplomb of a swan. If performance of the first model caused a German private's heart to beat a little faster, the potential in the later car must have sparked his imagination.

Below, an old soldier writes fondly of days with the *Schwimmwagen* . . . If the American reader finds the German writer carried away with enthusiasm for war incidents and campaigns that may, in the light of history, be considered quite unfunny to all sides concerned, it should be noted that the personal pronoun here may be identified as a *Schwimmwagen* speaking to another *Wehrmacht* vehicle.

THE *SCHWIMMWAGEN'S* AUTOBIOGRAPHY

First of all, may I introduce myself. As you can see from the accompanying photo I am a *Schwimmwagen* of the Germany Army. My speedometer passed zero twice, gave up the ghost, and was replaced. But, as always, I feel bright and cheerful, especially with my present master.

I've seen a lot of the world since that day in '43 when I left the VW assembly line for the front. There were proud days and times of deepest humiliation. My wheels ground the sand of North Africa, the mud of Russia and, at the end of my military career, the German soil of my homeland. I was at Tobruk and El Alamein and accompanied our brave *Afrikakorps* almost to Cairo. At that time my dress was the color of desert sand, and my hood bore the insignia of Rommel — a palm tree, bending in the wind. Sometimes I still hear our proud song:

Heiss ueber Afrika's Boden die Sonne glueht,
Unsere Panzermotoren singen ihr Lied . . .

My activities often brought me under enemy fire. I was even hit a few times: once in the gas tank, another time in the tire. As to the first wound, I didn't leave my men in the lurch, but quickly switched to the second gas tank and went right on. The next time it was the other way around: my soldiers didn't leave me. We just drove on till the tire was in shreds and I was behind the lines all in one piece.

After a short stay in an *HKP* (*Heimatkraftfahrpark,* meaning sanatorium for sick vehicles), where I had a great time, they got me going again, this time in an easterly direction. I had a hunch then that the sunny days were over. Those fellows in the *HKP* dyed my nice tan dress. To my dismay, I saw myself disfigured by brown, green, yellow and Heaven knows what kind of spots. Camouflage, that's what it was, my driver explained to me. In time I got used to my new makeup and even learned to appreciate its use. It protected me from enemy sight, and who knows if I would still be alive today without it.

Russia was quite a bit different from Africa. The streets and roads alone gave my people a lot of trouble, though they didn't bother me. Whether in deepest snow or mud I was always ready to go and (if you don't mind my saying so) never failed. No hole was too deep for me, no hill too steep and I was especially adept at cross-country drives. I am equipped with four wheel drive, besides which I have an extra low gear that enables me to climb any hill up to 65°.

But now back to my story. When I was sent to Russia, retreat was inevitable. My soldiers wore the same camouflage as I; their equipment was the finest. I did my best for them. Sometimes I was in spots that were nearly hopeless. Surrounded by the Soviets, under heavy fire, I still found a narrow way through swamps and lakes and out of their deadly grasp. It was then that I, the little amphibious VW, brought honor to my name. Into the lakes I splashed, lowering my propeller, and with the speed of a motorboat I would rush through the water, bringing my soldiers safely to the other shore. Even though I'm a car I can also swim. In the water I move ahead with a propeller located in my stern, which I can retract when I feel ground under my wheels. That surprises you, *nicht wahr?*

Under those conditions it is a wonder I am still alive. But I am not a German *Schwimmwagen* for nothing. My present owner enjoys telling people that soon I will be old enough to vote, and I am still completely in good order. And, as you know, war years count double.

The Russians took me in 1945 as booty. After various detours I arrived in Vienna as an item of trade, and was "civilianized." But as a soldier (that is what I still feel I am, since my coat is still the same) I hold my own in civilian life, hearkening back to the old times whenever I hear this song, which my master has changed a little for me:

> *"Obs stuermt oder schneit, ob die Sonne uns lacht,*
> *Ob heiter der Himmel ob eiskalt die Nacht,*
> *Verstaubt sind die Gesichter*
> *Doch froh ist unser Sinn, ja unser Sinn.*
> *Es braust unser Schwimmer im Sturmwind dahin!"*
> ("Whether it snows or storms, whether the sun shines for us
> Whether the sky is blue or the night cold as ice.
> Our faces are dusty
> But joyful are our thoughts, our thoughts.
> Our swimmer roars on into the stormy wind.")

Alfred Lanschuetzer
Pfc. Ret., German Army

Vienna

One heavy German command car with a classic look of solid function was the powerful 1½ ton Horch which carried free-rolling spare wheels midships to prevent sinking in mud ruts and assist in negotiating rough ground.

Porsche's staff continued during the war to design heavier military vehicles for the German armies.

Hitler kept Dr. Porsche busy all during the war with orders to develop various things for the *Wehrmacht,* including gas generated vehicles, a two-stroke diesel engine, tanks such as the famous "Mouse," and other rolling stock, including a high-clearance truck intended for the swamp areas on the Russian front. It reached only the prototype stage. One point of concern was the wheel design most suitable for marshland; several styles were tested.

Each *Schwimmwagen* was equipped with a length of rope, two paddles, two shovels, and a three-meter pole for depth soundings and *gondoleering*—all important where the very sound of a motor, or even the paddles, might betray presence.

Unlike the U.S. built amphibious jeep, which relied for navigable buoyance on massive built-in air tanks, Porsche designed the lightweight *Schwimmwagen* with none. It relied completely upon its boat-like design to stay afloat, and proved like a cork, breaking the water with a comparatively high freeboard (water line to deck). While the car performed admirably in sheltered waters, and could be relied upon even in rolling lakes, having no keel the Schwimmwagen never was intended to compete with an ocean liner on the open sea.

Fully laden the *Schwimmwagen* was capable of entering and leaving the water at sharp inclines. Its remarkable buoyance led to surprising performance underway—and brought many a surly Prussian officer around for a moment of light-hearted conviviality.

HOW THE *SCHWIMMWAGEN* SCHWIMMS

The *Schwimmwagen* incorporated many technical advances over the initial *Kuebelwagen* design. It retained the use of the same proven, slightly enlarged (from 995cc to 1134cc) version of the original sedan powerplant and the same suspension as the *Kuebelwagen;* but in addition it had four-wheel drive on land. Construction was even lighter than the *Kuebelwagen,* and a single man reportedly could lift the front of the vehicle.

The *Schwimmwagen* moved through the water by means of a special reduction-gear-driven propellor in the stern of its boat-like body shell. The hinged three-bladed prop on the rear of the *Schwimmwagen* could be flipped down to engage a drive clutch from the crankshaft whenever the vehicle was ready to enter the water. Carburetor air intake and exhaust outlets were positioned high and dry on the stern deck.

In the absence of a rudder, navigation was accomplished by steering the front wheels in the usual manner, thereby bringing a measure of direction to the water-treading Volkswagen. It sloshed through the water fully laden at approximately walking speed — four miles per hour — and, under ideal load and water conditions at up to 15 mph. Maximum speed on land was well over 50 mph.

Bild 31. Schraubenstellung für Land- und Wasserfahrt

1 Schwenkwelle	5 Schraubenwelle
2 Kettenrad	6 Bügel
3 Klauenkupplung	7 Schraube
4 Ketten	

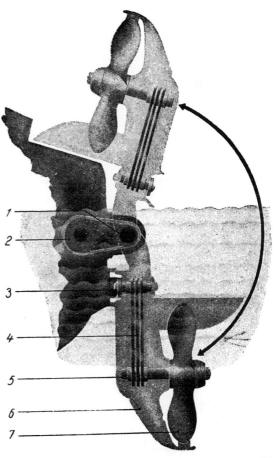

Several interesting schematic drawings follow. These illustrations, and the action photos at the left, along with companion photos (as well as the dimensional drawings) on several previous pages of this chapter, are taken from a now quite rare publication—the *Schwimmwagen* operating manual distributed among vehicle operators in the *Wehrmacht.* Reproduction quality is less than excellent here since the original printing was on rough, newsprint paper stock. While photos and phantom views (overleaf) depict the straight-side, prototype body style—reasonably the only thing around to photograph when the handbook was being prepared in advance of series production—the dimensional drawing also appearing in the handbook represents a last-minute up-dating before printing; it shows the notch-side, production model.

Native nomenclature captions have purposely been retained with the illustrations on this, and the two pages following, to offer a German language sampler to the American reader. One moment he may pass over them as a curiosity, the next accept them as a translation challenge.

Gesamttriebwerk, Durchsicht

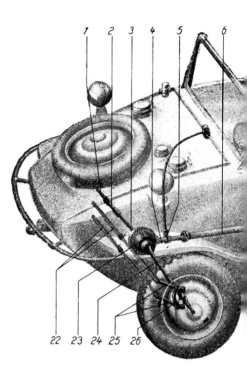

1 Radwelle
2 Zwischenwelle
3 Seitenwelle, rechts
4 Vorderes Antriebskegelrad
5 Antrieb für Geschwindigkeitsmesser
6 Vordere Gelenkwelle
7 Lagerbock für Getriebeschaltung
8 Schalthebel für Straßengänge
9 Schalthebel für Vorderachsantrieb
und Geländegang
10 Schaltstange für Vorderachsantrieb
und Geländegang
11 Schaltstange für Straßengänge
12 Hintere Gelenkwelle
13 Stoßdämpfer, rechts
14 Wechselgetriebe
15 Ausgleichgetriebe, Hinterachse
16 Anlasserritzel
17 Schwungrad
18 Luftgebläserad
19 Lichtmaschine
20 Kurbelwelle
21 Zwischenwelle für Schraubenantrieb
22 Drehstäbe, Vorderachse
23 Ausgleichgetriebe, Vorderachse
24 Seitenwelle, links
25 Längslenker, Vorderachse
26 Lagerbügel für Achsschenkel

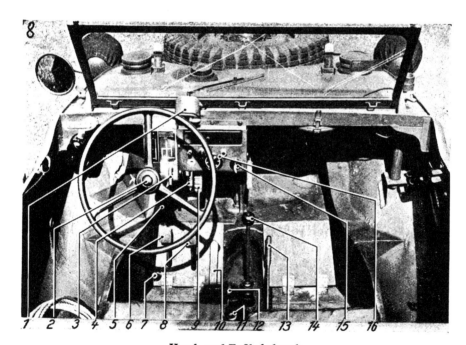

Hand- und Fußhebelwerk

1 Scheibenwischer
2 Signalknopf
3 Hebel für Kraftstoffhahn
4 Kraftstoffilter
5 Kraftstoffhilfspumpe
6 Kupplungsfußhebel
7 Fußabblendschalter
8 Bremsfußhebel
9 Hebel für Zentralschmierung

10 Fahrfußhebel
11 Schalthebel für Vorderachsantrieb
und Geländegang
12 Hebel für Luftklappe
13 Bremshandhebel
14 Schalthebel für Wechselgetriebe
15 Zündschloß
16 Geschwindigkeitsmesser

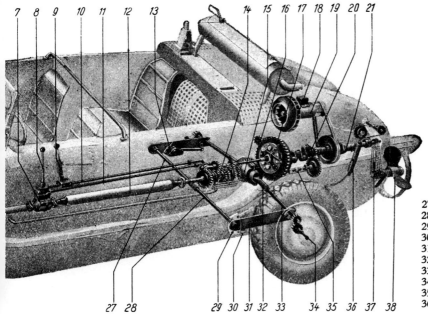

27 Federstab, rechts
28 Federstab, links
29 Deckel für Längslenkerlager
30 Längslenkerlager
31 Längslenker, links
32 Seitenwelle
33 Achswelle
34 Zusatzgetriebe
35 Nockenwelle
36 Spannfeder für Schraubenantrieb
37 Ketten für Schraube
38 Schraube

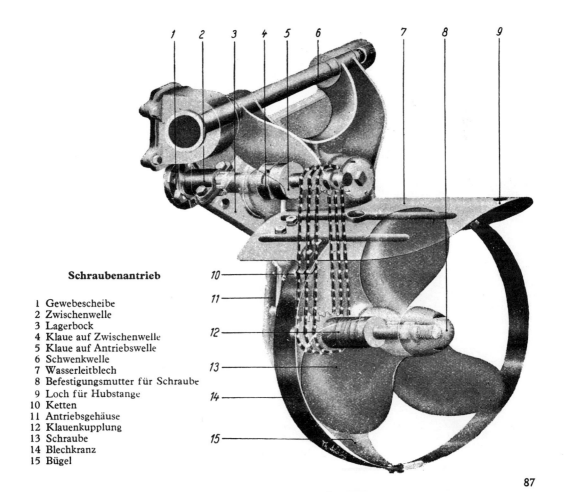

Schraubenantrieb

1 Gewebescheibe
2 Zwischenwelle
3 Lagerbock
4 Klaue auf Zwischenwelle
5 Klaue auf Antriebswelle
6 Schwenkwelle
7 Wasserleitblech
8 Befestigungsmutter für Schraube
9 Loch für Hubstange
10 Ketten
11 Antriebsgehäuse
12 Klauenkupplung
13 Schraube
14 Blechkranz
15 Bügel

WARTIME WOLFSBURG

Like other German industrial establishments which used imported forced labor in order to produce at breakneck capacity, the Volkswagen factory in Wolfsburg was witness to tragic Nazi brutality during the war years and in the period just before the war.

Hitler's works and armaments programs had relieved unemployment so completely by 1938 and 1939 that insufficient local labor could be found to build the huge VW factory. *Der Fuehrer* logically called upon his partner in the Axis to the south. In some parts of Southern Italy at that time only 10% of the labor force was employed, and *Il Duce* was quick to ship thousands of unemployed sons of Italy up to Wolfsburg to assist in the construction of the monumental factory for the People's Car — and at the same time ease his own unemployment problems.

Italians found life in rural Wolfsburg a rather dull existence compared with the busy night life of Naples, Rome, and Palermo. The transplant was slow to take; certain incidents occurred in which the local populace suffered. Before long some of the fair-haired local Wolfsburg *Maedchen* bore sturdy, dark-haired offspring. The imported workers soon found their temporary barracks surrounded by jack-booted SS men, placed there for the "workers' protection." Numbers of the Italian workers died from overwork, disease, and "disciplinary action" by the SS guards. However, the Government Employment Offices in Sicily and Southern Italy were quick to replace any of these less fortunate workers who "had sacrificed their lives for a national project"; and new Italian workers made the trip north to Wolfsburg every month.

The initial stage of the factory and a portion of the planned city of Wolfsburg were completed in 1939 as war clouds thickened. Then as the years passed, most of the Italians were replaced by hapless prisoners of war who happened to have survived the *Blitzkrieg*. Poles were the first group of workers to staff the Wolfsburg arms and auto works, followed by Frenchmen, Belgians, Dutchmen, Danes, and finally Russians. Estimates of the number of foreign workers in the Wolfsburg prison camps at the peak run as high as 11,000.

Primitive barracks rose along unpaved, concentric streets around the new factory in the 1938-41 period, as plans for a classless city took shape on an agricultural plain where fewer than 150 people had lived, with a Count for a neighbor in an ancient castle named Wolfsburg. Electricity, heat and light for the town, was supplied by the factory powerplant. As the tide of war began to roll against Germany, development of the town became aborted, and the homes of workers took on the pallor of a prison camp.

The roof literally caved in on production of *Kuebelwagens* and *Schwimmwagens* with Wolfsburgers and forced laborers alike sharing shelters for survival, as the plant became a target of Allied bombing attacks in the final days of World War II. The great factory ultimately was 60% destroyed.

This view from a postwar British report shows the main frontage still largely intact, while the production area behind it lay crumbled in desolation. Remarkably, the powerhouse, rising at the distant end of the canal frontage here, stood unscathed. The split-second error in releasing a string of bombs, that had allowed this very "heart" of the plant to stand untouched, would later have a profound effect on the economic recovery of West Germany and on motor transportation everywhere.

Reams of documents have been compiled about the sadistic deeds perpetrated in the name of the German People by Nazi officials and guards at these wartime prison camps, and Wolfsburg was no exception to the Nazi *modus operandi*. There is, however, a more heartening side to the wartime Wolfsburg story.

Both Germans and foreign workers employed in the plant during the war still tell stories of kind and humane actions on the part of many German civilians on the Wolfsburg scene. Some French and Dutch prisoners assert that they would never have survived their stay in Wolfsburg had it not been for food, drugs, and clothing given to them secretly — virtually right under the noses of the SS guards — by German technicians and workers acting independently of their country's political policy.

Former prisoners of war, returning to Wolfsburg years later, have managed to locate wartime friends and benefactors still among the Wolfsburgers of today. Moving scenes of reunion and thanks follow, restoring the faith in basic human values among people of many national origins who lived through the war in Wolfsburg.

From early 1940 until the last days of the war the VW factory rolled out about 55,000 *Kuebelwagen* and some 15,000 *Schwimmwagen,* in addition to aircraft components, mines, and other arms. The factory did not receive the early bombardment meted out to other prime industrial installations — perhaps because Wolfsburg was not then shown on most maps of Germany. What damage it did shoulder, even so, was to appear as a mortal wound for many months to come. Surrender found the factory 60 percent leveled to the ground; and that which was left standing had been plundered by the foreign labor forces working there during wartime production days. The gutted factory was turned over to British Occupation troops within a month after its surrender to American forces.

Hitler had ordered the Volkswagen to perform an "oblique march," when he diverted production from a product of peace to a product of war. But all he really accomplished was to march the VW and all Germany to destruction.

As the Allies closed ranks on Berlin, bombing raids were concentrated at Wolfsburg with increasing fury; 850,000 square feet of production area were leveled in the early days of May, 1945. With the plant at Wolfsburg lying in waste, one could only have concluded that Dr. Porsche's long-nurtured People's Car was destined to become extinct at last.

6

THE IMAGE VANISHES

For those whose war had ended in humiliation and disgrace the Volkswagen dream was as dead as its horned financial angel.

The market place at Breslau, Silesia (now in East Germany) typified the shambles of the cities where trade was reduced to bartering in the clearings.

After the Third *Reich* had been laid to waste through concentrated pounding by Allied bombs, Germany's once great cities were nothing more than mountains of brick, mortar, and mud. Few urban areas escaped destruction by bombing; one-half of all Germany's dwellings were in ruins.

Transportation and communication facilities above all had served as Allied targets, and at war's end they existed in a state of virtually complete ruin. The Nazi central government and various local jurisdictions had owned and operated all power plants, telephones, telegraphs, radio, railroads, buses, and other media of transportation and communication. When surrender came on May 7, 1945, these services, already reduced to skeleton performance, ceased to function at all. The only power available came from firewood; communications were by word of mouth; transportation was by foot.

Even the air was foul midst the chaos in historic Paris Square, Berlin, where even the French Embassy (at right) had been reduced to rubble. Proud Brandenburg Gate by a quirk had been spared.

Upended segment of *Autobahn* bridge, near a resort spa (Bad Oeynhausen) in Westphalia, served irrepressible youth (at left) as a great slide. Children, the forgotten generation of wartime, were quick to adapt their pursuits to reality.

Sunken vessels blocked the harbors of Hamburg and once-proud Bremen, from which had come the U-boat fleet that terrorized the Atlantic only a few months before. The Rhine system of waterways was choked by the remains of bridges, locks, and derelict craft, resting in the mud of formerly navigable channels. More than one mile in five of all mainline railway trackage in the U. S. Zone was damaged; and in all of Germany 885 railway bridges had been destroyed. The renowned *Autobahn* system of freeways was so heavily damaged that it was useless for inter-city transport.

Moral destruction among some of the German people was no less severe than the material destruction around them. It was a grim and desperate time, harsh to the human spirit. In a society where even the drinking water was polluted, mothers sought scraps of food from the gutters for their babies. Men looted brother from brother in order to exist until tomorrow. Some sold their souls or bodies to the occupying troops for bread or a Hershey bar.

The German economy was destroyed as well. To a great extent money had ceased to function either as a medium of exchange or as a standard measure of value. Normal consumer goods were in short supply, whereas old Reichsmarks were in plentiful, though varying, supply. Barter was the rule of the day, and American cigarettes became more stable as an exchange medium than the Reichsmark. Government economic regulations had collapsed with war's end.

The toll on Germany's capacity for production was total, with the old Daimler-Benz works at Cannstatt no exception.

Germany's banking system was *kaputt*. The result of this economic chaos was two-fold: an extremely slow recovery of industrial production, and a wide disparity between comparative plenty in the countryside and starvation in the cities.

As the Reichmark lost its value as a medium of exchange, lively currency in black market exchange became food staples and American cigarettes. The trader offering soap or pepper could name his own price in other goods.

Into this dismal picture marched the troops of the occupying powers, bringing with them new problems amidst the beginnings of law and order. In the very first days after the collapse of Germany the occupation continued to act, almost as by reflex action, under the influence of the terrible years of wartime destruction perpetrated by the Nazis. Their primary concerns were revenge, security from further offensive action on the part of Germany, and limitation of Germany's future war-making capabilities.

The last life blood of Germany's productive capacity was let at the direction of occupying governments; the heavy machinery, which might otherwise have led to an earlier recovery for Leipzig, Dresden, Chemnitz, and other East German industrial areas, was immediately uprooted by the Russians from factory sites.

At beck and call of occupation forces many former German soldiers were kept busy dismantling and loading factory machinery for reparation shipments to the Allies. Demands from the USSR were the most crippling.

RUSSIAN INABILITY TO MAKE USE OF GERMAN MACHINERY

Russian delegates who had come to Potsdam were awed by modern German industry. They concluded that the best way to reestablish the Russian economy would be to dismantle German factories *in toto,* then rebuild them inside Soviet Russia. Soon Berlin railroad yards were swollen with freight cars on their way to Russia, heavily laden with German factory equipment.

Possession of machine tools, the Russians were soon to discover, was but one aspect of factory operation. Buildings, transport facilities, access to materials, layout, skilled labor, and management "know-how" all were equally essential for the success of any factory; Russia could supply little or none of these. The Soviets found they could not reconstruct these factories as readily as they had uprooted the tools; in fact, they could hardly put any of the machinery to use at all.

Reports, documented with photographs, poured into Western Allied intelligence offices, telling of the machinery's sad fate. Numberless railroad sidings in East Germany, Poland, and Russia were choked with idle railway cars, still packed with the machine tools that had once been the heart of Eastern Germany's industrial might. The machinery rusted into ruin during the winters of 1946, 1947, and 1948.

Although Western reparation demands came second to the need of providing food for the German people, few plants in the American, British, and French Zones were left complete enough and remained organized sufficiently to produce anything at all. Those which were partially operable were swiftly dismantled by local black-market operators, if not by the conquering troops. Reparations activity caused German production potential to drop to an all-time low, as 744 key industrial installations were dismantled and removed from German soil, shipped off to the west and to the east.

At Schweinfurt, in the American Zone, facilities of Fichtel & Sachs, a prime motor-parts producer and Volkswagen sub-contractor (clutch parts, etc.), had been reduced to a brickpile.

Western Allies came to realize that the policy of plundering the defeated had to be replaced by one of assistance toward Germany's self-sufficiency once again. Distribution of vast foodstuffs was the first step. Here seed potatoes arrive in Berlin by rail from the Western Zones.

While the program of reparations also spelled out territorial losses beyond the Oder-Neisse line and in East Prussia, it was this dismantling and removal of industry, ironically, that eventually paved the way for the ultra-modern, super-efficient industrial plant which would one day be the symbol of a fully recovered Germany in the world market.

During the time of occupation German economic life was further handicapped by shortages of power and raw materials, and the occupying powers could not agree on unified policies of economic recovery. The flood of Germans who had been thrown out of their homes in Eastern Europe aggravated the already-existing situation in Western Germany. These overwhelming problems stifled the best intentions of individuals in the occupation forces and in the German economy.

RUSSIA'S REPARATIONS POLICY IN EAST GERMANY

The Western Allies' first break with the USSR in post-war Germany came over reparations policy, as the Russians began to remove the facilities of production even from East Germany's deficit economy. As the U.S. and Great Britain poured food and supplies into their Zones, Russia withdrew huge quantities of raw materials and whatever finished products it could find from its Zone, all the while causing the people of the area to subsist on the remaining resources. The East German population existed on a starvation diet. The victors' joint Allied Control Council seemed unable to persuade Russia to cooperate with the three Western Allies; and Russia's program of systematic plunder, begun in 1945, continued until the founding of the East German puppet state, the *Deutsche "Demokratische" Republik,* in 1949.

LACK OF ALLIED COOPERATION

The conquerors of Germany found it much more difficult to work together after the war than during the conflict. While they cooperated toward a common goal during the fighting, the differences in their peacetime goals magnified a hundredfold the hour that hostilities ceased. Each of the occupying powers acted at first like a small child turned loose in a candy store. No one wanted to give up his spoils.

"After one year of occupation," General Lucius D. Clay wrote in May, 1946, "zones represent air-tight territories with almost no free exchange of commodities and ideas. Germany now consists of four small economic units which can deal with each other only through treaties . . . Economic unity can be obtained only through free trade in Germany and a common policy for foreign trade designed to serve Germany as a whole. A common financial policy is equally essential . . . Common policies and nationwide implementation are equally essential for transportation, communication, food and agriculture, industry and foreign trade, if economic recovery is to be made possible."

Later the Western Allies met pointed obstructions in carrying out mutual constructive policies in their Zones of Germany as Russia made increasing use of delaying tactics to unified Allied action. But even after it had become clear to most observers that Russia was bent upon creating a communist state in the Eastern Zone, a lack of cooperation among the Western powers themselves for a long time hindered the reforming of a strong, free Germany.

The first major step towards a unified, better organized Germany came when the British and American Zones were fused in September, 1946. Then after two years of scarcity, black markets, ill-conceived controls, and Russian vetoes of proposed policies, the three occupying powers in the Western Zones decided to proceed with a positive economic and political program without Russia's cooperation. As the Eastern Zone, now looking to the dole of an expanded socialism to ease its economic difficulties, still existed in virtual starvation, the occupation forces in the Western Zones saw the need for restoring West German industry to free-enterprise production.

This turnabout in Allied policy evolved as it became increasingly evident that a strong, free, denazified, and democratic German nation would be a greater defense against Communism than a Germany in serfdom. Germany's previously throttled economy was now encouraged to grow. The new stress was on recovery, political autonomy, and democracy for the German people.

Even in the darkest postwar days of 1945 the German *Volk* in the Western Zones had wasted no time in their personal efforts to remove the visible scars of war from their cities. Grinding, monotonous, back-breaking labor was the only ready means of moving rubble aside to form a pathway; eventually the pathway became a road once again. Much of the highway and rail systems was restored by this method in the immediate postwar period, with the cooperation of the Allies.

Few of the people whose war had ended in humiliation and disgrace could dwell long on the fate of the *KdF* dream in those days. There was no time to stop and think — and nowhere to drive. This hungry people had to pay primary attention to the necessities of life, and remorse for the automobile that savings stamps had once failed to buy was remote from the thoughts of the German people. To them the Volkswagen was as dead as its horned financial angel, buried in the ruins of his Berlin bunker.

Der Innenlenker, Preis RM 990.- ab Werk Fallersleben

Only a few years before RM 990 had been promoted by the *KdF* as full price of the elusive People's Car, but by early 1948 the *Reichsmark* had become so debased that this same sum, procuring food in the illegal black market, would buy no more than five pounds of butter. The Volkswagen could hardly be farther from reality.

As 1947 and 1948 passed, the victors and the vanquished united ever more firmly against the rising threat of Communism, which confronted all with increasing pressure from the East. The energetic and resolute German people faced their task now with redoubled effort, heartened at last by a more reasonable attitude from Allied Occupation.

Currency reform in the middle of 1948 furnished the platform on which an economic comeback could be constructed.

NEW MONEY FOR OLD

Observers of the German scene concur that the 1948 Currency Reform signalled the beginning of a new era for post-war Germany. It marked the beginning of Allied policy designed to strengthen the country, rather than to punish her. Coupled with simultaneous redevelopment of the German banking system, the currency reform created a sound financial structure indispensable to economic recovery.

In the spring of 1948, France, Britain, and the United States had invited the Netherlands, Belgium, and Luxembourg to develop new economic and political policies for Western Germany. These powers decided to establish a republic, to reform the money-credit system, and to end inflation by killing off the old Reichsmark and introducing a new Deutsche Mark to take its place as hard currency.

The new currency law, put into effect June 20, 1948, incorporated four separate measures. The first permitted each person to exchange up to 60 old Reichsmarks 1 to 1 for the new Deutschemarks, and established a four-day moratorium on credit transactions. The second law authorized the *Bank deutscher Laender* to issue currency up to DM 10,000,000,000. The third and fourth laws, dealing with credit balances, made DM 6.5 of new currency available for every tax-clear RM 100 on deposit. On August 10, 1948, a tax reform reduced the anti-inflation income taxes and the excise taxes on tobacco and coffee.

Historically, initial reaction to currency reform has always created a difficult time for many people. While the new laws wiped out much of the life's savings of millions of German families, they also safeguarded these same people against the terrible, disheartening inflations of the Weimar period — when a wheelbarrow of bank notes bought a quart of milk. The Germans responded to their new currency with fresh confidence. Owners of speculative inventories of goods were forced to sell. Goods came out of hoarding; merchants reopened their stores; and the supply of raw materials increased. Factories and workshops began to produce whatever they could amidst their sometimes still rubble-heaped surroundings. Farmers became more willing to market their produce, and the improved supply of both food and industrial goods increased the people's incentive to work.

This favorable circular response to currency reform affected industrial production dramatically. If statistics may be taken at face value, production rose by nearly 50 percent during the second half of 1948. By then the recovery of Germany as an economic power was well under way.

Free enterprise was encouraged at every level, and economic assistance under the Marshall Plan brought the tools of manufacturing capacity back into German industry. The basic plans for the German Federal Republic were set in motion. Germany was at last on its way toward recovery and respect in the eyes of the Free World.

Reconstruction was hastened objectively among factories that had been base producers of hard goods. In turn, as their products were made available again, recovery efforts received further boosts. The Robert Bosch works at Stuttgart, electrical parts supplier for most car manufacturers, underwent a transformation even before surrounding rubble (background) was cleared.

7

VOLKS FIND A
SPORTING COMPANION

In circumstances remote from those *der Fuehrer* had once promised, the People's Car came into private hands for the first time, and through grinding competition proved once more the stoutness of its heart.

Stripped of top, front doors, and even the original lighting
equipment, this decommissioned *Kuebelwagen,* duly identified as Volkswagen on the rear quarter to calm the
curious, was pressed into service as a hospital staff car in
the American zone.

The efforts of the German People to reestablish normal social and economic conditions soon after the war became a difficult struggle, both for the
Allied occupation and for the local populace. Clearing and reconstruction
centered around moving away rubble and bringing in building materials.
Families pushing wheelbarrows and pulling sleds were able to accomplish only
a pitiable amount of work. The Germans needed trucks and cars, yet the
occupying forces had commandeered every piece of rolling stock for patrol and
staff use.

Outfitted anew with a set of American jeep tires, and bearing the insignia of
the U. S. Army, this *Schwimwagen,* once pride of the *Wehrmacht,* stood ready
to roll, or to launch, only at the discretion of occupation forces.

The scavenger with a vivid imagination scored a distinct advantage. Hesitation over the merits of an abandoned carcass sometimes permitted a less discriminating hunter to move in from behind and establish prior claim.

Derelict military vehicles, which had been standing as forlorn monuments to a lost world, were given a second look by the people. Those ambitious and skillful enough to attempt repair and restoration saw these vehicles as symbols of new hope. The occupation appointed agents within each geographical area to locate and tow into central depots all usable trucks and automobiles, but private individuals were also privileged to join in the search. The sharp-eyed, quick-acting scavenger had a field day.

Memory of a warm *Wehrmacht*-days interlude, when the VW somehow had proven a trusty personal companion, spurred many a former soldier on in his search to acquire even an incomplete skeleton he might hope to restore to private service.

In the early days after surrender anyone with trucking capacity was king. The average *Wehrmacht* VW under private license was rushed into service as a beast of all burden. This day this "beast" labored under a load of the real thing from a wild boar hunt.

From under rubble and out of forests all kinds of war vehicles were unearthed and hauled into the depots for an official assessment. By paying the price thus established a person could have a vehicle recorded as his personal property. Among the lighter cars reclaimed by these scavengers were a great number of the then ubiquitous *Kuebelwagen* and *Schwimmwagen* VW's. The long-promised "People's Car" was in the hands of private German *Volk* in some volume for the first time — in circumstances quite remote from those which *der Fuehrer* had once promised.

Though he rolled on tires instilling little confidence, and reserved a spare offering even less, the hard-pressed Munich owner of this ragged, home-enclosed *Kuebelwagen* found the VW so endearing that he picked up a paint brush and, with a twinkle in his eye, christened it "Henry the Sharp-Cornered, from the House of Rolls Royce (of the old line.)"

Few cars were complete; far fewer were in running order. Parts swapping became a valuable, highly skilled art, in which the life or death of a potential vehicle depended on successful barter. Some newly mobile car owners were content to straddle a bare chassis fitted only with bucket seats as long as they could achieve a self-propelled state. Others displayed great ingenuity in covering the war-weary VW frame with aluminum skin and body panels salvaged from aircraft and trucks. This practice re-ignited the spark of motor competition; soon it was to fire a whole new sport.

The combination, of VW chassis + aluminum body of original design, quickly became the formula for most sports cars of the period. Each unique creation, with only the familiar platform chassis from a *Wehrmacht* vehicle in common with its competition, reflected its builder's own theory of aerodynamics. Execution was always a compromise with materials and tools at hand. But spirit was never more intense. Huschke von Hanstein's #53 Special pushed to successes at Karlsruher and Köln in the summer of 1948. Rules were at a minimum; the nearest thing to regulation was a police effort to keep the race course clear of spectators.

Raced by Gottfried Vollmer in 1948 with some success, this interesting original concept, with its dominant individual front fenders, departed deceptively from the usual general profile of the VW Special. Only the intake scoop, rising high across the deck behind the driver, revealed immediately what lay beneath.

Officially the German automobile industry had no interest at this time in building for competition. Politically, manufacturers would have found little support from the occupying powers if they had sponsored a revival of racing; and they were in no financial position to underwrite the expense of this promotion themselves. The car makers were dedicated to resuming production of cars for the primary purpose of providing the country with some form of mechanized transportation. All available motive power was needed for the job of cleaning up.

Fresh from wartime experience in aircraft construction and maintenance, creation of a VW Special body was a natural extension of the familiar to popular driver Kurt Kohnke. Completed early in 1947 this was considered the first fully-enclosed original sports car built in Germany from VW parts and aircraft scrap.

Good VW sports car designs, after translation tempered by the inadequacies of improvised hand construction, seldom bore a finished look. It was a sport picked out of the rubble, piece by piece, and given the breath of life with "liberated" fuel. The Specials reflected a unique character to the introspective racing fan: every hour's work, every part that went into them, had been rendered only at the sacrifice of constructive labor and barter which otherwise might have brought bread to the family table.

In the absence of the usual factory participation — traditionally the backbone of motor racing — the sport revived in those days immediately after the collapse of Germany out of a human craving for contrast. The Germans sought escape from reality with an all-consuming intensity. Although there was hardly enough matériel available for the vehicles of basic transportation, true racing enthusiasts already were tinkering with their pieced-together cars in improvised workshops; the Germans were striving to reestablish their beloved motor sport. The People's Car of wartime vintage became a People's Toy, an object of joy for the first time in its existence.

Among the earliest supporters of the new sport was Petermax Mueller who built this deftly reshaped speedster in 1947. When he climbed through the field to prominence in post-war *Kuebel* racing he pressed on to further fame as an auto racing figure that stretched back to the stock car (DKW) Auto-Union factory team days, and to motorcycling before. Yet Mueller's greatest fame lay ahead. Vollmer, Kunhke and Mueller had dug deeply into their pockets to attain the degree of professionalism in their cars that they did achieve.

General configuration expressed in the styling of the Delfosse body, of the barnstorming period, proved precursor of the racing designs of several cars, notably among them the Alfa Romeo *Disco Volante*.

When the new currency was established in 1948, widespread consumer purchasing power again became a reality. Hard money brought increased life-span and vitality to competition cars in the form of new replacement parts; more and more complete machines could be seen among the motley racing stock.

Contests among these strictly home-built automobiles were both weird and wonderful to a people so recently stripped of all material possessions. Race interest was torrid as late as 1951, and the post-war period produced the largest crowds in German auto-racing track attendance history.

It was primarily the VW chassis that afforded prewar racing personalities this opportunity to renew their enthusiasm for speed; and it furnished a generation of new drivers with the basis for developing their driving form. Some members of this informal grass-roots level racing crowd later attained prominence with the Volkswagen in a much more dignified fashion as they became affiliated with the VW distribution, sales, and service organizations.

A few months before Delfosse produced this aluminum-bodied racing car, in 1949, Dr. Ferdinand Porsche and his son, working modestly in a small garage in an Austrian village, had shaped up a "Sunday sports car"—the first of a new breed that one day would bring new motor racing laurels to Germany.

PETERMAX MUELLER

An outstanding figure in German auto racing from 1946 to 1951 was Petermax Mueller, whose long-standing enthusiasm for the motor sport played a major role in reestablishing auto racing in post-war Germany.

Petermax spent his youth in Potsdam, just outside Berlin, where his father owned several boats; and as a boy young Mueller participated in numerous outboard motorboat races on the many lakes and streams in the Berlin area. His racing interest did not remain confined to motorboats, and he entered his first regularity runs on Zundapp and NSU motorcycles in 1931 — just days after he had received his first driver's license. Giving advance notice of his later fame as a long distance driver, he won the gold medal in a 1250-mile drive in 1934 on a BMW side-car machine as the only private driver in his class. Soon after he took over the Auto-Union dealership in Potsdam in 1937 his racing interest turned to automobiles. Auto-Union soon made Petermax one of its racing team drivers, and in 1938 he won the class victory in the Rallye Monte Carlo in a DKW — the first German driver ever to accomplish this feat. In 1939 he won second in his class in the same event, took third in the overall competition in the Liege-Rome-Liege run, driving a two-liter Wanderer special. Mueller's fame as a long distance specialist grew in the pre-war period as he aggressively participated year in and year out in the well-publicized East Prussian and Alpine runs.

After an adventurous escape — by swimming the Elbe River — from the Eastern Zone in 1945, Mueller settled in Velpke, near Braunschweig. Shortly after, he began work on his first VW-based special streamliner, which is credited with being the first of its type after the war. Mueller's success as designer and driver of specials built around the VW chassis and engine reached its high point in 1948 and 1949, when he became two-time German champion in the 1100cc class.

Mueller's interest in the VW became more formal in 1950, when he moved to Hanover and assumed the Volkswagen and Porsche distributorship there. In spite of his business interests, Mueller continued to race for a time; and in 1951 and 1952 he drove Porsche factory cars in the Liege-Rome-Liege and Le Mans events. He has since retired from racing, but Mueller remains one of the most vital figures in automotive Germany.

With a series of successes in a progression of VW Specials behind, Mueller put in an appearance, with countrymen Walter Glockler, Helmut Polensky and Huschke von Hanstein also driving in his stable, at Montlhery, a speedway near Paris. Here he recaptured a place for Germany in international racing by breaking the class records with an average of 76 mph in his VW Special for a distance of 6200 miles.

A brief interlude as an English car dealer (MG-Riley) in Germany in 1950, during which Petermax Mueller found himself very much out of his element, punctuated his career between the rough and tumble VW Special racing days and a more formal station as VW-Porsche distributor in Hanover.

These desperate years in the history of German automobile racing were a continuous trial for the valiant little VW. The car proved its mettle in grinding competition; the vanguard of post-war German race drivers found the Volkswagen a hard car to kill. Their punishment of the VW rendered a peculiar twist to Hitler's old slogan: Strength through Joy.

Huschke von Hanstein leads the way out of the pits in one of Mueller's Volkswagen Special team cars. Like Mueller, he was to cap a long racing apprenticeship by achieving great favor with Porsche in days to come. For both, days with the Specials proved the perfect prelude to brilliant driving for the Porsche factory team in days to come. For 1951 Porsche records would be credited directly to Mueller's resources. Von Hanstein went on to become racing and publicity director of Porsche in Stuttgart.

8

WHITE ELEPHANT, LTD.

**"We do not consider that the design represents any special brilliance
... It is not to be regarded as an example of first class modern design
to be copied by the British Industry."**

At War's end, remnant pieces of the big plant at Wolfsburg were sprawled in what was to be established as the British zone. Almost immediately the site fell host to commissioners who had been assigned to rend law and order out of chaos and rubble. The reincarnation of VW began on a summer evening in 1945 when a British Major stood before the motley assemblage of former workers at Wolfsburg and concluded his introductory remarks with "We may even produce a few cars." It was to be a valiant but restricted effort, for grand scale know-how would be lacking.

Under British direction former workers, who had been grubbing around the ruined factory ever since surrender, were put to work. Some machine tools and dies that had lain buried under piles of rubble or exposed to the elements were reclaimed. Car parts were exhumed from the tangles of wreckage, then fitted to war-damaged vehicles to get them rolling again. These pieced-together VWs were then used to support the cleanup and reconstruction campaign around the factory. Soon the VW plant was serving as a maintenance depot for the British motor pool.

Nearly all of the VWs in the area had been "liberated" by the commissioners for official use. Most were used without incident. But from the beginning one officer's fascination with the vehicle was almost out of character for a British officer. He had arranged for a crew of British Army mechanics to hand assemble a *Schwimmwagen* from various new and used components for his personal use. He refused the services of a driver, preferring to be behind the wheel himself.

While the *Schwimmagen* made headway to the particular delight of British VW factory overseers when they plied the Canal running through Wolfsburg . . .

. . . little headway was made among top administrators back in England toward acceptance of the Volkswagen as a design worthy of concerted production under British control. Even effort to attract an American manufacturer to consider operating the plant as a subsidiary resulted only in dismissal on a dismal note. A top executive from Dearborn closed the discussions by saying, "I don't think what we are being offered here is worth a damn!"

This Major's appreciation of the car's capabilities was all-consuming, and much time was spent demonstrating the amphib to visiting officers. After he navigated the little vehicle across mud holes and churned his way along water ditches, passengers usually were pleading for the demonstration to end. It was then that he would perform his finale — a spectacular leap into the Mittelland Canal from a running start. His enthusiasm for the VW proved infectious among the British staff.

Examples were sent back to England for examination, along with recommendations that the factory be confiscated, rebuilt and set up to produce VWs under British control. But top men in the British motor industry, fantastic as it may seem today, after extensive testing, declared the car to be unworthy of British consideration for manufacture under their control.

As front lines sometimes changed possession quickly, back and forth, on occasion vehicles fell into the hands of the enemy along with other matèriel. Early in the War the English captured an army VW, complete with operation manual, tested it extensively and published the results in a British Intelligence study.

British motor company examiners, in their reporting, gave
no credit to the obvious advantages of the *Wehrmachtkue-
bel's* rear engine location, which simplified chassis layout
and affected a substantial saving in over-all weight. Only
dissenting voices among the British acclaimed the VW as
a respectable concept.

THE BRITISH CONDEMN

Initial Allied policy in Germany after surrender made various German industrial
establishments available to occupying powers for dismantling and removal; and the Volkswagen concern was among those offered to the conquerors. No American, French, or
Russian manufacturer was recorded as having shown any interest at all in the vast VW
plant and its unorthodox product. In contrast, various representatives of the British
automobile industry did make the trip to Wolfsburg. But they found that most of the
plant was rubble and its equipment so badly damaged it would be unprofitable to repair
and ship to Britain.

Nor did the British industry have a very high opinion of the VW design. Sundry
military and civilian VW's were captured by British troops during the war, and the British
Intelligence Objectives Sub-Committee had the British Motor Industry carry out thorough
tests and examinations of the captured cars.

Typical British Industry opinion was expressed by Humber, Ltd., in its test report
for the BIOS:

"The design is particularly interesting because it is quite uninfluenced by any
previous traditions, and it is doubtful if the question of whether the public would
or would not like a car with an air-cooled engine positioned at the rear was considered
by the designer. This model has departed almost entirely from the conventional
motor car . . . In spite of the assumed freedom of the designer and the unconventional
vehicle produced, little or no special advantage has been obtained in production cost,
neither does it appear that any improvement in performance or weight compared
with the more conventional type of vehicle known in the country has been achieved.

"So far as materials are concerned, no signs of the use of any ingeniously applied
materials have been found, in other words the material specification is, with few
exceptions, very parallel with what is already well known in this country . . .

"A study of the engine indicated that the unit was, in certain details, most inefficient. The design of the inlet manifold makes it clear that the designer did not
intend the unit to produce power proportionate to its capacity, and from a study of
both the design and condition of the crank bearings it is very doubtful whether it
was even capable of giving reliable service had it produced a performance com-
mensurate with its size.

"Looking at the general picture, we do not consider that the design represents
any special brilliance, apart from certain of the detail points, and it is suggested that
it is not to be regarded as an example of first class modern design to be copied by
the British Industry."

And certainly to this day none of the conservative British auto manufacturers has
copied the VW design, despite the continuing inroads on British auto sales made by
the VW.

Favorable remarks came not from the manufacturers, but from their less-biased trade association executives, who concluded for the record that the car offered a potential as cheap transportation. Even so, and after reconsideration, officially, Great Britain turned "thumbs down" to the project of turning Wolfsburg into a British automobile manufacturing outpost.

Other British auto authorities belittled the car's "sluggish performance," and the "excessive engine noise of the unconventional air-cooled engine." Some asserted that the VW would only be popular with the buying public for two or three years, then the fad would wear off.

British army officers, however, had come to different conclusions about the car. They considered the military VW an excellent vehicle for its purpose, praising most particularly its ease of maintenance and repair. The VW required only a minimum of tools and equipment for field repairs, and its light weight allowed repairmen to use all sorts of improvised jacks and hoists.

There were exceptions to the prevailing negative opinion of the VW within the British Industry, too. Maurice Olley, Chief Research Engineer for Vauxhall, in BIOS Overall Report No. 21, published in 1949, later proved himself clairvoyant when he stated:

"Although a number of the reports give space to the Volkswagen, and one report is devoted exclusively to it, one doubts whether they convey a true idea of the possibilities of this car. They refer chiefly to captured military equipment or to staff cars hastily 'run up' from pre-war stocks for the military government, and subjected to military usage. We have yet to see what the makers, left to themselves, can make of this car in the way of a vehicle suitable for normal civilian use."

"Perhaps the critics of the vehicle forget that large areas of the world are still looking for cheap transportation and that the Model T Ford, which started world motorization, also had technical faults.

"This car, at its pre-war selling price of RM 990, was certainly a challenge to the whole motor industry."

Even though an investigation committee of the Society of Motor Manufacturers and Traders, Ltd., in another BIOS publication favorably reported the following:

"It is suggested that a very close investigation be made of the design of this vehicle as it would appear to offer, with perhaps a few modifications, a possible solution of the cheap utility vehicle which would be acceptable in this country and in the overseas markets."

Still, the prevailing judgment among the English held that the car was not up to British standards, and concluded that it would be very foolish for Great Britain to concern herself with the VW at all.

When the plant was singled out as a target for Allied bombing raids in the closing days of World War II, production lines at Wolfsburg were knocked out in every stage of assembly. Complete and near complete engines lay under the ruins in one bay, chassis in another, and wheels and tires under other debris. Even a shipment of *Kuebelwagen* bodies, fresh from the Ambi Budd Pressworks in Berlin hunched derelict nearby. Some assemblies lacked only final attention to roll out as finished automobiles. It was a condition that challenged scavengers and Occupation alike.

Commissioners stationed at the outpost Wolfsburg, in contrast, hoped England would change her official mind about adding the VW to the ranks of British cars after she had seen more of the little beetle. Work-hungry refugees, and the scant Wolfsburg populace, who had nothing left but their dreams, were standing ready to support any effort to revitalize the great plant.

With a select number of former employees the British commissioners began the seemingly hopeless task of setting up some sort of VW output, almost entirely without sanction. Workers' only rewards were a noon meal, a few cigarettes (then worth at least one hour's hard labor) and the hope of securing some sort of compensation in the future. It was not a very business-like arrangement. Parts on hand were inventoried; a few more tools and machines were unearthed from the ruins and put into working order. The men freely "obtained" supplies wherever they could be found. The first coal came from two barges drifting derelict nearby. Assembly of a few cars amidst the shambles began to appear possible.

Virtually hand-tooled *Kuebelwagen* and *Schwimmwagen* models began to take form along a motley production line. Some of the finished cars fell into the personal possession of soldiers, who prized the VW highly as booty; others remained in the official service of the Occupation staff.

Nine hundred seventeen units were assembled in 1945; then the back-log of pre-manufactured parts, from which the cars were being assembled, dwindled to nothing. Shortages of body panels and finished transmissions brought a halt to one man's valiant effort to revive the Volkswagen.

But England was not finished with the VW. As occupation continued on into early 1946, the British authorities in Germany found that they needed some source of motor vehicles within the British Zone if Britain was to speed her recovery at home. The VW factory was the only automobile plant in their Zone which could practically be redeveloped to produce cars in quantity. The military government also saw the need to establish normal working conditions in Wolfsburg, thereby providing employment to the people of the area and creating a greater degree of law and order.

The British Occupation resumed production of VW's early in 1946. From this point on, producing cars entailed manufacturing parts and sub-assemblies, rather than simply bolting together pre-finished components reclaimed from the rubble. The Occupation now received official British government backing, but it proved far from adequate to rehabilitate the VW plant fully. As a result, the efforts by the British Military Government at grand-scale VW production were ineffectual; only about 9,000 units were produced in 1946, and slightly less in 1947.

At first British Army forces absorbed nearly all of this production; but later the Occupation put a few VW's up for sale, even exporting a shipment of cars to Holland in 1947. Very few German civilians were able to purchase cars

This historic moment in October, 1947, marked the beginning of an export program at Wolfsburg that one day was to dwarf every other export achievement on the Continent. Ben Pon, Dutch importer, at left, accepts the first six Volkswagens ever sold for distribution outside Germany. Beside him are K. Schmuecker, P. J. Kock, F. Novotny (VW Press Chief), Dr. Feuereissen and K. Th. Martens. (Earliest postwar assemblies were marked with hub caps of the same nippled style used on *Wehrmacht* VWs.)

Soldiers of American Occupation, through their Post Exchange system, were able to purchase the British-sponsored production by counting out approximately $645, if they were lucky, demand being so great that buyers had to be selected by lottery. Even so, the car proved a disappointment to many U. S. troops, who had been accustomed at home to bigger engines, smoother shifting and less operational noise. Sometimes it might have been the other way around, with the VW becoming "disappointed" with its owner —as might have been the case with this well-lit VW bearing an American Occupation license. (Sphere-section hub caps with giant VW emblem marked the first change in hub cap design since 1939.)

during the time before currency reform; the VW factory required payment from buyers in cash in order to cover future production costs. Occupation soldiers were usually the only persons with enough hard cash to buy.

As the Western Allies gradually reached agreement that economic re-development of Germany, and not economic revenge, was the wiser policy, the great unrealized potential of the VW factory became a source of embarrassment to British authorities. Great Britain had shown little interest in producing the small car for herself, but to continue on in the current half-hearted manner would merely be senseless.

In 1947 the British began a search to find a qualified new industrial leader who could bring the struggling VW works out of stagnation. After some searching they selected Heinz Nordhoff as the man who might be able to do the job. They had undoubtedly invited the best man for the position — perhaps the only individual in all Germany with the peculiar training, understanding, capability, and drive to make a success of the challenge he was asked to face.

The British Occupation Authorities had chosen Nordhoff as the man to restore the VW factory and to create normal conditions of employment in Wolfsburg; but in selecting this man, the British officers had unwittingly set the cornerstone for the competition which eventually would put the whole export market of the British motor industry in jeopardy.

9

THE RELUCTANT PHOENIX

"Up to this moment I had never even driven one of the cars."

If Germany pinned its hopes for recovery in the post-war period on free enterprise and on natural resources, it was no less counting on its industrial leaders; and Heinz Nordhoff was outstanding even in this country noted for its brilliant technical and industrial men. Through his broad experience as a worker as well as an administrator Nordhoff was extraordinarily well equipped for the monumental task of managing the postwar Volkswagen factory.

Born in Hildesheim in a rural area of Lower Saxony on January 6, 1899, he was the second of three brothers, the son of a small-town banker. As a schoolboy he recognized the wisdom in the old German saying: "The future belongs to those who prepare for it." Heinz was already preparing; he had decided to become an industrial engineer. His productive genius developed from that time onward.

Young Nordhoff accompanied his family in a move to Berlin in 1911. In the capital city he attended classes at the Polytechnic Academy, and he continued his engineering studies with unswerving ambition until World War I interrupted his study. After service as a private in the German Army, during which he received a knee wound in action, Nordhoff began work as an apprentice in the historic Bavarian Motor Works in Munich. He eventually became an aero-engine designer with BMW, and he served there until 1929.

His tenure with BMW was interrupted when he decided on an action which, perhaps more than any other, was to prepare him for automobile manufacturing leadership. Nordhoff had concluded that experience with an American auto company would further his training, so he left BMW to apply for a position in Germany's Opel plant at Ruesselheim, which had recently been purchased by General Motors Corporation of the U.S.A. The interview

Aircraft engines of the *Bayerischen Motorenwerke A.-G.* displayed at the International Paris Exhibition in 1928 in part reflected Nordhoff's hand. (Note that center background display showing mounted prop is from an adjacent exhibit.) By its nature, aero engine design dictated a distillation of the finest practices known in internal combustion engineering. During the period at BMW Nordhoff grew to appreciate the virtues of functional understressing to achieve absolute reliability, and designing with simplicity to effect weight saving. He advanced in the skill of combining the two in engine design. It was an experience that would peculiarly fit him one day to bring absolute maturity to the evolution of the VW engine.

Heinz Nordhoff became progressively more valuable to Opel. After a time as director of the service organization he was advanced to technical consultant to sales management. During the 1930's he spent considerable time at General Motors in the U.S. studying production and sales methods. His service at Opel led to the truck making installation at Brandenburg where he became director. Here Nordhoff's experience served to crystalize his stature in automotive administration, production, and sales, for the monumental job that was to lie ahead.

with his prospective employer, an American, was friendly and casual; and Nordhoff became aware of the cordiality then existing in America between management and workers — a relationship he one day would bring to his own administration.

Nordhoff's initial assignment for Opel was in the service organization, where he wrote technical service manuals. He chose to work a seven day week; and even his vacation was invested in Opel's production lines, as he got to know the workers and their problems. Only his marriage in 1930 to his sweetheart, Charlotte Fassunge, followed by a brief honeymoon, took him temporarily from his intensive work at Opel. Occasional trips to Michigan to keep abreast of American production methods were "vacation" enough for Nordhoff. In 1930, at 31 years of age, he became head of Opel's service department. He reflects of his days with Opel: "Work was not a duty, it was a sporting challenge to show what you could do."

Nordhoff stayed with Opel many years, eventually becoming a member of their board of directors. In 1940 he assumed the helm of Opel's Brandenburg truck factory, then the largest in Europe. His responsibilities there included the diplomatic task of dealing with the Nazis, whereas he personally was not in sympathy with the Party Line. His able administration at the plant, which turned out three to four thousand heavy vehicles each month for the German Army during the war, was highly respected by the Hitler regime; and he was never pressured into becoming a party member.

Former plant directors from German industry were probably the least sought after of all personnel in the labor market at war's end. Brandenburg, like the rest of Soviet-controlled East Germany, was being looted of its industrial tools, and the Russians did not spare the mammoth Opel plant. Prospects for recovery seemed nil; and Heinz Nordhoff's future as a motor car administrator appeared bleak.

A SHOVEL OR A BROOM

While Opel's giant Berlin truck plant had fallen into Russian hands and was being dismantled, its last chief executive, Heinz Nordhoff, still held hopes of returning to the GM fold once conditions had eased. For immediate survival after the war he held his family together with a mechanic's job in a Hamburg repair shop. The home and possessions of 25 years had been left behind when the family had slipped into the Western zone. Only when Nordhoff's application for a position with GM was rejected, as coldly as though he had once been no more than a stock boy, did he know that his future lay in some other direction.

General Motors had officially taken the position that employees who had also been wartime enemies were not to be rehired in the wake of the war. At that moment when this international corporation, like other foreign companies with subsidiary operations in enemy territory, had okayed its sites as targets for bombing, it had written off these properties and cut off their people with brutal finality. As far as his future was concerned, the gate back to Brandenburg or to any arm of GM was closed and locked.

Even worse, as director of a war matériel plant he had served the Third Reich well, even though he had never become an actual Nazi Party member. This record was the supreme blackball with American occupation powers and he was barred from any but menial hand labor.

"Yes," said one U.S. officer, "we'll give you a job, and even a choice...you can have a shovel or a broom. But you can never build cars again." The officer's remark was dead wrong. But at this time, and in this place, his word was The Law.

But Heinz Nordhoff was not defeated in spirit. He lived as best he could during those hard post-war years, confident that he would one day find a place to build cars in a new Germany. He was destined to perform a national miracle for his people.

10

TOMORROW IS TOO LATE!

"I am with it heart and soul. The future begins when you cut every tie with the lost past."

With vivid recall of the grandiose promotion a once omnipotent Nazi regime had engineered to steam-roller the Volkswagen into a position of unfair competition with Opel, Nordhoff was firmly reluctant to associate himself with the post-war straits of the Volkswagen, which he regarded as "a poor thing, cheap, ugly and inefficient." But he condescended to admit of himself "The motor industry *has* gotten under my skin."

When the British approached Heinz Nordhoff with their job offer in 1947, he was not immediately attracted to the Volkswagen proposition. Trained in the American automotive tradition by GM, he held little regard for the small car concept; and in his administration at Opel, he met Hitler's nationalized *KdF* car project with scorn, branding it as "cheap and unfair competition." Even without his particular background it would have been natural for Nordhoff to share the distrust of the VW common among all German auto manufacturers. The beetle car had challenged the whole industry at its original price of RM 990 —. It had been a deeply disturbing thought for any car maker to see the taxes on his free enterprise being used to build up a state-owned competitor which would have first choice of capital, machinery, materials, and labor.

Nordhoff's distaste for the VW was no more pronounced than that of other motor makers who once had faced the probability of competition with the State-financed *KdF* in a most unfair price climate. The People's Car had been tagged to *undercut* their free-enterprise-based prices many times—in the case of Nordhoff's small Opel, as well as this 1938 DKW, by a clean *two-thirds.*

When Nordhoff was approached by British Colonel Charles Radclyfe about coming to Wolfsburg, he could not have dreamed that he would express his gratitude to the old gentleman posthumously one day by presenting his widow with a milestone British market Volkswagen sedan. But he listened as the Colonel painted his proposal. He was challenged with a review of the enormous potential of the Wolfsburg plant, and with the prospect of lifting himself and his family out of a day-to-day existence. The British Occupation Commission, with more naiveté than good business sense, was insistent. Nordhoff's ingrained reluctance transcended to an attraction for this car nobody wanted. "I saw that there was no going back to GM — and nothing but laborer's work for me in the U.S. zone. I decided that what the British were offering me in their occupation zone was better than nothing.

"I accepted and became director at Wolfsburg — and up to this moment I had never even driven one of the cars."

The little auto that Petermax Mueller's crowd had proved so tough was going to be revived yet again.

Once he had accepted the British invitation, Heinz Nordhoff never looked back. "I am with it heart and soul," he reflected; "The future begins when you cut every tie with the lost past."

The problems facing Nordhoff in 1948 were staggering. Though the British had cleared some sections of the VW factory for their sporadic production of the VW, the great mass of what was once Europe's most modern industrial plant was still a shambles of wreckage and deterioration when Nordhoff stepped upon the scene. Only one happy fact encouraged him; somehow the immense powerhouse had escaped any direct hits by bombs.

Heinz Nordhoff's image of the pre-war VW as a monster of unfair competition first began to lose its significance when he considered that any future production would receive no government support and would sink or swim on its own merit in a free market. He began to reflect on how he might materially improve the product. His prejudice against Volkswagen dissolved, and the rebuilding of Wolfsburg by democratic principles became Nordhoff's passion.

The city of Wolfsburg, which had been only partially completed before the war, had suffered damage from air raids and vandalism. The original populace and numerous bands of refugees still existed in improvised huts. Nordhoff was thus faced with the responsibility of providing housing and employment for tens of thousands of people. And since no one was ready to subsidize the VW factory with unlimited, interest-free capital, as was the case during the Third *Reich,* Nordhoff had to establish a selling price and a rate of production for his car which would enable him to finance VW's operations realistically. He had to bring the war-gutted plant up to a commercial level of operation and efficiency.

The lost time of the dead days became only a remote memory, as Nordhoff threw himself into his work with demonic energy. For many months he was back on a seven-day work week; he slept on an army cot in one corner of his wind-swept temporary office.

Nordhoff's experience in American industry had taken from him all the superior airs of the traditional German works director, and he worked side by side with his men to clean up and rebuild. Amidst the desolation of Wolfsburg, his warm and understanding ways with his workers established a closer relationship between labor and management than the Germans had ever experienced before. Nordhoff was able to keep before his workers the belief that man holds the course of destiny in his own hands, that for both the workers and himself there were but two alternatives: to succeed or to die.

When the big signs reading "WOLFSBURG MOTOR WORKS," which the British had erected along the main frontage during their tenure, mysteriously were replaced by others restoring the original name VOLKSWAGENWERK, British overseers quietly let Nordhoff's change stand. His prime condition in accepting the directorship had been "No interference." Privately, the British probably were relieved to find themselves disassociated at last with what had become for them a very white elephant.

One of the most pressing needs for workers in the area was for a place to live. Nordhoff's design and development of 4,000 company housing units in Wolfsburg paralleled his enterprise in redevelopment of the factory as a production force. One required the other.

Construction of a special residence was announced by Nordhoff to offer single apartments for the workers without families, in 1951. Speculation arose at the time that the comforts of this home "where workers would feel just as though they were at home with mother" would decrease the marriage rate in the area proved without foundation. In years to come even the number of children per Wolfsburg family was to rise above the national average.

NO! TO A RUFFLE IN THE IRON CURTAIN

By the time the British called upon Nordhoff to "Make something of it, if you can" they were already at the end of their royal rope. They had previously attempted with embarrassing lack of success to administrate the plant themselves. They had offered the plant to any Allied government that might want it. All had declined.

Soon after Nordhoff had taken the helm they were confronted with a new problem. This time they performed to their everlasting credit. The Russians one day proposed acquiring the factory as a reparation by simply moving the border about five miles to the west in order to append Wolfsburg to the Eastern zone in a sort of peninsula. The British voice had been loud and clear in the negative. No further Russian efforts to put this ruffle in the Iron Curtain were recorded.

While the original Type 38 engineering design was basically worthy, a pattern of faults and weaknesses appeared as the VW finally got into a semblance of mass-production under Nordhoff. Complaints of short engine life, excessive noise, underpower, weak braking, and stiff riding qualities became legion. Nordhoff knew that for total acceptance with the public the car had to satisfy the owner mechanically and also as an investment; it had to look lively and perform in accordance with its appearance. It should be made to appeal to the heart as well as to the pocketbook.

Without altering the basic Porsche concept, Nordhoff and his designers set to work to correct the car's gross faults. Under his close direction teams of engineers redrew Porsche's original drawings as many as ten times, and eventually no single part in the VW corresponded exactly in its dimensions to the original pre-war Series 38 design. Then the engine was strengthened and pepped up; its noise level was reduced; the braking system was improved; the hard ride was softened; the life of parts in general was lengthened.

Production of the improved VW was expanded slowly, but at last the VW was on a firm foundation. The beetle had come of age.

Volkswagen "Type 11," first actual production after the war, depicts details long since altered. At this time engineering development had not been advanced beyond that of the Hitler era; production was an almost literal duplication of the prewar and *Kuebelwagen* model engine and chassis. Illustrations are taken from an operator's manual which was bilingual, in German and English, confirming that a principal market for the original post-war product lay among occupation troops from England and the U. S. A. Soon after, under the direction of Nordhoff, the Volkswagen was to undergo a virtually total engineering overhaul. People had said, "We like it technically, but we can't afford to be seen in it." Nordhoff's efforts were bent to take the car out of the atmosphere of austerity, for he had said, "Austerity touches neither the heart nor the pocketbook." Engine and fan noise were decreased, longevity of component parts was substantially (if not phenomenally) extended, horsepower was elevated from 25 to 30, and ride and braking force were improved. The whole automobile began to bear large and small changes reflecting Heinz Nordhoff's fruitful experience with Opel.

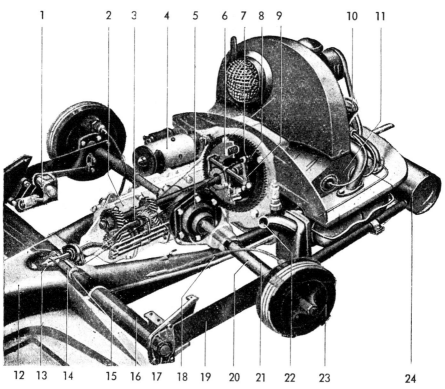

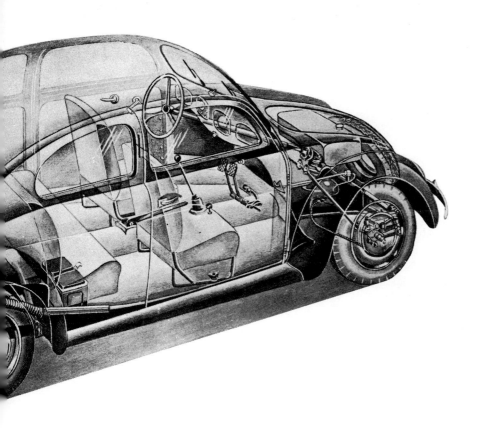

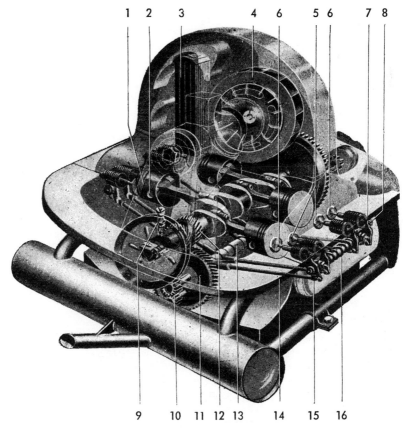

While Nordhoff was able to reclaim some 1,600 milling machines and other heavy tools that had been hauled from the plant site to the relative safety of nearby farm buildings in the later days of the war, every new precision machine for his production program had to be purchased outside Germany with hard cash. Shipping the VW abroad provided this currency. Many heavy pieces came from the USA like this battery of fully automatic camshaft grinders.

FINANCING NEW MACHINERY

Perhaps the most urgent task which confronted Nordhoff in 1948 was modernizing and equipping the VW plant with adequate machinery. Many of the tools which had been installed in 1939 had been destroyed in the war, others had been looted or vandalized. The cars produced since the war by the British had been tooled almost by hand, and the limited machinery they had been able to restore to service was already obsolete.

Much of the new heavy machinery which Nordhoff needed in order to set up grand scale production could only be purchased for hard currency in overseas markets. Under the Federal Republic's free enterprise policy, however, German manufacturers could obtain foreign currency only by exporting finished products. Nordhoff had to produce a quantity of cars for export if he were to carry out his plans for modernization and expansion.

Nordhoff rationalized his existing facilities as much as possible, then concentrated his attention in 1948 on certain export markets where currency was freely convertible, as in Switzerland and Belgium. (The very first export of VW's was before Nordhoff's time, when the British sent fifty-six VW's to Holland in 1947.) The next year Nordhoff expanded export operations to include Denmark and Sweden.

Increasing production taxed the output of the plant's Klingelnberg gear cutters. Additional tools, sorely needed for modernization and expansion, were imported as rapidly as receipts from Volkswagen exports afforded the ready funds. Transmission gears came also to be profiled on American-made Gleason machines.

Almost from the beginning Volkswagen dealers were given the ability to supply any feasible order for spare parts from immediate stocks. Dealers laid in 8,400 items from complete bodies to contact points. Parts in this warehouse of the Porsche-Hof, distributor in Austria, were considered a four months' supply. An old-style top panel (pre-March 1953) may be seen amidst a predominant stock of the succeeding style, then current.

A confirmed belief, dating from his Opel service department days, in the principle that "A car is no better than its available service facilities" brought Nordhoff to establish an extensive sales and service organization in every country to which he intended to export Volkswagens, even before the cars arrived in a volume to warrant the installation.

This policy of pre-service was unprecedented in the history of the industry, and no sales promotion could have done more to popularize the car. Even in countries where the people retained animosity towards any German product, motorists recognized that the VW was the only car available with a sales and service organization comparable to those of the largest American auto companies. The VW was enormously successful as an ambassador of good will; and many Europeans soon lowered the barrier of anti-German feeling through their need for and enjoyment of the little beetle.

Export sales soared beyond all predictions. By 1950 Nordhoff's export program had been so successful in foreign markets that export production had increased four times over the previous year; total VW production was up by a factor of two. Nordhoff was able to purchase with hard currency the machinery he had needed for expansion, and in turn he could offer the world markets an expanded volume of VW's. The circular response that followed was one of success spawning more success.

Depots sprung up in way stations of 83 countries throughout the free world by 1952. An African agent in Tangier, where proverbial ships of the desert peacefully intermingled with their Wolfsburg-bred successors, was typical of many outposts where VW helped to bring contemporary contrast to a distant, historic age.

Encouraged by the transformation taking place around them, and inspired by the man who stood shoulder to shoulder with them in their effort, the workers responded to Nordhoff with a contagious enthusiasm. There had never before been such rapport in Germany between labor and management; and to this day Heinz Nordhoff's office door is open to any worker with an occupational or social problem.

At the 1953 Stockholm Chamber of Commerce, Nordhoff said:

"The worth of making one-third of the places on the VW Board of Directors available to representatives from the body of the workers has proved itself, and especially so, in that we have turned from the Functionaries to the true Personalities in the firm — and more than anyone else the workers of the firm belong in this category."

During the early stages of VW production in 1948 no one knew exactly how much a completed car was costing. Nordhoff installed a strict cost accounting system on the stream of raw materials flowing into one end of the plant, another on the man-hours expended inside, and a third on the finished product being shipped out at the far end of the factory. He was soon able to tell his workers that four hundred man-hours were required to produce one car. He asked them to cut that time to one hundred man-hours. His critical study and improvement of production methods reduced the number of workers required to produce 1000 VW's from 744 in 1946 to 100 as early as 1953.

When the British Occupation authorities turned the plant over to the German Federal Government and the State of Lower Saxony in September, 1949, the Nordhoff family at Wolfsburg numbered ten thousand. More than double the number of vehicles of the year before had been produced so far that year, including over 5,000 for export. It was only the beginning.

KdF offices once had promoted the vision of cars popping off the end of an assembly line like peas falling out of a pod. Now under the free-enterprise leadership of Heinz Nordhoff it was coming to pass.

Assembly lines in Ireland, South Africa, and Brazil, as well as North Germany, were producing the familiar beetle by 1954, with more plants abuilding. Production had reached such a rate that it was dwarfed only by the American big three. Volkswagen appeal to the world's heart and purse had hardly begun.

11

MAD DASH TO RENOWN

"I wish I could have nailed the gas pedal down, then my right leg
wouldn't have fallen asleep so often."

Volkswagens participated in motor racing events all over the globe in the early 1950's with remarkable success. These competition achievements greatly enhanced the car's worldwide reputation. The VW never disappointed racing backers under even the most trying conditions, from the Giant Rally across North Africa to the rough Round Australia Rallye. But of all the VW sporting triumphs, perhaps the story of the car's participation in the *Carrera Panamericana Mexico* of 1954 is the most exciting and widely praised. The first person story of the VW role in the Mexican road race is told by Prince Alfonso de Hohenlohe, Captain of the Volkswagen team.

A short time after I had taken over the Volkswagen agency in Mexico City I happened to overhear a conversation between our sales manager, Señor Vera, and one of our prospects on the floor. Señor Vera, an excellent automobile salesman, had been able to satisfy his potential customer, Señor Gonzales, on all points of discussion save one: Señor G. would not believe that one can drive this 30 hp. *tortuga* (turtle) on Mexican country roads and across mountain passes exceeding 10,000 feet without breaking down. I quote his words:

"I drive a 240 hp. Cadillac and I don't believe that you can get across the mountains with only one eighth of this horsepower. Besides, you will overwork a small motor like this on long distances and ruin it, since it cannot stand to be driven at top speed for long, etc., etc."

A test drive through the city is sufficient to convert most prospects to customers — but to convince Sr. Gonzales would have required a trip far beyond the city limits. This problem of selling the VW's rugged qualities harassed me throughout the day, and as I fell asleep that night it was still unsolved. Soon the problems of Sr. Gonzales were replaced by others still more distressing. In my dreams I was a driver in the approaching Panamerican Road Races, racing wildly through the Sierra Madres. Past Oaxaca on the second leg of the race, my car went out of control on one of the many precarious turns. Leaving the road completely, it took to the air. As we flew along I turned reassuringly to my co-driver: "Don't be afraid, I have a pilot's license." We aviated for some time in the VW till a sudden jolt brought me rudely to my senses.

Awakening, I found myself on the floor. Through the window the first pale light of dawn cast an eerie shadow across the bedroom. Disappointed, I rolled back into bed and tried to drift off into sleep again. But my mind was already at work and tackling a challenge. From the hazy realm of my semi-conscious the specter of Sr. Gonzales commanded my attention. I was awake now and wrestling with the problem: "How can I convince the *nativos* that the Volkswagen is up to long distances and mountain roads?"

In a flash I recalled the dream: "Why not start a Volkswagen in the next *Panamericana?*" But no — the factory is against any participation in automobile races, and besides that, could the VW hold the average speed of 50 mph? My thoughts shuttled feverishly back and forth, finally resolving themselves: "I am responsible for the representation of Volkswagen in Mexico City and therefore must do everything that I consider advantageous for its promotion. I shall plan a test drive and arrange a thorough discussion with Mr. Manuel Hinke, the business manager of *Volkswagen Mexicana, S.A.*"

I called Mr. Hinke's office very early. "Don Manuel," I fairly shouted, "I have a million dollar idea!"

"Why a million *dollars* today; usually it is just pesos?"

"We'll enter three cars in the Fifth *Carrera Panamericana*. What do you think of that?"

It took him a little while to reply, "Where are the million dollars? All I can see are costs and a very great risk, and besides, you know the opinion of the Company."

After detailing my plan to Mr. Hinke and assuring him that a success in the *Panamericana* could mean much more to the company than a million dollars, since the sales in America would rise correspondingly, I let him have the clincher. I declared myself willing to bear the costs, place three cars at our disposal, drive one car myself, supply the servicing, and take over the registration fees. That convinced him.

Wherever the car was exported enthusiasts soon made it a part of the racing scene. The wealthy and titled sportsman Alfonso de Hohenlohe barely had settled, after becoming the Volkswagen agent in Mexico City, before his confidence in the durable nature of his product was expanding without bounds. By privately financing a racing team in the *Carrera Panamericana* he hoped to popularize the VW as "right" for Mexico.

A few weeks before the race four famous Mexican race drivers also decided to take part in the *Panamericana,* driving Volkswagens. After I had tested their driving ability on some hairpin turns and sandy roads in the *Parque Chapultepec,* the palace park in Mexico City, I agreed to their participation.

Rules were fixed for the team, with no competitive racing or chasing allowed among team members. On November 16, after the cars had been released by Customs and had received the usual customer-delivery servicing, the Mexican group, composed of Juan de Aguinaco, Axel Wars, Ara Arakelian and Alfonso de la Pena, left. The route to the starting point led through Oaxaca to Tuxtla, a distance of 800 miles from Mexico City. Hinke, Wyers, and I were detained in Mexico City with business for another day, forcing us to drive the entire 800 miles without interruption in order to arrive on time for the start.

After a fast but uneventful journey we arrived in Tuxtla. The only damage was a shattered windshield on Hinke's car, which had broken from following too close on a curve, compelling him to drive 400 miles without a windshield. By the time we reached Tuxtla his car resembled an insect showcase in a museum of natural history, with hundreds of flies, mosquitoes, butterflies, and even a colorful colibri exhibited on the rear window.

The cars were inspected by the Race Committee and found to be in order. When I requested the oil filler caps be sealed, because we wanted to drive the whole of 1900 miles without an oil change, there was much surprise. But then most race drivers are considered not quite normal anyway, so the oil filler caps were duly sealed to the accompaniment of some shoulder shrugging.

We were awakened at 5 a.m. after a rather restless night, filled with worry lest we should fail to maintain the set minimum time in the first leg. All of Tuxtla was up for the events; everybody wanted to be present at the start. The town roared with the noise of 200 engines.

I was the first of our team to leave and my speedometer soon advanced to 45 mph. I shifted into fourth and felt the tenseness and nervousness of the previous hours subside. Relaxed, I took the first curves and considered: More than 1900 miles are before us. Will we make it?

Hoping to gain a few seconds, I opened the throttle at every curve, for I knew that the minimum time was determined very closely. Shortly after the start I took off my crash helmet, as it was most uncomfortable. After brief consideration I put it on again: I had just seen the first accident, and remembered the two Argentines who had crashed fatally during training. It was established later that they could have saved their lives had they worn their helmets instead of hanging them on a hook in the car.

The VW ran superbly, and its roadability was just as outstanding. It was a joy to cut around the curves. As I came to the first straightaways, an Alfa Romeo, driven by Mancini, passed me at about 110 mph. It had started three minutes behind me.

More curves followed, leading downhill to the plains of Tehuantepec, and I closed in on the Alfa Romeo as the VW demonstrated superiority in the tight winding stretches. The speedometer never dropped below 60 mph. At every *Peligro* (danger) sign I gave it more gas. On one downhill stretch I brought the VW up to 85 mph. Once on the plains, however, the Alfa Romeo disappeared into the distance.

Thick rows of people stood alongside the road, where they had been waiting hours for the passing of the cars. From the mountains and the remote villages the Indians had come, for they, too, wanted to witness the *Gran Carrera*.

I glanced in the rear view mirror, hoping to find Wyers' red VW. Instead I found a grey dot, steadily growing larger and larger as Alfa Romeo No. 265 approached and roared past.

Close to Tehuantepec, midway between Tuxtla and Oaxaca, I glanced at the clock and noted with alarm that it had stopped. To maintain our average in the mountains we had to be in Tehuantepec in less than three hours, but without a clock I couldn't figure my time.

There was no sign of my comrades. The air was aglow; perspiration streamed down my forehead. Thank goodness I had affixed an oil temperature gauge to the dashboard. But the motor ran evenly and cleanly. According to my estimation I had driven about three hours. It would be impossible to stop or drive slowly to question the spectators. I had no choice but to go on as fast as possible.

I wish I could have nailed the gas pedal down — then my right leg wouldn't have fallen asleep so often. Later, on the endless straights leading to Durango, as my right foot was completely numb, I operated the accelerator with my left foot.

Far ahead a gleam of light appeared. As I approached it proved to be an American car — a Ford — its radiator spouting steam. By and by I counted 18 disabled cars. Some had crashed into roadside ditches, others had dropped out because of motor failure. Among them were my good friends, the Marquis de Portago — whose Ferrari had burst an oil line, and Bracco — whose Ferrari was crippled by a broken water line in the radiator. After the race he confided "Only air-cooled engines for me!" The Alfa that had passed me also lay at the side of the road. I was told by signs that the drivers were safe, but the engines were gone.

Now we entered the Sierra Madre. In many curves we climbed from sea-level to 6600 feet. I shifted quickly back to third. The speedometer skidded from 70 mph to 45. There seemed to be no end to the curves; minutes turned to hours in my impatient mind.

I intended to stop briefly at the Alfa Romeo box to ask the time, but then I thought that if their watches were not accurate to the second it would be useless to waste precious time. I sped on through the most dangerous stretch of the race. With neither a map nor any other clue I could make only a rough guess as to my whereabouts.

THEN — all of a sudden — THE ENGINE MISSED. Blood surged to my head! "Is this the end?" flashed across my mind. An ominous silence followed; the motor had stopped. The VW rolled forward on its own momentum. In a last ditch attempt I switched over to the reserve fuel tank. After a few suspenseful moments the motor coughed, then ran again. I hardly had time to relax before new worries beset me. "How far is there still to go? Will I get to Oaxaca?" I was on pins and needles. Finally I reached the highest point of this leg — 7300 feet — and descended into a valley in long, sloping straights. I recognized the country again and calmed down a little. But at racing speed you can't run forever with a gallon and a half of fuel — even in a Volkswagen!

But civilization lay ahead. The way was becoming more crowded; more and more people stood at the roadside. Hundreds of cars were parked on the meadows. Everybody waved and called out to me. The Mexicans saw their champion in the VW and thrilled to the performance of the little car. I had passed quite a few Americans on the curves who had started some minutes ahead of me. The public must have liked that. The smallest American car had four times the horsepower of the little VW.

"At long last I spied the distant spires of the Old Spanish colonial town of Oxaca, founded by Cortez. In my enthusiasm I believe I must have shouted aloud!"

At long last I spied the distant spires of the Old Spanish colonial town of Oaxaca, founded by Cortez. In my enthusiasm I believe I must have shouted aloud: "Only a few more miles! I hope the gas supply will last. If I make it in time what will my average be?"

Then, through a long corridor of cheering humanity, I saw before me the sign *Meta* (finish). With my foot jammed to the floor and my horn singing joyfully I dashed to the finsh line of the first day's leg.

Two hundred yards past the line I handed over my *Libreta de ruta* (log). A little farther down a Volkswagen flag waved to me, indicating the way to our service station. We only had one hour before the cars were due in the closed parking lot, where hood and trunk would be sealed for the night.

I was received with stormy applause by our mechanics. Without waiting to stop, I eagerly questioned them about my time and average. Nobody could give me an answer, since the official times had not yet been released. These would be determined later from the entries in the *Libreta de ruta*.

Senor Alvarez Murphy, our VW partner who had organized the quarters and servicing in this race, came rushing in, embraced me in typical Latin style and told me of our good fortune. "You came in one hour and 11 minutes *ahead* of time and your average for today is 63 mph. How did you do it? It is simply unbelievable!" With that he slapped my shoulder so hard I almost choked.

We refueled in a rush — only a little over one quart remained in my reserve gas tank — and checked the oil as a precaution — it stood 1/4 inch higher than at the start. It certainly didn't mean that the Volkswagen had suddenly turned into an oil well! This condition was due to expansion caused by higher temperature.

In 35 more minutes my car was in the closed parking lot. I returned to our service station to help my comrades. Within an hour all seven Volkswagens stood in the parking lot.

Our business at the station completed, we trooped happily to the hotel. There we found Hans Hermann, a German racing driver, who handed me 500 pesos. He had wagered that I couldn't hold the average. At the start earlier in the day, as I wished him *Hals und Beinbruch* (good luck) he had yelled to me, "I'll see you in Oaxaca, and I hope I lose the 500 pesos." I told him to wait and pay off at the end of the race.

That night everyone slept better than the night before. At six the next morning we were ready to go again. The next leg was Oaxaca-Puebla-Mexico City, the most tortuous part of the race. This time the starting order was set up according to total time driven, instead of in categories. Naturally it looked quite strange to see the Volkswagen standing among cars of the *Torismo Especial* class.

Of the Volkswagens, again I was the first to start. Since we had agreed to drive in closed groups of three and four cars each, I drove very slowly after the start to allow time for Hinke and Wyers to catch up. Wyers' windshield had been smashed the first day as he was being "pulled" by Hinke. We called it "pulling" when one car drove in the slip-stream of another, almost bumper to bumper. This "Pull Theory" was to serve us well in the northern straights, as will be seen. Because of the danger involved, race officials had ordered Wyers to install at least a thin wire netting in place of his damaged windshield for the rest of the race. It seemed doubly advisable, since Wyer's wife, the only feminine participant, was co-driver. Rules forbade any repair whatsoever after a car entered the closed parking lot so the netting could only be attached after the start. This meant a further delay of two to three minutes.

At last I saw the two Volkswagens approaching, close together. I accelerated in the lead and our *Dreier-Fahrt* (triple file) began. Uphill and downhill, in a series of close curves, relieved now and then by a few longer ones, we moved on in tandem.

In addition to motoring pleasures, the race thus far had afforded much in the way of scenic variety. The road from Tuxtla led us through the dense tropical jungle of Southern Mexico, then across barren mountainous stretches dotted with towering organ cactus, and finally into the neatly cultivated outskirts of Oaxaca. Beyond we climbed through pine forests almost to the snow line, from whence we descended to the sugar cane plantations and orange groves of Atlixo, only to rise again into the alpine regions between Puebla and Mexico City. Charming, too, were the many small towns along the way, whose narrow streets were lined with curious onlookers.

"Wyers' windshield had been smashed the first day as he was being 'pulled' by Hinke . . . race officials had ordered Wyers to install at least a thin wire netting in place of his damaged windshield for the rest of the race . . . the netting could only be attached after the start. This meant a further delay of two to three minutes."

"We knew that more than 300,000 spectators from Mexico City and Puebla, without counting people from the surrounding country, would be lining the route . . . Crowds cheered us as we whizzed through the curves. Often the curious had to pull their heads back to keep from being grazed by the cars."

The only incident worth mentioning occurred just past Matamoros, when swirling dust obscured my comrades from view. But we soon re-established contact and in a short time arrived in Puebla.

Our friend Wenzel, the VW agent in Puebla, already was waiting for us. The wheels were quickly checked; we had only thirty minutes. After a quick Coke we headed for the starting point.

Ahead lay the shortest but most interesting leg of the race. Everybody in Mexico knows the run from Puebla to Mexico City as a type of comparison stretch for all motorists. It was important for us to make good time. I agreed with Hinke that everyone should go as fast as possible. From former years and the day's radio announcements we knew that more than 300,000 spectators from Mexico City and Puebla, without counting people from the surrounding country, would be lining the route.

Exactly thirty minutes after my arrival in Puebla I got my signal to start. "Ten-five-four-three-two-one-GO!" Mentally I reviewed my driving over the familiar stretch as I wheeled away. "Full throttle here. Take this curve nicely — don't slow too much or there'll be a loss of time getting into the straight." The course ran 80 miles, over a pass 10,000 feet in altitude. At first the road ran in long, slightly rising straights, and the VW lost ground to bigger cars for about 48 miles. The second stretch consisted of steep curves through a forest up to the very crest of the pass, followed by a run of 32 miles downhill.

The following data will give an idea of our speed in this most dangerous section of the race and show just what the VW's remarkable roadability permits. We took just 58 minutes to reach the summit of Rio Frio, averaging about 49 mph — and from there to the terminal point in Mexico City only 15.25 minutes. To our left were sheer drops of up to 2000 feet and to our right soared the snowclad reaches of Ixtachuatl and Popocatepetl.

Crowds cheered to us as we whizzed through the curves. Often the curious had to pull their heads back to keep from being grazed by the cars. Nobody can imagine my inner excitement when I approached the finish. Mexico City, my second home! About one mile past the finish we handed in our log book. A motorcycle policeman, his red light flashing and siren screaming, escorted us at full tilt through town to our Volkswagen workshop.

"This was the day of the longest racing stretch of our lives—600 miles with only a half hour's break in Leon. The road between Mexico City and Toluca wound a gaily curving path over a pass of 10,000 feet . . ."

Our people were impatiently awaiting our arrival. Sixteen minutes later all seven VW's were in. The worst was over; but two-thirds of the race remained in the last three legs to come. The two following runs concerned us most because they demanded such high average speeds. Who would have believed at that time that we would meet such averages, thanks to our new *Knackwurst* (sausage) driving method.

Our workshop lies in the center of town, on the main avenue, Paseo de la Reforma. Fortunately it is very close to the closed parking lot. Our trained mechanics checked the cars completely and begged to change the oil; but we stuck to our original plan and would not permit it.

To compensate for the delays of city traffic the race management allowed two hours for repairs instead of one. However, 35 minutes sufficed for us to put everything in order.

That evening, after a hot bath, I sank into a deep, sound sleep, relieved that the most treacherous stretch lay behind us and that all seven VW's had come successfully to Mexico City. This is not to say that the North held no dangers.

We were awakened at four o'clock, had a hasty breakfast — our first in three days — and left at five to secure the cars from the parking impound.

When the cars were all lined up on the Paseo de la Reforma, we set out on our noisy way down its eight-mile length to the starting point, accompanied by roaring police motorcycles, howling sirens, and loudly cracking exhaust pipes. I doubt if our passage left a single soul still sleeping, despite the early hour and the fact it was Sunday. From partly lighted windows people in nightgowns waved to us; but I can imagine that among those who waved were many who swore. Nevertheless, the general enthusiasm at this early hour was admirable.

By 3 a.m. great crowds of people filled the stretch between Mexico City and Toluca 46 miles away. Warmed by campfires, Indian blankets, and the fruit of the vine, their wait was not lacking in comfort.

Before our departure from Mexico City my father stopped by to wish me luck. I shall never forget his solemn plaint, "Next year I shall drive, and YOU listen to the race on the radio!" One can easily imagine a father's feelings when his son takes part in so dangerous a race.

At 8:46 a.m. the starting flag waved for me. Only 97 cars were left of the 180 that had started at Tuxtla, but all our Volkswagens were still in the race. This was the day of the longest racing stretch of our lives — 600 miles with only a half hour's break in Leon. The road between Mexico City and Toluca wound a gaily curving path over a pass of 10,000 feet, then sloped swiftly downwards to what we knew was the most dangerous curve of the race. I carefully applied my brakes and went into third gear. A spectator waved a yellow jacket in caution. Skidding slightly, I charged into the "ball-bearing" curve. Considerable gravel from the roadside had been scattered onto the dark asphalt and all the outer curbstones were missing. Terrific skid marks were visible. One of my predecessors must have had bad luck — and sure enough, a Pegaso had only minutes before hurtled off the curve, after blazing downhill at 125 mph. The driver had assumed that after a slight dip the road would go straight on. This beautiful handbuilt supercharged car, costing $29,000, was burning among the *agaves*.

The motor of my Volkswagen hummed monotonously as I came out of the mountains into the plain of Queretaro, the town in which Emperor Maximilan was shot. Now came the long straights through a country called El Bajio, with only an occasional curve slightly changing the course.

Cautiously I proceeded through Silaco. Here the road was crossed by many *vados* (flood channels), creating unexpected hazards. In this spot the unforgettable Bonetto was killed a year before in his red Lancia, when he was leading in front of Taruffi, Maglioli, Fangio and Castellotti. In the Volkswagen, however, it was pure delight to jump over those ditches.

At Leon a time check revealed my average to be 62 mph for 215 miles — quite satisfactory. I passed beyond town and waited for my comrades, Hinke and Wyers. We then proceeded bumper to bumper, enabling us to achieve speeds of 70 mph and more. I checked the exact speed a few times at the kilometer signs and established that for every mile we needed about 50-52 seconds, which indicates a speed of around 70 mph.

In triple tandem we drove through a treeless desolate region, only sparsely settled. An occasional ranchero on horseback watched from the roadside, cheering us with a wave of an enormous sombrero. Apparently these observers thought we were trying to pass each other, not realizing that this was our slip-stream tactic.

In Zacatecas, the silver capital of Mexico, the monotony was broken briefly by winding terrain — a real pleasure after the endless straights. Between Zacatecas and Durango the road resumed its bee-line course and we entertained ourselves by passing one another. As an added diversion, Wyers' wife nonchalantly peeled oranges, then handed them through the window to Hinke, who was driving very close to the Wyers' car — all at 70 mph! This disregard for safety angered me so much that when she offered me some orange slices I indignantly declined. Despite their unquestioned driving ability, an accident could have happened through the smallest unevenness in the road.

". . . we entertained ourselves by passing one another. As an added diversion, Wyers' wife nonchalantly peeled oranges, then handed them through the window to Hinke, who was driving very close to the Wyers' car—all at 70 mph!" ("Cream and sugar?")

**PAN-AMERICAN
HIGHWAY SYSTEM
IN MEXICO**

Shortly before Durango this playing around was cut short by sudden and terrifying danger. We had just crested a hill and on descending were confronted with a jam of thousands of cars. A police patrol had just passed through and the spectators, thinking the race over, had streamed onto the road to drive home. Most of them had spent the whole day outdoors toasting the passing cars with tequila (the national beverage distilled from *agave* juice), with the end result that they all drove homewards at racing speed. Slowing drastically, we careened right and left among their cars, with almost continuous bleeps from the horn. Several times we were forced to leave the asphalt and experienced the greatest difficulty in maintaining our course. The fact that we had many minutes ahead of schedule did not diminish our fury at this inexcusable added delay. A Borgward and a few American entries had the same bad luck. This had been the most dangerous moment in the whole race.

In Durango we protested violently to the race management, warning that such a thing should never be allowed to happen again. We had driven the near 600 miles in 8 hours, 52 minutes.

At six o'clock in the morning we were jarred awake by a blaring radio which was announcing the arrival of the cars at the starting point. A background noise of engines filtered through the voice in confirmation. In a flash we were on our feet, dressed and off to the parking lot. All the cars had been picked up save the seven Volkswagens, which stood in lonely rank and file awaiting their masters. Quickly we started the engines and, not even bothering to warm them up first, tore to the starting area. Luckily we were near the end in order of departure, ahead of a few Fords and Chevrolets.

Before long we were off again. Outside of Durango we regrouped in *Knackwurst* formation and forged ahead together. Our equanimity was suddenly shattered by a roar from above. A two-engine aircraft flew barely twenty yards overhead. Friends of ours were aboard. They circled and returned at a very low altitude. As they passed one could distinguish the waving people in the cabin. They photographed us, apparently amused at our way of driving.

At various stages of the race planes had followed the cars. In some ways this is more dangerous than competing in a Ferrari. During the *III Carrera* I followed my friend Karl Kling in my plane, taking still photos and movie shots. Several times I was compelled to tug desperately at the joystick, in mortal fear of hitting some other craft which had appeared from nowhere in front of me.

About 85 miles past Durango the road narrows, and very sharp curves force a slower pace. Just around the first of these curves an Argentinian Chevrolet lay upturned 60 feet below the road in a little ravine. Twelve miles further on a yellow Studebaker lay totally wrecked on the slope. The steering mechanism had broken. Both occupants survived unhurt, I learned later.

This dangerous stretch of curves leads to one of the longest straights in the world. I stopped at the entrance to read the sign at the side of the road: *"Empieza la tangente 90 km. longitud, conductores prueben la velocidad de sus automobiles"* (Here begins the "Tangente," 60 miles long, drivers check the speed of your cars). At that moment I wished I were driving a 550 Porsche. On this straight the Porsches were reputed to have attained a speed of 145 mph. We were content with slightly more than half, and after 42 minutes — clocked — we too had the 60 miles behind us. After some fast downhill stretches we arrived as a group in Parral, so close together that the control official, who was swinging a check-ered flag to mark each arrival, could not keep up with us.

Behind Parral the road climbed a little, then passed through arid regions in long straights and very slight curves to the cotton country. Approaching Chihuahua again there were mild changes in our course. On this stretch, I am sorry to say, both VW teams had bad luck. Two windshields cracked because of close following. But the important thing was that the engines kept going. The seals on the oil fillers still were untouched!

Following closely together as we did amplified greatly the exhaust noise so that it sounded like the roar of a three-engine airplane, announcing our approach from afar. Wherever we passed we received sincere applause, which we encouraged by driving near the side of the road, stirring up great clouds of dust to effect an illusion of speed and danger. In Chihuahua we were hailed vociferously by the local cowboys, whose enthusiasm for the Carrera fully equalled that for the rodeo.

One hour after our arrival all seven Volkswagens stood together again, beside a notice-ably shrunken number of American cars. Our admiration for the Volkswagen was un-bounded; the public, too, showed great enthusiasm for the little car. While we didn't want to tempt Fate in Chihuahua, we were all but convinced that the VW's would make it all the way. The next day there were only 210 miles to drive (minimum average 63 mph), and if the tires played no last minute tricks on us, we should easily finish.

In Chihuahua we feasted on their famous T-Bone steaks, and retired soon after to the wonderful Hotel Victoria. The following morning, November 23rd, we slept in, for the first cars of a field now reduced to 87 were not to start before 10 o'clock.

An atmosphere of apprehension drifted among the ranks of drivers on the morning of that final start. Each one was possessed by a single wish — to have arrived already in Ciudad Juarez; and a single fear — to be cheated out of success in the last moments by an accident or automotive failure.

I was as excited as at the beginning in Tuxtla. At 11:18 I received the signal to start. I drove fast for a few kilometers to make a good show for the public, but once out in the desert I waited for my comrades. Then off we went in our *Knackwurst* formation, which by now had become famous.

The last stretch of 200 miles seemed uncannily short to us. The dark blue sky and the red desert sand contrasted beautifully with the dark asphalt road. Except for 18 miles of curves the stretch was straight as a die. We were followed again by planes. This time they were principally Americans who had flown to the race from Texas, New Mexico and California. One aircraft loaded with members of the press tried to catch Maglioli in his Ferrari, but without success.

With an average of approximately 120 mph for this leg, he arrived in Ciudad Juarez the overall winner. In the big race he won the grand prize of 200,000 pesos (about $17,000) plus many other prizes totalling altogether more than $25,000. Phil Hill in another Ferrari was second, after a well-driven race. Hans Hermann, in a Porsche, was third in the over-all classification; first in his own.

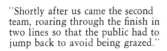
"Shortly after us came the second team, roaring through the finish in two lines so that the public had to jump back to avoid being grazed."

Tears of joy welled up in my eyes as I approached the finish line. In my preoccupation I took no heed of the crowds bordering the avenue. With barely a kilometer to go I was fervently praying "Please, good little car, keep on going, 500 yards, 250 — 100 — 50 — HURRAH! In graduated formation, close behind one another, we crossed the long awaited line. Shortly after us came the second team, roaring through the finish in two lines so that the public had to jump back to avoid being grazed.

Seven cars started; after 1,800 grueling miles without an oil change, without a tire change, without any repairs whatsoever, the same seven cars crossed the finish line. It was a feat unprecedented in the history of the *Carrera Panamericana*, the toughest road race in the world.

—Alfonso de Hohenlohe

By his mad dash to renown the Team Captain, shown here with his co-pilot, had demonstrated the Volkswagen as an able performer to the once dubious Senor Gonzales —with two continents looking on. After this success, peoples all over the Americas knew that the letters "VW" stood for reliability.

The driver with a cast-iron constitution held the advantage, for paved stretches were the exception and not the rule. Much of VW's success was attributed to the sturdy design of the car itself, which negotiated roughest mountain terrain, then soft sand or mud, then cruised the long, flat runs at a respectable average speed.

AROUND AUSTRALIA

Another impressive demonstration of Volkswagen's fine road-handling ability and endurance came in the famous Round Australia Rally. Taking its name from the sponsoring oil companies in various years, the rally lasted 21 days and 10,000 miles, was reputed to be the world's longest and roughest reliability run. Since the object of the competition was to test the reliability of stock cars, the only modifications allowed on participating vehicles were bucket seats, safety belts, first aid kits, and food supplies.

The competition cars ran every gamut of driving conditions: desert heat, fog, choking dust storms, hail, and rainstorms — which turned primitive dusty roads into treacherous hub-deep mud. Tires became shredded through miles of driving over roads "surfaced" with rock splinters; one terrifying stretch of "road" had 58 creek fords in 62 miles. Drivers often took along hammers and axes to make the necessary body "repairs." Many of the legs were difficult purely on the basis of distance, as some of the check points lay 500 miles apart.

Tire failures played no favorites and were not uncommon even with the best rubber. Other contestants often were dogged by overheating, sometimes complicated by vibration-caused radiator leaks, while the aircooled Volkswagens charged on. Some other cars dropped out when they had shaken literally into pieces.

Three harried weeks later, bearing battle scars of 10,000 rough and tumbling miles, the Volkswagens moved nimbly down victory lane in Sydney—confirming a dauntless mechanical nature that irrevocably endeared the car to the Aussies.

VW took first and second places in 1955 in its class, winning the manufacturer's team prize as well. 1956 saw VW in the first *six* places in its class, and in places 1, 2, and 3 in the manufacturer's team competition. When it was run again in 1958, VW came in 1, 2, and 3 again. The VW's durable design and the thorough maintenance by VW mechanics repeatedly proved themselves in this rugged trip around a continent.

Over a torturous route of the most trying and varied terrain and weather Volkswagen established itself as heir-apparent for the role of *flivver* to the people of a continent still accustomed to getting the good out of the Model A and even the Model T.

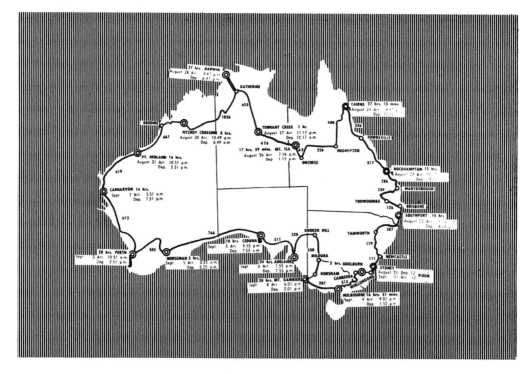

12

THE BEETLES SWARM

Today all free civilization knows the buzzing of the beetle by ear . . . "It doesn't have anything to do with miracles — only with work, consideration, and the knowledge how to go about doing something."

Door fit and fine detail in the trim appointments, coupled with an unkillable motor chassis, established a quality for the car quite unknown among economy models. VW excellence of construction became legendary wherever the car was known.

Since 1948 Heinz Nordhoff's advanced production methods have brought the VW to markets all over the world. When the Volkswagen became available to the German public in quantity for the first time acceptance was immediate. It had already cherished a desire to own the car for a decade. The Rhineland jeweler and the *Schwaebisch* baker, who had thrown their *KdF* cards away in disgust, responded to the VW as if they were welcoming home an old friend of the family. Their expectations were rewarded, for the VW was quick to prove itself handier and more helpful than a host of other cars designed for the same use.

When Heinz Nordhoff became
General Manager, the Volkswagenwerk had been under the direct
control of the Control Commission
for Germany and was subject to
law No. 52. By the end of
September, 1949, the Commission
withdrew and Nordhoff was
encouraged to run the factory on a
private enterprise basis. "Our own
workers will always benefit from our
efforts" he promised his employees.
This rather than a lot of grand
words demonstrated the spirit
behind his actions—were they for
the factory, his employees, or the
German economy.

Looking across the Mittelland Canal the factory at Wolfsburg is landmarked to the East by its great power plant—which by a miracle escaped destruction during Allied bombardment, to stand as the incentive for revitalizing the plant after the war. In the distance rises the fourteen story administration building which has been added in recent years. Between the power house and this building stretches nearly a mile of canal front bays which outline the largest automobile factory under a single roof in the world. As barges convey raw material into the area in one section, trains loaded with the finished product, now ubiquitous in more than 130 countries of the free world, pull away from another.

THE FACTORY

Contrasting the first postwar scene — when more than sixty percent of the factory lay in rubble and the remainder was in shambles from looting and neglect — with the edifice that stands at Wolfsburg today accents the recovery known to an awed world as the "German Miracle." Many people question whether any other nation, faced with this mass of destruction, lack of tools, scarcity of power, and the psychological hurdle of a seemingly hopeless future, would have accomplished so much so fast.

To pick up, sort, and rebuild anew from almost nothing would not have been the American way. The impatient Yankee probably would have bulldozed everything, including the remaining 40 percent, and started fresh. But that would require money and machines, and the Germans had neither. They had only time, energy, and the will to lift themselves out of chaos.

After all these years of postwar effort the Volkswagen factory today has become what Professor Porsche had once dreamed it would be: the most modern automobile factory in Europe, with Detroit-style assembly lines spewing forth low-cost cars for everyone. The original *KdF* plan had been for 30,000 employees to produce 2,700 cars per day within six million square feet of factory. But the roof in 1939 covered less than three million square feet, and only 100 Volkswagens had been built when Hitler switched production to war machines. Today, under Nordhoff's direction, the original plan has been surpassed: over 92,000 employees produce over 6,700 vehicles every day.

When the capacity of the power plant was advanced recently a new landmark was added. Three great smoke stacks now rise 409 feet into the Wolfsburg sky, towering nearly two and a half times higher than Niagara Falls.

Literally miles of overhead conveyors carry sub-assemblies through the plant. Here bodies are trimmed and completed. Soon they will be joined to running gear, which at this moment is being finished in another section of the plant.

The Mittelland Canal, running east and west across Germany, is used to bring many supplies to the factory, including coal from U.S. mines. South of the waterway spreads the prosperous city of Wolfsburg, home to 90,000.

Other European automobile makers long ago conceded that Nordhoff had become the most successful car manufacturer in the Old World. What his administration at Wolfsburg wrought between 1949 and 1955 almost exactly paralleled the production triumphs of Henry Ford between 1909, when he produced the first Model T, and 1915, when his issue of this single model totaled up to its first million . . . Production increases at the Volkswagenwerk were forged against immense difficulties in obtaining raw materials. Even as Nordhoff's VW earned a well-deserved reputation for its uncompromising quality in both construction and materials, non-essentials at the plant were compromised to bring this reputation to flower. In this 1953 aerial view of the unexpanded original plant skylight roofing all over the plant still revealed an unpoetic varigation from a patchwork repair of war damage.

The Wolfsburg factory represents a great example of production efficiency. In the present plant, rebuilt from the original foundations, work is done according to one plan and under one roof. Trucks and trains loaded with material enter at one end of the mile-long building; finished VW's leave at the other end. Numbers of material handling vehicles buzz through the huge complex; their drivers never see the sky during working hours. The production machinery, arranged with military precision in neat, efficient rows, is unique in Europe. As in Porsche's time, under Nordhoff much of the machinery was purchased from American tool manufacturers. Mills, cutters, presses, and boring machines are almost exclusively automatic for the utmost in mass production, while conveyor automation routes the correct number of parts to their proper location at the exact moment of their need.

The splendor of this fortress-like factory, rising amid the fields of Wolfsburg, is a manifestation of the new, self-made prosperity of West Germany. It is the pride of the community and the country — and the envy of the world. It is Nordhoff's National Miracle.

Down-to-earth Heinz Nordhoff, however, has a slightly different opinion of his own National Miracle. As he said in a VW factory workers' meeting in 1959: "It annoys me greatly when people speak of the miracle of the Volkswagen factory. It doesn't have anything to do with miracles — only with work, consideration, and the knowledge how to go about doing something."

As styling changes never were made for annual change's sake, the body stampings enjoyed a seasoned precision brought about by refinement of the same tooling over a long period of use. Automated handling throughout the plant later replaced much of the man handling required with body panels.

Each worker, whether mounting a principal part, or only setting a tolerance in millimeters, treats the assembly before him with the care he would lavish on it were it for his own personal VW. This view from the early 1950's would be considered primitive when compared with engine manufacturing procedure today.

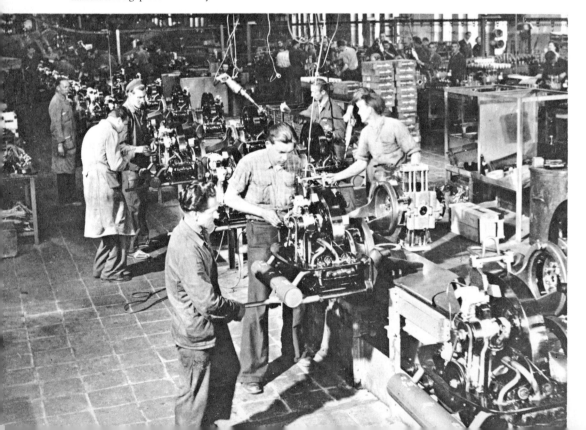

Even a production rate of one car every 11 seconds at Wolfsburg does not preclude exercising "tender loving care" on each vehicle as it makes its way along the line. Here a worker using an abrasive wheel grinds off rough edges on a windshield frame, assuring the final "finish" for which Volkswagen is justly famous. Below, a 13-minute supply of front end assemblies, each prepared to perfection. The only lemons at Wolfsburg are in the lunchpails of the workers.

Front end panels for the sedan are jigged together at the first station of a roundabout welding rig which progressively welds them together as it rotates the assembly through fully automated stations.

A similar merry-go-round is used to erect the rear body section for the sedan. Panels are automatically welded together at 318 points as the assembly passes through nine welding stations.

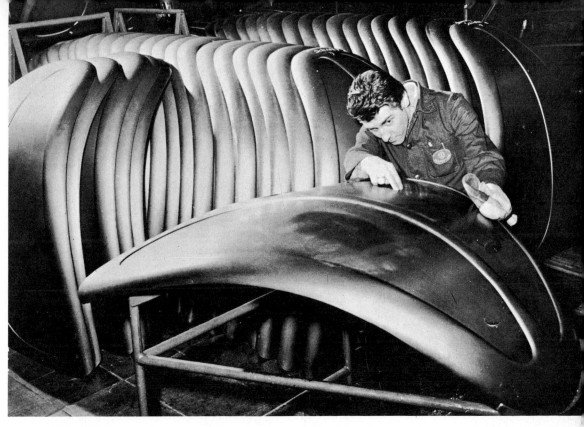

One of nearly 6,200 inspectors at the Wolfsburg plant casts an all-seeing eye across a hood panel. Inspection crews are an independent part of the Volkswagen factory family, second to no other department.

Each body is submerged completely in a primer paint bath to impart a firmly non-corrosive surface to every area—including those inaccessible to standard paint spray treatments. No matter where the VW goes after it leaves the factory, its owner is assured of superior body life. Three other coats are sprayed on before bodies leave the paint shop. With usual corrosion thoroughly discouraged most Volkswagens go on sparkling like new for years and years.

More than 100 miles of overhead conveyor lines are used in VW's five factories in Germany. But none is more important, and dramatic, than the section leading to the drop where the body slips down to join its chassis and become a complete Volkswagen at last. A whole battery of final body drops are employed at Wolfsburg to maintain the present output pace.

Soon after the body drop the mated body and chassis is conveyed once again by monorail to have its wheels fitted. An automatic wrench fits and tightens all five lugs on a wheel at the same time.

A shipping manager works at the pay-off end of the assembly line as VWs spew into daylight for the first time. Each car bears a coded shipping ticket which designates its customer in one of more than 130 Free World markets . . . The factory makes 26,000 ash trays like the one in left foreground each working day, though most leave Wolfsburg as hub caps.

Production of the millionth Volkswagen was commemorated in the first week of August, 1955, establishing a European production record within ten years after the war—substantial proof of the outstanding quality of the car. In years soon to come, *annual* production would eclipse this achievement.

THE CITY

When Lafferentz was scanning the Lower Saxon landscape from his airplane in 1938, Wolfsburg was no more than a huddle of huts occupied by the peasants of Count von Schulenberg's feudal-like estate. Today it is a modern community of well over 90,000 people. This transformation is a living legend of the new Germany.

By European standards conditions in modern Wolfsburg are almost idyllic. The comparatively high wages earned at making a product with an ever-increasing worldwide demand has given Wolfsburg a living standard far above the German average and above that of most all other European communities. Wolfsburg has fine schools, churches, a new hospital, a community swimming pool, and other recreation facilities; row upon row of sparkling white apartment buildings have been built since the war; and a cultural exchange program brings in the arts and intellect of other cities and nations.

Smart company-owned apartments rose early under Nordhoff's direction, where clapboard barracks once had offered workers little beyond primitive shelter. By 1950 living standards at the factory town had outdistanced those in other parts of Germany. In conversation a Wolfsburger's proud reference invariably was to "our Volkswagen" and "our factory."

Wolfsburg lies 110 miles west of Berlin, but only five miles from the barbed wire that marks the border between the East and West. In 1937 it was not even a town, but only a cluster of farmhouses around a castle—built in 1344 by a knight whose crest bore a wolf—from which the city gained its name. It is a new city in a new Germany and most of the construction has been since 1955.

Although the VW plant is Wolfsburg's single major source of income, the town retains a separate identity unlike the coal towns of England and the steel towns of America. City decisions are made by an elected council, and the factory administration wisely avoids exerting influence on city government. There are, of course, some natural signs of the impact which the Volkswagen has had on life in Wolfsburg. As Alistair Horne describes in his book *Return to Power:*

"Over every inch of it [Wolfsburg] prevails the ubiquitous spirit of the golden goose; the main street with its luxurious shops is called Porsche Strasse after the designer of the Volkswagen; even in the churches and schools the little beetle-like car appears incorporated in mosaics or murals."

The town of Wolfsburg has in fact taken on something of the personality of the Volkswagen. They both exemplify the favorite words of Heinz Nordhoff: "Work hard, don't boast, and be bigger than you appear."

Wolfsburg is young, active and still growing—a city of 90,000 whose activity is solely the production of Volkswagens. It has more cars, and more children per capita than any other German city. *Kinder* of the town enjoy recreation activities as international as the automobiles their fathers produce.

Twice a week an open air market blossoms out in front of Wolfsburg's contemporary city hall. In the foreground a stall advertises another name recognized around the world . . . Looking to the north from a vantage above the market the factory's familiar facade may be seen beyond the city across the Canal. Almost completely new in recent years Wolfsburg rates as one of Germany's most modern cities.

Looking into one of six parking lots provided for employees at the Wolfsburg plant a salting of several odd makes may be seen—just enough to comprise a democratic employee body. Rebels have a common cause: each is able to walk right up to his own car at closing time.

Even on the stormiest night the fourteen story administration building is alive with light against the winter sky. There is power from the plant to spare and the whole city is lighted by the factory. Volkswagen's own administration building, a landmark of the new Germany, is never darkened.

In recent years additional floorspace has been developed to the north of the original factory—doubling the square footage at the Wolfsburg plant. Over 100 miles of conveyor lines now speed parts along more than three miles of assembly lines from which come 5000 cars every double-shift working day. More automobiles are produced in the Volkswagenwerk at Wolfsburg than in any other single factory in the world—at a rate of one VW every 11 seconds.

WHO OWNS WOLFSBURG?

The long-standing problem of who owns the VW factory was finally settled in 1959 after much legal squabbling and bargaining; the German Federal Republic and the State of Lower Saxony announced that they would privatise the company, putting stock up for sale beginning in January, 1960.

When the British Occupation turned the factory over to the Federal Republic in 1949, it became the nominal property of a trusteeship set up by the Federal Republic and the State of Lower Saxony until final ownership of the concern could be determined. The growth of VW operations during this period of trusteeship is unique in corporation history; VW financed its own expansion without any support from the two governments or from capital stockholders.

As VW continued to make increasing profits through the 1950's, the VW management elected to form a trust fund made up of excess profits until the German courts decided on the claims of the remaining *KdF* card holders. In 1956 the German Supreme Court decreed that the card holders had no justified claims to ownership of the VW factory or on presently-produced cars.

This decision, however, only cleared the way for a long legal battle between the Federal Republic and Lower Saxony over ownership of the firm. This struggle was finally settled amicably in 1959; each government agreed to retain equal ownership in the form of 20% of the stock, while the remaining 60% would be sold to the public under certain restrictions. The two governments have set up a foundation to aid German education with their share of the profits, while small, private stockholders benefit from the remaining stock.

First opportunity to buy stock was given to Volkswagen employees. Of the 65,000 at the time all but 1,000 subscribed for shares; hence the VW factory has the largest percentage of employee-stockholders of any firm in the world. The 1,000 non-shareholding employees all had incomes above the legal limit set up by the government for purchase of VW shares. Employees were allowed a maximum purchase of 10 shares; the tenth was a gift from the company, whereas the employees were allowed to finance the purchase of the other nine shares.

The stock not purchased by employees then went on sale to the general public. The maximum which any one individual could buy was five shares; but since the original sale of 3,600,000 shares, at the offering price of about $83 per share, was 84% over-subscribed, each private purchaser was allotted only two shares. The balance of unsold shares was then distributed by lot. Certain reductions in initial price up to 25% were allowed to young people with lower incomes and/or with three or more underage children. The same income ceiling applied to private purchasers as to employees, so that the VW factory will continue to be owned by large numbers of small holders and foreseeably will never fall into the hands of large industrialists.

After a period of time all stockholders were free to buy and sell VW stocks on the market with other German citizens, but with the restriction that no one person may ever own more than 10 VW shares.

The VW company, which originally was built on a foundation of socialism, stands today as a great symbol of the free German people and their new prosperity — a uniquely democratic example of free enterprise.

Before Nordhoff's time Volkswagen shipped the first export cars to Holland in 1947. Since that date a significant portion of production has gone overseas, and recent times have shown exports ranging from 55% to 63% of total production. VW is now the best selling import car in such diverse countries as Sweden, Switzerland, Holland, Canada and the U.S.A.

Volkswagenwerk accumulated capital after the war solely from the sale of its product, since there were no stockholders. The government had no money to subsidize the plant and acted only as trustee for the property. Until mid-1948 three out of four cars produced were supplied to the Forces of Occupation, almost the only parties around with cash to buy. A provisional contract was made with Dutch car dealer Ben Pon, in August 1947, to export the VW for the first time. Exporting was to become Wolfsburg's key to success. By 1964 there would be nearly 130 countries on the list. About 63% of production is now earmarked for export. Twenty percent of production is slated for the U. S. A.

§ 17.   Erfüllungsort und Gerichtsstand

Erfüllungsort für alle aus diesen Vereinbarungen für beide Teile sich ergebenden Verbindlichkeiten ist Wolfsburg.

Als Gerichtsstand wird das für Wolfsburg zuständige Amts- bzw. Landgericht vereinbart.

§ 18.   Änderungen und Ergänzungen dieses Vertrages bedürfen zu ihrer Gültigkeit der Schriftform.

Nachtrag: Dieser Vertrag ist ein vorläufiger; er soll ehestens so ergänzt werden, daß er das gesamte Volkswagengeschäft in HOLLAND beinhaltet. § 2 wird bereits jetzt dahingehend geändert, daß dieser Vertrag vorläufig bis 31. Juli 1949 Gültigkeit hat.

Wolfsburg, den 8. August 1947

PON-s AUTOMOBILHANDEL
AMERSFOORT

VOLKSWAGENWERK GmbH.

Der Fuehrer probably never envisioned the *KdF* as an *international* success. After the war it was do or die. Materials and new machinery could come to VW only from favorable trade balances created by sales abroad. Ben Pon stands before one of the earliest of his wares from Wolfsburg, historically the first to make Volkswagen international.

VOLKSWAGEN GOES INTERNATIONAL

Volkswagen's first general exporting contract was signed in the summer of 1947 when shortages were the rule, the car was a novelty with the public, and Heinz Nordhoff had not yet appeared on the horizon at Wolfsburg. Today Ben Pon, who signed the first provisional contract with VW to export cars to Holland, August 8th, 1947 has imported more than 250,000 cars and trucks and would like 250,000 more to meet the demand in the Netherlands, which constitutes the fourth largest export market for the car (next to USA, Sweden and Belgium).

Enterprise and initiative of a high order were necessary in the grim postwar days when even civilian movement was restricted. Many times, to obtain cars, he would climb into the uniform of a colonel in order to cross the frontier to Wolfsburg with the least difficulty.

"If everyone sweeps in front of his own door the whole world is clean" goes an old Dutch saying. That early post-war administrators at VW had elected to begin making friends abroad with the Hollanders proved a good omen, for the business-like details of the transaction established a formidable tempo for the vast exporting relations to come.

The Pon organization rose to national prominence as it became inseparably associated with the superb character of the little car it had chosen to represent in Holland. Service and facilities were expanded to keep pace with this foremost reputation. This artist's impression depicts the new Pon headquarters in Amsterdam.

To bring much-needed dollars for plant development Nordhoff hoped to develop the USA among the first export markets. Ben Pon, acting at his request, became VW's ambassador to the States. Early in 1949 he arrived with the first VW officially exported to the U.S. and began a tour of the country seeking dealers who might see a future for the car. Every automobile man he met saw VW only as a no-reputation, no-name product, in itself devoid of any redeeming features. Pon sold his sample in despair and returned without a single contract.

While over a hundred different makes are imported to the Netherlands from all over the world, of all cars in Holland today about one in five is a VW. Ben Pon and his brother now head an organization with over 150 dealerships and 165 repair stations.

In Holland only one in twenty of all the population owns a car. In Germany the figure is 11, and those for others on the continent are: Switzerland 10, Belgium 11, Denmark 10, Luxembourg 9, Great Britain 9, France 8 and in Sweden as low as 6. (In the USA the figure is three.) It would appear that Holland would offer a very favorable climate for more sales; but the domestic tax load, even greater with colonial losses, still makes motoring in Holland a relative luxury.

Soon after Nordhoff's arrival at Wolfsburg, sales everywhere became inseparably linked with service in a manner unparalleled by any other car maker in the world. Parts and service *first*, cars to sell *second*, became the order of VW business in every market. This aerial view of the facility in Amsterdam shows the main parts warehouse for Holland.

Old *Kuebelwagen* and *Schwimmwagen* models helped satisfy the immediate call for VW's in Austria more than anywhere else. Even today cars of the *Wehrmacht* period swing into the Salsburg facility for minor attention almost daily.

Everyday folks in over 130 free-world countries embrace the Volkswagen as though it were a native. As a matter of record their demand for VW outstrips distribution volume, and a waiting list for delivery has been common ever since Nordhoff has managed VW. Customer demand has exceeded supply year after year, even though no arbitrary style changes have been made to obsolete existing cars; so the owner finds himself enjoying a uniquely gentle rate of depreciation. Someone, somewhere always seems ready to buy the used VW at a relatively high price.

Special two-level railroad cars, built by the thousands to dispatch VW's to market, provide a common sight all over Europe. 95% of VW production is forwarded by rail. Looking closely, about 290 Volkswagens appear in this view at the factory's rail yard—about 70 minutes of production at Wolfsburg. U. S. exports leave via the ports of Hamburg, Bremen and Bremerhaven.

In South America, where no automobile is better than the service and parts tributaries that support it, the VW quickly was embraced with an enthusiasm shown no car since the days of the Model A Ford. In Sao Paulo, the Panambra House supplies Volkswagen users in Southern Brazil, a country where the car takes form along a local assembly line. German-built parts comprise only part of the Brazilian car.

To encourage acceptance under varying export-import laws, VW has set up assembly plants in Australia, Belgium, Brazil, Ireland, Mexico, New Zealand, the Philippines, Portugal, South Africa, Turkey, Uruguay and Venezuela. Some simply assemble German parts, others combine these with locally-produced components. Programs to develop greater mixes of native materials are continuous. By early 1966, the Mexican-made car, for example, will roll out at the rate of 2,500 per month with 70% local content. Subsidiary import corporations are active in Canada and the United States.

The emblem appearing here on an agency in Lima, Peru, added a new letter to the alphabet of Spanish-speaking people. Through the local prominence of VW, they came to recognize and pronounce the letter "W" for the first time. The letter does not appear in the Spanish alphabet.

A NATIONAL BLUNDER FORGOTTEN

The unorthodox little beetle car which Great Britain once had tested, nominally manufactured, and officially found too wanting to bother with, today is greatly admired in the Commonwealth, even though its positive personality has pushed the whole British motor industry to the sidelines in many of the world's markets. Wherever a Volkswagen stands in England the envious gather. Against stiff competition, and under backbreaking import regulations — which impose a £90 ($250) import duty to discourage disloyalty to the cars of the Crown (which in turn raises the compulsory purchase tax) — Volkswagen has sold over 110,000 cars in the British Isles. Each purchaser staunchly chose the VW's virtues over those of many larger British cars for the same money. J. J. Graydon, the import concessionaire explains: "It's *value* that makes the VW so desirable — the frugality of the car, its service organization and its high resale price." Of 30 distributors and 225 dealers in Great Britain two distributors and thirteen dealerships can be found in London, alone.

British Isles importer J. J. Graydon stands before a map pinpointing the some 225 dealers of his Volkswagen territory. Maps of nearly every country in the free world came to be dotted with similar concentration of service support for the once improbable little beetle.

Volkswagen assumes an everyday part in the colorful scene before the exclusive Mayfair Hotel in London, as its West End showroom lies across the street from the hotel and even the neon letters spelling its name are reflected in the Mayfair's plate glass facade. Customers enjoy associating the elegance of the neighborhood with that of the car.

A reversed negative? No, only the usual cockpit appearance of a Volkswagen built for use in an area of the British Commonwealth.

Volkswagen Australasia, while only an outpost, when compared with the parent plant in Wolfsburg, has become much more than a simple facility for assembling components shipped from Germany. The Melbourne plant now presses its own body panels and is moving toward the day when even the engine and transmission will be manufactured completely in or near this capital city of Victoria.

VW'S DOWN UNDER

Volkswagen has adapted its distribution and marketing policies to local market conditions everywhere in the world; and in a land where local manufacture is encouraged over importation, Volkswagen became one of Australia's four major auto makers less than a decade after the first VW's were imported down under. Ever since the beetles landed in Australia in 1953 the car has proven itself ideally suited to Australian driving conditions, and sales have increased severalfold in the last few years.

Volkswagen (Australasia) Pty. Ltd., which is controlled by the Volkswagenwerk, G.m.b.H., was established in 1957. Production and assembly of VW cars takes place in a new factory in Melbourne, Victoria; 70% of the components are locally manufactured. A huge new press shop in Melbourne, built at a cost of $4,500,000, turns out all necessary VW body panels. Only the motor, transmission, and parts of the suspension are imported from Germany. As production and sales of Australian VW's grow enough to warrant further expansion, the parent company plans to invest additional capital in Australian plant and equipment. Ultimately, at the rate the Australian VW market has expanded, the car will likely be fabricated completely from Australian components. Projected VW plans include Australian-made Transporters as well. The Volkswagen makes a significant contribution to the Australian economy and motor industry through the development of local resources, creating jobs, and providing economical transportation for Australians. The VW, in a land far distant from its home, is as much as ever the People's Car.

Volkswagen commemorated production of the sixth millionth vehicle since 1945 only a year after rolling out the fifth millionth car. Earlier milestone units took longer. The first celebration was on August 5, 1955; the second followed on December 28, 1957. The third millionth VW, heralded here, coincided with completion of the 500,000 Transporter at Hanover, August 25, 1959.

GERMAN VW EXPANSION

In its efforts "onward, upward" to keep ahead of world VW demand the Volkswagen-werk continuously carried out extensive expansion and modernization. This was to be known to an awed world as the "German Miracle." New production lines, larger areas of production floor space, psychological incentives to workers, and more modern machinery — purchased in part from the U.S.A. – then raised Wolfsburg factory production rates almost nine times during the 1950's. VW invested $50,000,000 in expansion during 1961 alone. This time saw VW as the first European auto maker ever to produce one million cars in a single year.

New VW plants have been established in Germany in addition to the famous Wolfs-burg factory. VW Transporters are now manufactured in Hanover, and in mid-1958 a special plant was established in Kassel for the reconditioning of engines, transmissions, and other VW components. In 1959 VW announced that engine production was being shifted to Hanover, and in the same year VW opened a new plant in Braunschweig for the manufacture of front suspension parts. A fifth West German plant, recently completed at Emden on the North Sea coast, raised total output of VWs by 450 a day for export. A former Auto-Union works at Ingolstadt became VW's sixth plant.

NEW ENGINES FOR OLD

As the years passed many older beetles had served their owners for several hundred thousand miles and were still being used daily. Often tight-bodied and well-preserved in appearance, these cars generally were roadworthy for mechanical renewal. VW management was not to turn its back on the owners and their veteran Volkswagens.

Were high-quality engine and transmission rebuilding services available, the factory reasoned the problems of the owner of an older, much-used VW could be alleviated; and at the same time it would become more likely that older Volkswagens might continue to be testimonial to the basic VW durability.

The VW rebuilding works at Kassel experienced much the same hard time in their history as did the Wolfsburg plant. Originally operated by the Henschel firm, famous builders of heavy machinery and steam locomotives, the factory buildings became a prime target for Allied bombs in World War II; and they emerged from the war as a pile of rubble. In 1945 British forces of occupation partially rebuilt the damaged factory and used it as a supply depot. While the buildings were eventually reacquired by Henschel after occupation, the machinery firm concluded the property was no longer financially profitable and offered it for sale.

Both 36 and 40 hp engines, as well as starter motors, complete clutch assemblies, carburetors, relined brake shoes, fuel pumps, generators and transmission-rear axle assemblies are reconditioned at the Kassel plant.

Nordhoff's industrial engineers revamped the plant. Old shops became mass-production, assembly-line work areas; several stories were built on the old foundations; housing was put up for the workers. The plant opened as a quality controlled rebuilding works in June, 1958; immediately mass-production methods began transforming worn-out VW engines and other parts into fresh components for the world market.

Well over 1000 workers presently rebuild nearly 500 engines, 150 axle units, and various lesser VW parts every day. All used parts first enter a line where workers with power wrenches tear them completely down. The floor of the disassembly shops is a grating, through which the dirty oil from the old engines can drain. All parts which fall below a certain standard in quality are discarded; all parts which meet or can be remachined to acceptable factory standards are preserved and put in supply pools for reassembly.

Various parts, such as engine heads, crankshafts, flywheels, etc., are sent to separate machining stations, where experienced craftsmen re-turn them to rebuilding specifications. All parts are then thoroughly cleaned in steam and solvent baths.

Engines are then subassembled, usually with a completely new set of internal parts; and final assembly follows, lasting about 20 minutes for any given engine. Rebuilt units receive full testing before being packaged and shipped to all parts of the world. Individual replacement parts are catalogued for distribution to dealers and repair centers. An engine block which did its service in South Africa may come back to Kassel, then put in 60,000 miles more in Sweden or Brazil.

The VW factory rebuilding service has been growing in popularity: it saves time and money for customers and dealers. A worn engine can be replaced with a factory rebuilt within an hour or two, while the local VW service center would require days to overhaul the old engine. Factory experience has lent extra value to the VW rebuilt; it is not only cheaper but considerably more reliable than the ordinary rebuilt engine.

Recently constructed, in the middle of a varigated quilt of intensively cultivated farmland on the outskirts of Kassel, the vast new transmission and replacement parts factory incorporates layout features more modern than the home plant. Its 13,000 employees work together in a model of efficiency.

For a number of years the Volkswagenwerk presented this medal along with a commemorative wrist watch to owners who had reached 100,000 km. (62,000 miles) without major repair to the original engine and drive train. The promotion proved well-founded as an instrument to encourage thrift and pride among VW owners, and the medal came to be nearly as common upon instrument panels in Germany as *Christophorus*.

At a 1954 meeting of the 100,000 km VW drivers in Stuttgart, Nordhoff said:

"The principle of free competition is respected in the U.S.A. without restriction and argument, whereas here in Germany competition becomes more rigidly restricted the more basic and important an operation becomes. Much has been said for and against the cartel laws; and this gives me occasion to say quite clearly that I am 100% an advocate of free competition. Without free competition we never could have raised our living standards to their present level."

In a 1957 factory meeting, Nordhoff said:

"Again and again the sophism that the State could help some enterprise with its money! The State only gets money from the taxpayers, and thus in the end everything that the State does is paid for together by all those who earn money. The State can only create money by printing it, which of course brings on inflation. The true economic value which raises our standard of living is produced by the *Economy*."

To the Society of German Auto Makers, Nordhoff said in 1956:

"The problems which concern me when I cannot sleep at night are not those of cash balances or new construction or investments or export or competition. The cause of my sleeplessness is only the fact that in a large industrial undertaking men are employed, in large numbers, in a small area, and men are not machines!

"If we began a long time ago to give a portion of our profits to our workers, we did so because we were convinced that it was a command of fairness and justice and that herein lay the only possible way to make the work of everyone connected with the plant meaningful and efficient. If love really operates through man's stomach, as the old proverb says, then you can be sure that a good relationship between labor and management certainly cannot be based on anything so insubstantial as words alone.

"However it doesn't appear to me to be right to give the workers a portion of the capital of the entrepreneur. The ownership of capital and its use involves risks to which the average worker is completely unfamiliar and from which we should protect him. On the other hand the worker is doubtless entitled to a share of the results of our mutual labor, and management should grant him this share because he has earned it."

The Bavarian State Mint marked Dr. Nordhoff's production of the five-millionth Volkswagen in December, 1961, by striking this special commemorative coin, which already has become a collector's item.

Through Dr. Nordhoff's vision and management a devastated factory that had never had a production line, along with an assemblage of shanties that had never been a town, became *Wolfsburg*, star symbol of the new Germany. Plaudits have come to him from many quarters, but none is more significant than the informal honor paid to their Managing Director by Wolfsburgers themselves in the success of a democratic relationship between management and labor which Nordhoff initiated in German industry . . . Hopes for a people's car had been a recurring dream of motor car industrialists in Germany from the earliest industry. But the stereotyped solution of making a conventional car small and cheap never had proven acceptable. With Porsche's concept came the first original answer—a chassis package specially developed for the light car. But till Nordhoff brought production organization to the plan and maturity to the engineering concept, VW, in all its lives up to this time, never had attained true production. Even the *Kdf* show cars produced in 1939 were constructed largely in shops outside Wolfsburg, a production line at the incomplete factory being more fancy than fact.

NORDHOFF'S DECORATIONS

During the course of his service to VW, Heinz Nordhoff has been awarded many of the highest honors which can be given to any German citizen. In consideration of the part he has played in the economic recovery of Germany, the Technical University of Braunschweig named Nordhoff as recipient of the degree "Dr. Ing. h.c." (Doctor of Engineering) in July, 1950, on the occasion of the University's 200th anniversary. In 1951 the Berlin Technical University conferred upon him the academic honor of Senator of the University, and in May, 1955, he was made Honorary Professor of the Braunschweig Technical University. On August 6, 1955, on the occasion of the production of the 1,000,000th Volkswagen, *Bundespräsident* Prof. Heuss honored Dr. Nordhoff with the *"Grosskreuz des Bundesverdienstkreuzes mit Stern"* (the Starred Service Cross of the Federal Republic), the highest distinction of the German Republic.

175

To further assure reliability in production design a complete proving ground was completed at Wolfsburg early in 1959. Weather and road conditions that might be encountered anywhere in the world are simulated there. One washboard section presents ridges one-inch-high with 27-inch to 31-inch pitch from crest to crest, the varying lengths arranged to reproduce all possible axle vibrations. A mile-plus oval for sustained runs at top speed is dished to permit speeds up to 93 mph without side thrust. The exceptional stability of the VW is particularly accented in the foreground by a right-hand-drive car.

Unlike most other cars, where full throttle operation should be avoided over long periods of time except in emergencies, the VW's top speed of 71 mph is also defined as its cruising speed, that is, the *ideal* speed for motor operation. Porsche wisely designed his engine to run slow at high speeds. Even at full throttle the Volkswagen engine continues to keep wear to a minimum and conserve fuel, for its rpm and speed of piston travel never rise above a leisurely rate little more than half that of many other cars.

Volkswagen's simple and forthright approach to the problem of dependable, low-cost personal transportation has keynoted its unlimited success. The philosophy reflected in the design of the car is carried over into all facets of VW marketing and servicing. A trained VW mechanic will fix the car using factory approved parts and work methods in the simplest, least expensive manner possible; he will never try to sell a new VW as soon as the motorist enters his shop.

Today all civilization knows the buzzing of the beetle by ear.

13

PATHFINDER ON MAIN STREET, U.S.A.

When two new Volkswagens were registered in the United States in 1949 only Noah would have cheered. It was against all the odds of Detroit's research to the American public. Then VW began to out-maneuver others on the streets, in sales and even in advertising.

What American car builders heralded as "functional design" dishonestly approached becoming the very opposite. Gimmicks, like enclosed front wheels, were given a fanfare in inverse proportion to their worth. The indelicately-styled number shown, with its blubberous outer form tied together underside by a forest of struts, typified this trend toward the "big package". Not only was the convenience of a tight turning radius sacrificed here to feature a dubious style note, but normal door opening was also arbitrarily short-stopped by a bulging, sill-high body section which added perfectly useless extra inches to the car's width along the lower doors. Design of the "low priced" car had begun a journey that would lead it far from basic practicality. Yet, auto-thirsty consumers, but for small imports, found nowhere else to turn. Haplessly they encumbered themselves with 142,592 cars of this 1949 design, a new high in sales for the maker, who, mistaking the new car shortage of the time for consumer approval of the styling, responded immediately by planning even more elephantine models to come.

The year 1949 was an exciting one for new-car-hungry Americans. Ford, Chevrolet and Plymouth, among others, signalled their concerted return to spirited competition by introducing all-new models — their first postwar.

Enthusiasm ran high. Buyers took little note of design innovations that short-changed them in efficiency as they were treated to the first of what would become in the late 1950's an unwieldy and all but functionless automotive package.

The alternative buy in a new car was the small foreign car. Among imports the Austin and Morris vied for a place in the Western sun that year, with the MG-TC becoming a classic in its own time among the sporting. If anyone had bothered to get a breakdown of the *pot pourri* lumped under "Miscellaneous Imported Cars" — which always brought up the tail of the list of official new car registrations — he would have come face to face with a remarkable moment in automotive history; and he wouldn't have given it passing attention.

Virtually unknown in the United States, Volkswagen was there, showing *two* new registrations in 1949. Only Noah would have cheered.

A New York City importer, Max Hoffman, came to be awarded importing rights for the United States in 1950. Volkswagen sales created no storm; registrations rose to 157. This franchise continued until the end of 1953, when 980 cars were registered. The price of the Sedan was then $1643. As the registrations reveal, the car still was little known in America.

When the Volkswagen was imported into the USA in 1950 the car appeared to most American car buyers very much like the many small foreign cars that had met initial success among the car-starved public in the early days after the war.

Unfortunately, for a newcomer among light cars at this date, the record of inadequate servicing and parts supply for many of these cars already had built a negative image for small vehicles in the minds of many. To the average American small cars had proven disappointing. He wanted no more of the pattern of grief so recently experienced.

The appeal for theoretical ease of handling and economy came to be negated by a spreading general knowledge among would-be buyers that there was, in the long run, no real savings to be made. Originally purchased to conserve fuel and therefor operation costs, too often one had discovered the savings more than washed out by a need for early overhaul and reconditioning—much of which in turn was inadequately performed, leading to greater frustration. The usual light car attained its power by high rpm's. Something had to give, and did.

EDITORIAL

THE FOREIGN CAR DEALERS ARE BIG BOYS NOW

Too many early import car agents after the war had emerged from the band of gypsy-like, low-end used car operators, who had competed with legitimate trade by digging into a carpet bag of shady tricks. These unscrupulous opportunists had carried their *buyer beware* tactics over into import car selling *in toto.* By the early 1950's the sharp practices endured by many light foreign car owners had become such broad fact that the import car in the U.S. was approaching doom.

For the past five years, *Road and Track* has been deliberately lenient with foreign, sports, and other out-of-the-ordinary cars.

In road tests and articles we have tried to give the imported product the benefit of the doubt, whenever there was any doubt. At the same time we have tried to maintain a high standard of accuracy and fairness. We adopted this attitude for a definite reason.

Road and Track has understood the problems of introducing an imported product into this country. The public prejudices had to be broken down. People had to be made to see that a car needn't be big to be comfortable, have a huge engine to be fast, or be sloppily sprung to give a smooth ride. *Road and Track* felt that it was important to draw a firm line between engineering and gadget development; between design and style; between quantity and quality. And most of all, we thought that many Americans would appreciate the chance to buy a car which was a little different, and maybe a little more fun to drive.

We think we have been right in our attitude. We think that it has been worthwhile to give the Italian, British, and French car a helping hand in getting acquainted with the domestic public. A large minority may now walk into salesrooms all over the country and buy an almost infinite variety of cars—from the super-finished Rolls Royce right down to the economical Morris Minor. You can have just about what your tastes and pocketbooks desire.

In its policy of helping the foreign car dealer, *Road and Track* has been more than once put in an embarrassing position. Readers have written again and again complaining about parts and service. These letters have told a lamentable tale of dealers who have failed to make good on guarantees . . . of dealers who have neglected to keep even a barely adequate supply of parts, or who have failed to order the parts needed.

All types of complaints have come in. Many dealers pursue an out and out policy of banditry when it comes to charging for repairs. One customer, in a well documented case, was told that it would cost him $250 to repair his gearbox. The difficulty was that the third gear syncromesh wouldn't function. The service manager told the distraught customer that the clutch was at fault and that the engine would have to be removed from the chassis in order to make repairs. On the advice of *Road and Track*, the car was taken to one of the oldest foreign car men in the vicinity. This authority diagnosed the trouble as a loose ball bearing in the gearbox and guaranteed a price of $30 for the job. Needless to say, the latter mechanic has more work than he can possibly take care of.

When such letters come in, *Road and Track* rarely prints them. We have believed that foreign car dealers needed every break possible to stay in business. Instead we have turned these letters over to the agency or shop concerned asking that the customer be given satisfaction.

The time has come, however, when it may be stated that foreign cars are here to stay. They have arrived. They are no longer in their adolescence in this country.

The time has come when *all* dealers—not just some—must see that their customers are satisfied. They must be sold a car that will stand up or the dealer must "make it good." The dealer must provide adequate service and parts. He must devote a certain percentage of his profit on each car to getting that car on the road in satisfactory running condition. (Naturally we are not referring to those dealers who *are* giving good service.)

It is understandable that there may be times of delay in getting parts from overseas; but there is never any excuse for charging two or three times what a repair job is worth.

The purpose of this editorial is to serve notice on the unscrupulous. If in the future our mailbag indicates that practices unfair to the enthusiasts are going on—these letters will be printed—let the chips fall where they may.

Each milestone VW was commemorated with a wreath of flowers and a brief ceremony —with a show of workers' enthusiasm characteristic of that accompanying car Number One's original journey down the final line. At Wolfsburg the 25,000 car for tiny Norway met with nearly the reception given the 200,000 car for Sweden. On another continent, meanwhile, Americans had hardly come to know what the letters "VW" stood for.

On this American scene the Volkswagen came to be offered in a limited way. Seasoned importers predicted that no matter how favorably received in other parts of the globe, the VW would never make its mark in the United States. The beetle's future in the country appeared bleak.

Other countries were receiving the VW with more positive recognition and the factory eyed the USA anew. By 1954 changes were brought about which eventually would turn the tide for VW. A branch office of Volkswagenwerk GmbH, was set up in the St. Moritz Hotel, New York, with a pilot organization so that VW distributors could be appointed around the country.

In Germany the circle of sports car enthusiasts had been first to boost the VW after the war. In many other countries the initial support also came from the racing brotherhood. Introductory experience in the U. S. followed this established form. On the West Coast, for example, John von Neumann, a dealer in British cars, had made an honest name for his car and himself by driving a dusty trail with an unblown MG-TD in competition racing. Like Petermax Mueller, von Neumann's competitive spirit led him to appreciate robust qualities in any automobile. In 1952 he blazed another trail—record sales of the little beetle car—as one of the first distributors for VW in the U. S. (Competition Motors, Los Angeles). Von Neumann's racing career continued in stride —behind the wheel of a Porsche 356 coupe.

Distributors were named in rapid fire order. Each distributor functioned as an independent importer. The Sedan was now listing at $1495. The dealer body spread and the year closed with 6,343 registrations — more than 500% increase over the previous year.

There was no advertising promotion, no concerted sales push, only word-of-mouth. But there was a steady effort to install and equip adequate servicing facilities and parts depots, just as Volkswagen was doing in other world markets.

To improve service for a growing band of owners and to broaden the owner circle more effectively *Volkswagen of America* was incorporated to succeed *Volkswagen United States,* in October, 1955, as a factory subsidiary of Volkswagenwerk GmbH. Even though an original staff of three was un-equally divided between offices in New York and San Francisco in the first days of this new set up, development and coordination of a distributor-dealer organization began immediately. Rapid build-up of the service organization with a high spare parts inventory was encouraged, laying the foundation for an aftersupply superior to that of any other imported car. In a few years it was to become the best parts stock for a single model either imported or domestic. By the end of 1955 the increase over the previous year's sales again approached 500%, as registrations totaled 30,928. The secret of VW quality was on many lips.

As days passed a strange story began to be heard among Americans who used cars most. Men who pronounced "Volkswagen" most diversely, and never properly, were telling the tale of a little car that could take anything that could be handed its way. A Ford Motor Company employee confided to a neighbor that in tests his company had conducted on every production car in the world the Volkswagen had come up with the top score for *structural rigidity*.

The car was rendering unfailing service wherever it happened to be in use. More of the heartier became owners. And more, and more. Always the story was the same: "You can't kill it if you drive flat out all day!" And people kept on trying all across the country. Porsche's low piston travel at high cruising speed, coupled with Nordhoff's refinements and production quality became a winning combination in yet another land.

While improvements were incorporated continuously in the motor, chassis and body, styling changes came infrequently, and only after seasoned study. The subtle metamorphosis of window areas in the sedan may be cited. In March, 1953, the rear glass was increased by removing the center-split, standard since 1938. In August, 1957, forward and rear vision both were enhanced when these windows underwent enlargement. Recently, in August, 1964, (shown) all glass areas were further enlarged, with pillars reduced to a slim look. The rear window was made nearly 20% larger and sills of the side windows were dropped more than an inch. The windshield adopted a slight curvature for the first time.

By the beginning of 1956 the changeover from individual distributor importing operations was completed and VW of A became the general importer for Volkswagen. Service fieldmen were brought from the factory to set up distributor service departments. In turn distributors then trained dealership service personnel. A move was made out of New York City to Englewood Cliffs, New Jersey. 55,690 cars were registered. Owner satisfaction had become a contagion all across the country.

WAGENING

Intense owner enthusiasm and loyalty have created Volkswagen owner clubs all over the Western world. The Volkswagen Club of America, Inc., typically reflects the VW contagion; it has claimed since its inception in 1955 to be the "fastest growing automobile club in the world."

Article One of the club's constitution defines its purpose:

The purpose for which this corporation is formed is for the exchange of information among owners of Volkswagen automobiles in order that each member of the association may help every other Volkswagen owner to enjoy his car to the fullest.

These VW enthusiasts band together to share various do-it-yourself ideas through their monthly publication, the *VW Autoist;* to help each other improve their cars' performance, handling, appearance, comfort, and usefulness; and to have a good time together in the process. Members schedule enthusiast activities ranging from an annual VW meet and convention to a caravan of VW drivers from Detroit to Costa Rica and back: the round trip of 9,000 miles encompassed every possible type of highway, from sea level to 12,000-foot mountain crossings, and included a 108-mile stretch by railway flatcar. Another enthusiast reported to the Club that he found it possible to use his VW to pull water skiers — providing the skiers did not wander too far out from shore! The *VW Autoist* also reports activities of member clubs all over the U.S., and it carries general interest items as well:

ROUND-UP TIME, VW STYLE

The huge King Ranch in Texas — so big that it takes several hours to drive across it — has turned to the Volkswagen. According to a newspaper report, the King Ranch has bought Volkswagens for its cowboys to drive on fence-riding patrols.

Yippee, Hans.

Substituting a Volkswagen for a motorboat may prove great sport for shoreline waterskiing. But it's an art requiring special care on the parts of both tow and tower—lest the skier become dry-docked, or the VW turn into a fish.

1956 Volkswagen Sunroof owned by Dorothy E. Rogginger
Villa Park, Ill. — Membership No. 1256

The car is a 1956 Volkswagen Sunroof, diamond green in color. It's been driven every day since it's been purchased, and at present is being driven between 60 to 70 miles a day.

The car carries the following extra equipment: VW hubcap tool kit, windshield washers, Blaupunkt AM-FM-Marine radio, compass, safety belts (quick-release) for all occupants both front and rear, fire extinguisher, flares, first aid kit, emergency parts kit, rallye equipment consisting of 2 stopwatches, a calculator, and a rallye board with a navigation light; an Abarth muffler, and a Ghia anti-sway bar.

Its competition record is as follows: its been in over 50 rallies (I stopped counting after I hit 40 and that was in Feb. of '58). It's been in 2 gymkhanas, 2 hillclimbs, 1 English trials, 3 acceleration trials, and 3 sports car races. (It's also picked up some iron along the way.)

Its concourse record is as follows: it won its first concours, placed 3rd in the next two which were antique car shows, and since that time, 1957, has never placed below first in class. It has won the VWCA concours in '58, and was also judged finest sedan in the show at the 1959 Courtesy Motor Concour d'Elegance. It has also placed first for two years in sequence at the Elkhart Lake Road America Concours. It has been on television, and most recently was judged a Midwest Champion and was placed on exhibition in the Chicago Coliseum.

Photo by Ray Bolot, Nile, Illinois

A feature from the *VW Autoist* illustrates the all but filial dedication to the beetle fostered by a typical member of the national enthusiast organization.

Local VW clubs have been chartered by the Volkswagen Club of America, Inc (Box 30 Willoughby, Ohio 44094) in every quarter of the U.S.A. Regional clubs have proven especially successful in providing members the opportunity to exchange information on an informal, fireside basis. Local clubs place special emphasis on driving safety, and they attempt by precept and example to spread the ideals of safe driving throughout the community. They also hold competitive programs of standard events, including rallies, *concourses d'elegance*, gymkhanas, and regularity runs; and local VW clubs sponsor occasional social affairs — progressive dinners, caravans, picnics, and the justifiably famous VW Club *Oktoberfeste* and *Herbst Festtage*.

The *Wolfsburg Trophy,* taking the form of a handsomely engraved silver tray contributed by Volkswagen of America, Inc., is awarded annually by the national VW club to its regional group proving most active during the past season. Miss Barbara Nordhoff, an active member of the Public Relations staff of the U. S. importer and, incidentally, the daughter of the General Director, traditionally presents the award at the Club's National Convention.

Insignia of a representation of local clubs depicts the pride of membership among Volkswagen enthusiasts everywhere.

Seventy VWCA members, with their families, hopped to Hanover by chartered *Lufthansa* recently on their pilgrimage to Wolfsburg, where they were graciously received by factory officials, who had arranged direct delivery of more than forty cars, and, of course, a special guided tour of the works. The group posed its fresh new Volkswagens proudly at the plant, bannered for all to see, before beginning a motor tour of Central Europe. The new fifteen-story administration building, marking the western end of the Volkswagenwerk's main frontage, rises behind the Clubsters' caravan.

The crowning function of the Volkswagen Club of America is an annual tour to Europe — including, of course, the city and factory of Wolfsburg. There members have the privilege of taking delivery on new VW's right from the factory, following which they spiritedly caravan for several weeks through Germany in their new cars.

VWCA conventioneers were duly impressed recently by this novel display provided by Import Motors, the Chicago VW distributor. Various amphibious demonstrations have been made with the car to dramatize its practically boatlike buoyance. Not long ago two English salts "set sail" for home in a VW off the French coast (Like the others they had selected the *sunroof* model, and for the same unspoken reason!) Ten miles out to sea their confidence in the craft as an ocean liner became severely dampened when their "boat", swamped by rough water, unceremoniously joined the Channel fish. It has been said that this is the only watercooled VW in the world.

Ouch! Accidents have many times demonstrated Volkswagen as a "smashing success". The protective strength of the VW body shell was reconfirmed in this freak turnpike encounter. While the top vehicle pressed the beetle's body down to the pavement, passenger headroom remained uncompromised by the crushing weight from above. In a way, this accident might almost be classified as an encore . . . Coincidentally, it was the manufacturer of this particular make of truck who some years before had structurally tested models of all production sedans for rigidity in body construction; and had quietly tabbed VW as the toughest of all.

By 1957 distributors had appointed 350 Volkswagen dealers. New problems were faced and solved. To assure transport for constant vehicle supply to meet a rising Stateside demand for the little car the Volkswagen company contracted for long-term leasing of ocean transports for their exclusive use. No national advertising had yet been used, yet waiting time was on an average nine months. 79,524 cars were registered in 1957. VW of A now numbered a staff of 74.

The following year, with the VW value story still being circulated solely by word-of-mouth, Volkswagen agents recorded the highest per dealer sales in the U.S. industry. Each accounted for 246 units. In years to come the lead was to become a yearly tradition with Volkswagen.

With her waterline high above the surface, the *M.S. Carl Trautwein* (previous page) has just begun to take on her cargo of cars at a berth in Bremen, while the *M.S. Konsul Schulte* (above), lying lower in the water from a partial load, hoists on more before embarking on her Atlantic crossing. At least one ship of the Volkswagen fleet docks at a port somewhere in the U.S. every working day. Each car is protected by a paraffin-like shell of wax, applied at the factory. At the destination this coating is removed with special solvents.

THE VW VOYAGE

Little appreciated, because it is not generally known, is the carefully scheduled transportation of the VW to the American buyer. Fourteen days after departure from Hamburg or Bremen the Volkswagen arrives at a U.S. port of entry on the Eastern Seaboard — an extra 14 days if the car is going to a West Coast port. A shipload of new Volkswagens reaches port somewhere in the U.S. every working day, carrying up to 1850 vehicles, to fill American orders . . . It wasn't always possible. Neither the shipping industry as a whole, nor the American ports, were prepared for the sudden emergence of autos as a major import commodity for the United States. Drastic improvements were hastened by Volkswagenwerk so the future expansion of the market in America would not be jeopardized. Vessels were time-chartered, the first carrying only 600 cars, despite the installation of wooden decks adapted to VW measurements. On her first voyage to Port Newark,

New Jersey, there was no suitable pier for her, and she discharged her cars into the main road running past the Newark Airport. She then waited ten days in Brooklyn before receiving a berth to load grain for the return voyage. Later, ship lines mustered the confidence to invest in special automobile carriers... In 1964 Volkswagen had to have a fleet of 29 freighters under contract for individual voyage time charter and 38 more under full-time charter — at around $3,000 per day. After the ships discharge their many layers of wax-coated cars, at a rate of close to 100 per hour, they proceed to other piers to pick up cargo for the homeward voyage. It may be coal, soya beans, grain, phosphates, or it may be U.S. steel, magnesium, or other raw material — a portion of which, one day, will be making a return crossing as a part of a new Volkswagen.

Volkswagen became a yardstick of serviceability among light cars, by which all other makes suffered in comparison. As VW prospered in the vast American market, dozens of other makes from the continent made fresh assaults to emulate this success. But even when contenders like Renault or Fiat became used cars they had lost appeal. Somehow the cluster of interested second buyers around the Volkswagen, who based their worship on an unsaid premise that "VW wears *in;* not *out,*" were not in evidence when these others came up for resale. Their values faded; the VW's remained all but constant. As the resale fell off among other latter day imports, with it went their chances of eclipsing Volkswagen's success.

Special triple-decker trailer cars and truckaways, tailored to accommodate the VW exactly, hustle the car to authorized dealerships across the U. S. at an ever-quickening tempo. Sales increased steadily even in the midst of a chaotic crumbling of sales volume among other import cars. Renault dropped its factory prices $200 early in 1961, followed by Hillman with slashes up to $250. A cooperative dealer ad for the latter, in the February 17, 1961, New York *Times,* blazed away with the following headline: "Sure you can buy a Volkswagen for $34 less . . . but look how much more value you get in a Hillman 4-door sedan for only $1599." The lead phrase, "buy a Volkswagen for $34 less" apparently seemed an attractive inducement to smart new car prospects: VW sales vaulted ahead, while Hillman sales tumbled by a devastating 75%.

These representative offers, assembled from the classified section of a national auto trade journal, document the magnitude of the wholesale traffic in "new" Volkswagens among non-authorized importers and car dealers during the peak seasons of this strange "grey-market". Each ad presents the pitch of a different independent import outfit; the mortality rate among bootleg operators was high.

BOOTLEG BEETLES

Since Volkswagen delivery by authorized dealer channels in the U.S. traditionally entailed a period of waiting, the condition of short supply was taken as a challenge by world traders. The car has been made available by enterprising operators for immediate delivery to the impatient buyer at an extra tariff. But the buyer of a bootleg VW must be willing to let his desire to take the wheel overshadow his desire for proper specifications and the obvious advantages of authorized agency delivery.

Total nationwide registration figures, when compared with Volkswagen dealer import figures, indicate that during the years 1958-60 traffic in this grey market in Volkswagens reached a peak in which the country's new VW population was about 20% higher than factory export figures reflect. One out of every six VW's entering first U.S. ownership appears to have been a bootleg beetle during this period. Today beetle bootlegging has subsided almost completely and represents only a very small percentage of the new registration figures.

Black market importers acquired the cars by threes and sixes from mercenary sub-agents abroad, imported them by the hundred, and unloaded them on the docks of each point of entry around the U.S. Then they sold them in small numbers to Renault dealers, Fiat dealers, used car dealers, Plymouth dealers, and all manner of other unauthorized outlets, who in turn offered immediate ownership to those so intensely possessed with the VW idea they could not wait for normal delivery at the authorized dealership across the street.

These Volkswagens actually were no more than *near* new, having been previously registered and most probably previously used. But a recent VW freshens well under polish and a little elbow grease, and the "near" appeared in small print in presentation to the prospective buyer. He did not seem to care; he had his VW, and his neighbor was still waiting.

While the profile of his car was identical with that of a factory authorized export model, it may have varied in details of lighting equipment, upholstery, outside trim, and more vitally, even in the type of brakes and transmission supplied.

Assuming ownership of a bootleg beetle invariably entailed paying appreciably more, and generally meant receiving less.

The durability and sheer usefulness of the Volkswagen, which had grown from rumor to established fact among American motorists, at first was only a bug on the windshield of the U.S. built product. Later it appeared more in the form of a lion on the hood . . . something a bit more difficult to overlook.

Detroit in the 1950's somehow had drifted away from the basic motorcar concept. Each successive model issued seemed more unwieldy to navigate intracity. Potential car buyers, taking note of this drew up short of buying. It was becoming increasingly apparent generally to consumers that a new car was not necessarily better than the old one.

Resistance took many avenues. A few die-hards even beat the bushes to locate and buy older models that somehow had escaped being used up. Others, taking icy note of the hollow investments they held, after several seasons, in automobiles for which they had paid four or six thousand dollars, vowed not to be quite so foolish again. Buick, the traditional heavy-weight badge of middle success in American life, lost ground and face in the market place. Would-be car buyers had ventured in other directions. A vacation trip abroad became a more measurable investment than changing cars. A swimming pool in the back yard became a more permanent asset.

America, where there is an automobile for every third inhabitant, is truly a country on wheels; Americans use up cars like shoes. Most people in the U.S. had gone along with the American car builders' outlandish concept of *the most car for the most money that the buyer can be induced to pay* because no worthy substitute had presented itself. They had footed the gargantuan bill of ownership which generally amounted to the equivalent of one week to ten days' income each month. They went along as best they could; some staggered under the load; others collapsed.

"Maximum package per package" had become Detroit's theme. Designers ventured almost into outer space with overhangs and square-corners to present that big, long car look. Except for lending this extra length in side appearance, however, the square-corner on an already extended overhang constituted a limiting and dangerous encumbrance for all normal use. When two square-cornered cars "touched" in the course of only slightly inept parking, suddenly it had cost $200 to repair. Collision insurance rates went sky high. Most owners suffered in silence. But they were clearly not keen to buy more of the same, for when one American producer, thoroughly out of touch with reality, came up with a new nameplate featuring the same old schmaltz, there were few takers. Resistance to the ridiculous was on the rise.

As new medium-priced American cars came visibly to offer less practical appeal than would-be trade-ins still possessed, prospects looked about for more tangible means of expressing their middle class success. Almost overnight the home swimming pool became one badge of this ascension.

The vanguard to embrace Volkswagen's honest concept discovered a contrast that was startling — and satisfying. Acceptance of the beetle swept firmly through the big country on a footing of unparalleled technical perfection and durability. Early models were still rendering daily service with only the usual respectful upkeep, racking up a reputation for long-life based on fact. People who could afford the most costly cars demonstrated good judgment by turning from land yachts to the Volkswagen.

After national U.S. media carried VW advertising for the first time in August, 1959, Americans everywhere knew the car. To many VW owners the forthright ads seemed to express their own thoughts with simple eloquence; some even preserved them in albums. Volkswagen was on its way to becoming an American institution.

Is Volkswagen contemplating a change?

Why the engine in the back?

We've gone places!

Ten years ago, the first Volkswagens were imported into the U.S.A.

These strange little cars with their beetle shape were almost unknown.

All they had to recommend them was 32 miles to the gallon (regular gas, regular driving), an aluminum air-cooled rear engine that could go 70 mph all day long without strain,

sensible size for a family, and a sensible price-tag too.

Beetles multiply; so do Volkswagens. By 1954, VW was the best-selling imported car in America. It has held that rank each year since. In 1959 over 150,000 Volkswagens were sold, including station wagons and trucks.

Millionaires buy them, so do working peo-

ple and college kids. Their snub noses are familiar in every state of the Union; as American as apple strudel.

Volkswagen is an honest car. We put as much as we can into it; and we think it the best car in the world for your money. We're glad so many other people agree.

© 1960 VOLKSWAGEN

Prominent professional advertising critic Harry McMahan wrote in ADVERTISING AGE: "We've commented before about Detroit's tired automotive advertising this season: with rare exceptions, it's dreadful. Volkswagen continues to outmaneuver most of 'em in the streets, in sales and in advertising. Agency: Doyle Dane Bernbach . . . against all the odds of Detroit's research to the American public."

Volkswagen had become a part of the daily American scene. By the end of 1959, 470 dealerships stretched around the United States. VW of A expanded its sales department to cover all phases of sales and merchandising. After setting up an advertising department, two advertising agencies were appointed – one for Sedans, one for Trucks and Service. Soon after, the first national ads appeared and the VW image of practicality and reliability was publicized aggressively in the United States for the first time. Previous sales records now became fractions, 150,601 Volkswagens appeared on the official registrations for 1959.

THE DISTAFF DELIGHTED

The "Diary of a Happy Volkswagen Owner" was written by a young mother of three. Eleanor Bruce also is a career girl working for "Kelly Girls," an organization supplying temporary office help. Mrs. Bruce has taken the time and trouble to compose a "diary" which excellently represents Volkswagen from the feminine point of view.

I am having more fun than I've had in years. The fun is driving my new VW. It responds immediately to my control — it moves easily and directly wherever and whenever I want it to.

"While other cars are cruising about looking for parking spaces . . . there always seems to be a resting spot for me."

Why are people buying Volkswagens faster than they can be made?

Aug. 17, 1959

198 lbs.
(why Volkswagen's aluminum engine is still years ahead of its time)

Aug. 24, 1959

Gerhard Baecker teaches Volkswagen
(Or why Volkswagen service is as good as the car)

Aug. 31, 1959

The only water a Volkswagen needs is the water you wash it with.

Nov. 16, 1959

What year car do the Jones drive?

Nov. 23, 1959

Repair 'em? I've got enough parts to build 'em!

Feb. 8, 1960

Think small.

Feb. 22, 1960

Can you name this car?

Mar. 28, 1960

Why are so many people looking into the Volkswagen?

Mar. 14, 1960

Lemon.

Apr. 11, 1960

"There is a certain camaraderie among owners . . . whose satisfaction is gained from the faithful service of the car."

I've found that there is a certain camaraderie among owners of VWs who talk eagerly about the amazing number of miles they've rolled on their first set of tires. They boast about the fantastic number of happy miles they've driven their VWs and that the only car for them in the future would be another VW.

I was delighted to find that while other cars are cruising about looking for parking spaces or resorting to high-priced parking lots, there always seems to be a resting spot for such a reasonable size car as my VW. Friends, who first teased me about my little car, now ask the most interested questions about it. They can appreciate its good features and many will make their next car a VW! Whenever *Life* and such magazines run the full page VW ads I always read them with pride and show them to my friends. These ads confirm my enthusiastic Volkswagen feelings.

Volkswagen has thought of everything. And this is especially important to owners like me who are both career gals and chauffeuring mothers. The service book of tickets tells me exactly at what mileage I should call for a preventive maintenance appointment. And the ticket tells me exactly what will be checked, lubricated, tightened — It's a comfort to know that I can put my trust in a company which takes an active interest that I get the best performance from my car for years to come — one that's not just interested in my trading it in as soon as the new models come out.

When ordering my Volkswagen, it was a satisfaction to find at least one car manufacturer who can appreciate that all gadgets are not essential to all people. VW made it possible for me to select what things I thought important instead of loading everything on and then setting the price to include the extras. And the salesman didn't try to force or shame me into taking options which I didn't want. I found, too, that Volkswagen, instead of presenting a whole host of models and body styles to confuse me — has concentrated on just a certain number of styles, thus eliminating the cost of variations.

And how nicely the family fits into the VW! The little ones climb eagerly into the back "pocket" where they consider themselves kangaroos. Safely contained in a comfortable compartment, they can easily see through the front, side or back windows, and can play with their toys.

"The little ones climb eagerly into the back pocket where they consider themselves kangaroos."

Why?

Apr. 25, 1960

The famous Italian designer suggested one change.

May 16, 1960

Who in the world seals the bottom? Volkswagen.

June 6, 1960

The oldest Volkswagen in America.

You might mistake it for the newest.

July 11, 1960

It isn't so.

Aug. 29, 1960

Why so many Volkswagens live to be 100,000.

Sept. 19, 1960

(1960)   **(1961)**

Can you see the 27 changes?

Oct. 3, 1960

Do you think the Volkswagen is homely?

Nov. 7, 1960

A Volkswagen, obviously.

Jan. 27, 1961

The '51 '52 '53 '54 '55 '56 '57 '58 '59 '60 '61 Volkswagen.

Feb. 10, 1961

The experimental X-93 Volkswagen.

Feb. 24, 1961

"Inside were parked two VWs . . . This garage would hardly have held just one oversize car."

Driving down the street the other day, I spotted one of the older, smaller garages so prevalent in established neighborhoods. And there, inside, were parked *two* VWs. It occurred that this garage would hardly have held just one of the over-size cars we often see today. Then I realized that our 2½ car carport, originally built with much larger cars in mind, would give our family more room now that we own a VW — with space for storing the children's equipment and room for them to play.

My greatest joy, however, is that this VW is the answer to all of my transportation qualifications. It doesn't pretend to compete in a pretentious race for prestige, startling new styling (obsolete in a period of months), excessive power (illegal anywhere but on the Bonneville Salt Flats), nor is it gadget-laden with gimmicks I don't want. *It does* provide me with a classic styling of its own, proven to be successful over many years. It does give me the power I need and can use, the mechanical improvements and other features which I consider important. It takes me out of the competitive prestige seekers' group and into that great fellowship of proud Volkswagen owners whose satisfaction is gained from the faithful service of a car offering good transportation for an unbelievable number of miles and years — My one regret is that I didn't save hundreds of dollars on depreciation and gasoline by buying a Volkswagen ten years ago.

—Eleanor Bruce

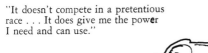

"It doesn't compete in a pretentious race . . . It does give me the power I need and can use."

Following the initial ad thrust with a greatly increased advertising budget the next year VW became a conversation piece among national advertisers. Some proud owners reassembled the ads in permanent scrapbooks and scouted to get every one. The value in Volkswagen was fast becoming a public fact among all automobilists. At the beginning of the year, one in four imported cars sold was a VW; by year's end, it was one in two. Registrations for 1960 were 191,373, ahead of Cadillac, Chrysler, Comet, Mercury and Studebaker. More than 621,000 Volkswagens by now had been registered in the United States since the token plurality in 1949.

Volkswagen overdoes it again: 4 coats of paint.

Mar. 10, 1961

Why you should open a window before you close the door of a Volkswagen.

Mar. 24, 1961

Our number one salesman.

Apr. 7, 1961

$1595.

Apr. 21, 1961

Last one to conk out is a Volkswagen.

May 5, 1961

You don't have to replace half the car.

June 23, 1961

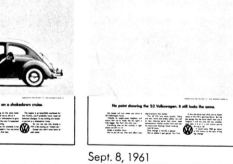

Impossible.

July 7, 1961

You don't have to take it on a shakedown cruise.

Aug. 25, 1961

No point showing the '62 Volkswagen. It still looks the same.

Sept. 8, 1961

Never.

Sept. 29, 1961

How can you be sure you're getting a '62?

Oct. 20, 1961

How to tell the year of a Volkswagen.

Nov. 10, 1961

This leading American award in the field of technology commemorates the achievements of Dr. Elmer Ambrose Sperry, pioneer in the development of the Gyrocompass and other navigational aids, as well as improved automobiles. It is the gift of Dr. Sperry's daughter and his son, to the engineering profession, and is awarded annually after a year's deliberation.

DISTINGUISHING U.S. RECOGNITION

Volkswagen's exemplary behavior on the international scene received formal recognition when the Elmer A. Sperry Award for ADVANCING THE ART OF TRANSPORTATION was bestowed at a joint meeting of the SAE and the ASME in New York City in November, 1958. President Nordhoff, on behalf of the workers of Volkswagen, was present to personally receive the singular honor. The citation read:

"To Dr. Ferdinand Porsche (in memoriam), Dr. Heinz Nordhoff, and their co-workers in Volkswagenwerk for the development of the Volkswagen automobile which, in concept, engineering design and production, has made available to the world an automobile of small size for multiple uses, with unique attributes of universality; of low initial and operating costs; of simplicity of design having ease of maintenance; comfort with adequate performance; and suitable for rural and urban use."

This distinguished award has been made only in recognition of outstanding engineering contributions which, through application in actual service proved to have advanced the art of transportation whether by land, sea or air. The first award, in 1955, went to William F. Gibbs for the concept and design of the *S.S. United States,* the fastest passenger ship in the world. In 1956 Donald W. Douglas was recognized for his DC series of airplanes, half the total of all aircraft operated by airlines throughout the world. In 1957 it went to developers of the GMC Diesel-electric locomotive, credited with helping revolutionize American railroading.

In naming Volkswagen, the Board of Award, composed of representatives from the American Society of Mechanical Engineers, American Institute of Electrical Engineers, Society of Automotive Engineers and the Society of Naval Architects and Marine Engineers, had commended a foreign engineer or engineering team for the first time. The vote for Volkswagen was a unanimous one.

At the awarding of the Sperry Prize in 1958, Nordhoff said:

"We are eternally indebted to the genius of Professor Porsche for the *creation* of the Volkswagen. But for the continuing constructive improvements in the VW, the maintenance of its high quality, and the continually growing production of the VW, we thank our outstanding engineers in Wolfsburg . . . but we don't build cars for our own ambition, but only for our customers, among whom the old and true VW drivers are every bit so dear and valuable to us as the new drivers, whom we hope to win over to VW."

Newspaper clippings from papers all over the country testify to the volume of U.S. labor and U.S. material that contribute to the manufacture of each new Volkswagen.

IMPORTED vs. DOMESTIC

In recent times Volkswagen has accounted for three percent of the total cars sold in the world's biggest, toughest auto market — USA. By 1962, of an estimated 400,000 imported cars entering the United States, VW accounted for more than half.

Although the imported car and the domestic car are pitted against each other in the minds of automotive writers and analysts they are really all one to the buyer. With only one market for automobiles all makes from all countries compete on the basis of value offered. The car buyer selects one make rather than another, not on the basis of where it came from, but on the basis of its value and its use.

The American seldom confuses himself by separating imported cameras or watches from domestic models. He simply buys according to design and function. Imported steel or imported machine tools cannot be separated either. The Volkswagen factory buys American machine tools and American steel not because they are American, but because these tools and this steel do the job better than other machines or other steel.

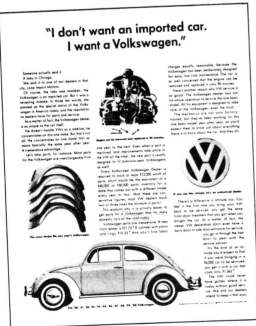

Made in USA? Foreign parts represent only a tiny percentage of the value of U. S. products, according to Federal estimates. Still it was an item of $48 million in 1961 American cars, up from $17.6 million in 1957. "American industry and European industry must . . . shop the world for the most economical values, not only in finished products, but, just as importantly, in parts, materials and accessories," declared Henry Ford II, chairman of Ford Motor Co., in mid-1962. Ford estimated that its purchases of parts for passenger cars and trucks from foreign sources for the 1962 model year would total about $3.4 million. Foreign parts used to fill a portion of its requirements included water pump and generator bearings, springs and connecting rods. Ford pointed out that its foreign affiliates were expected to buy $68.4 million in production parts from the U. S. during the same period.

More than fifty heavy-duty presses from the United States—the biggest operating at 1600 tons psi —form about 170 tons of American sheet steel into doors, roofs and fenders at Wolfsburg every day.

While U.S. wages are from 2 to 4 times those paid anywhere else, raw materials, fuel and power are still more expensive overseas, made so by lesser facilities and shorter production runs which are geared to smaller markets. Producing a ton of finished steel takes 21½ man hours in France, and 17 in Germany, but only 12 man hours in the U.S. Price advantage in export markets is sometimes less important than the quality or special characteristics of the material. Volkswagen discovered that the United States makes the best deep-draw steel for shaping roofs and fenders. In 1961 the Wolfsburg factory bought 10% of all its sheet steel from the U.S. It also added $2.8 million worth of U.S.-made presses, gear gutters and other highly specialized machines to its ever-expanding production capacity, during the same period.

With appearance of news like this Volkswagen's pre-eminence among all makes became historical fact. VW dealers outpaced every make in the U.S. industry, in terms of average sales per dealer, from 1958 through 1961. The crown was recaptured for 1963, with 327 new passenger car sales per dealer, and nailed on with a record average of 343 sales for 1964.

Meanwhile, in Las Vegas . . . In commercial rental, where rates directly reflect durability and depreciation, the bug went out for half the price of the compacts.

DEALERSHIPS WANTED

VOLKSWAGEN OR CHEVROLET DEALERSHIP. Young, experienced, aggressive man looking to buy either a partnership or complete agency. Your reply kept strictly confidential, Box 3017, c/o Automotive News, Detroit 7.

COLLECTIONS, REPOSSESSIONS

DEALERS, FINANCE FIRMS, BANKS,

Dual billing of VW with the traditional U. S. sales leader in this little want ad appearing in the trade paper of the U. S. automotive industry eloquently testified to VW's desirability as a dealer property.

Ten percent of the free world's output of magnesium goes into engine and transmission parts of Volkswagen. Most of it comes from the United States and Canada. Not long ago Continental made a big thing out of the fact that its upholstery leather came from Scotland. The purely domestic automobile no more exists than the purely imported one.

Some old-line domestic agents, suffering a sharp decline in traditional public favor, moved out of their plush facilities into lower overhead quarters as an economy measure—only to witness the blossoming of a VW agency at the old stand. Across the country, agents for low-volume U. S. offerings sacked their domestic ties altogether to take on the beetle franchise. Even among dealers for American favorites some sought relief from a long romance with factory drumbeating for unrealistic sales volume. Among the latter was one dealer prominent along the Atlantic seaboard as exclusively Ford since 1934. This agent was only too happy to spend $73,000 to remodel a less than five-year-old facility, as only one qualification toward obtaining the VW franchise, where once again automobile selling could be practiced as a service to the customer.

VW Tops Per Dealer In Sales

MARCH 7, 1960

SELLERS of imported cars played "follow the leader" again last year in the sales-per-dealer derby. As usual, the leader was Volkswagen.

Volkswagen's victory wasn't news, but its sales-per-dealer total was definitely an eyebrow lifter. VW retailers delivered an average of 292 cars apiece in 1959. That was far and away the best performance of any dealer organization in the nation last year. By comparison, Ford led the U. S. makes with 215 sales per dealer, and Chevrolet was second with 196. Volumewise, of course, Volkswagen is a long way from the U. S. pacesetters. Both Ford and Chevrolet registered more than 1.4 million new cars last year, compared with VW's 119,899.

Even when the U.S. industry could feel the heat of the VW brand, as a Volkswagen dealer opened in Detroit, publicly it acted as though smaller cars were a passing fancy. But behind this neutral facade Detroit was hell-bent in tooling for cars intended to stop the import down to a decimal in total sales. By the summer of 1959 motor chiefs confirmed the rumors and estimated that 10% of production devoted to the new lighter models would turn the trick.

Most flattering to VW of all new light cars to appear was GM's Corvair, which emulated chassis layout right down to adoption of an air-cooled, flat-opposed engine "in the rear where it belongs." Changes in the big land yacht series cars were even queued to the trimmer trend, being billed as *shorter* than before. For the moment, Americans were getting a measure more of efficiency in all their new automobiles. Volkswagen, the "unmentionable" in Detroit, had set the new pace.

JUNIOR GROWS UP

An understanding of how Detroit thinks and acts in its car building is necessary to comprehend what happened next. Cars brought out to steal VW's thunder would not be allowed to stand or fall on their comparatively pure merits. A yearly progression of face-lifts was scheduled to move the compacts away from the efficient car field literally before public introduction. "Upgrading" of the original 1960 models began when "marketing engineers" — respecting the more than two years of lead time required for changes in U.S. carmaking — pre-judged that the smaller cars *would not sell*. Even as these "experts," who had come up with a sour pre-sale guesstimate of 10% of production, saw sales begin at 20% and almost immediately soar to nearly 50% of some segments of the industry, they continued to be motivated by a blind allegiance to their system's overpowering dedication to maximum-sale-per-sale design. With the sole exception of Corvair, each succeeding season brought models to confirm their official presale prejudice against lesser profits. Extended overhangs gave way to increased wheelbases, and "big engine" options further widened the gulf between the all-car VW and the profit-oriented American concept. Detroit's efforts to capture Volkswagen customers had been abandoned.

One smaller U.S. maker by economic necessity had breasted the trend toward unwieldy bigness by doctoring its comparatively narrow 1953 body shell for too many seasons with a progression of fore and aft sheet metal extensions. By 1958 the car's inept proportions had grown openly ludicrous. The model was walking in its own blood in the market place by the time its maker wakened to this suicidal premise. Just as industry experts were predicting a quiet funeral, management surprised all with the product of a bold decision—historically significant in the industry for its open faced honesty. For 1959 Studebaker appeared as "a new concept of automotive transportation". Almost literally a meat axe had been taken to the cold potato. Outstretched sheet metal had been lopped off drastically; the remaining approach and departure angles became trim and practical. Though bobbing operations were scabbed over by only the barest styling tricks, with resulting appearance far from esthetically winning, the turnabout frankness of this model found new friends, and the old body found acceptance for several more sales years.

No other event could have served more convincingly to endorse the unorthodox Volkswagen engineering concept in the United States than the introduction by America's volume leader of this "car created to conquer a new field" for 1960. The "field" being referred to could not have been mistaken by the dullest motorist reading this initial newspaper announcement: "America's only airplane-type horizontal engine . . . independent suspension at all 4 wheels . . . air-cooled aluminum engine . . . in the rear where it belongs." Details were, indeed, "revolutionary," as the ad stated, by domestic standards. But on an intercontinental basis, they emulated the Volkswagen feature for feature. After the fanfare of this promotion Volkswagen reached an acceptance in the U.S. on a par with apple pie.

Think Small

18 New York University students have gotten into a sun-roof VW; a tight fit. The Volkswagen is sensibly sized for a family. Mother, father, and three growing kids suit it nicely.

In economy runs, the VW averages close to 50 miles per gallon. You won't do near that; after all, professional drivers have canny trade secrets. (Want to know some? Write VW,

Box #65, Englewood, N. J.) Use regular gas and forget about oil between changes.

The VW is 4 feet shorter than a conventional car (yet has as much leg room up front). While other cars are doomed to roam the crowded streets, you park in tiny places.

VW spare parts are inexpensive. A new front fender (at an authorized VW dealer) is

$21.75.* A cylinder head, $19.95.* The nice thing is, they're seldom needed.

A new Volkswagen sedan is $1,675.* Other than a radio and side view mirror, that includes everything you'll really need.

In 1959 about 170,000 Americans thought small and bought VWs.

Think about it.

Envious of Volkswagen's snowballing popularity, more than one light car competitor came openly to use VW as a point-of-reference in promoting its own *marque*. The most sincerely flattering of all was one low-volume importer who elected to follow up the catchy "Think Small" ad with a double-page spread in leading U.S. magazines in which half the space—one full page—was obligingly given over to a gratis boost for the beetle. Of sales later netted from this ad, very likely the majority were Volkswagen.

First you thought small.

Now think a little bigger.

No sooner had it appeared as the starkly simple theme of a Volkswagen ad than tones of the new moderation crept into everyday language all over America. Not only was it proper to accept the challenge to "think small" in various pursuits, but it became the height of fashion—and political device—to bear evidence of having followed the trend.

California to Buy Only Compacts for $200,000 Saving

FEBRUARY 5, 1962

SACRAMENTO, Calif.—Gov. Edmund Brown said his state is "thinking small" this year and expects to save almost $200,000 by buying only compact cars for its agencies.

Brown announced that all 1,838 new passenger cars the state plans to buy will be compacts. Last year, the state bought 75 percent compacts for its fleet.

Purchasing officials said savings on initial cost would amount to $93,283 and they expect to save another $100,000 on operating expenses.

They expect that eventually the state's entire fleet will be made up of compacts. The Highway Patrol was not mentioned in the announcement and presumably it will continue to use standard-size models.

VW FORMULA FOR U.S. SUCCESS

As Volkswagen led the way and Detroit followed nearly half of the car buyers in the United States came to buy cars smaller than those they had bought before.

Strangely unlike other makes Volkswagen sales have not shot up and zoomed down with the fad of the moment. They have been consistently increasing in every area of the USA. VW's steady sales seem to confirm the merit of satisfying a basic need among automobile offerings. As long as Volkswagen continues to do this it will continue to be bought by Americans.

Volkswagen has never had plans to become a major competitor of Detroit. Like other automobiles the car has certain limitations that restrict its potential; it was never designed specifically for America, or Sweden, or Brazil, or any other country. VW is built for all these places and many more. It does not aim at dominating, but at satisfying a portion of the buyers in every country.

U.S. compact cars are not considered by VW of America as direct competition, even though sales of other import cars tumbled in this country as the various compacts appeared in the market. Dr. Nordhoff maintained in an interview in 1959 that the U.S.-built compacts are not truly "small," and that they fill a different market from that of the Volkswagen. He even predicted that as the European market develops in its desire for higher-priced, more comfortable, and larger cars, these American-made compacts may do very well in export sales.

The sales success of the VW seems as independent of other import car sales as the VW is different from other cars. In 1961 when sales of all imports fell off in great measure, VW sales continued to rise. Today, close to half of all imports sold in America are Volkswagens.

Volkswagen does not claim to have any mysterious secret for success either in America or in the world. Its broad acceptance has been based on the underlying fact that VW performs its function economically and dependably.

The Volkswagen makes a significant contribution to the American economy. Outlays for advertising and promotion by VW of America now annually total more than $7.5 million. Each VW sold in the U.S.A. also adds approximately $1,000 to the U.S. economy through duties, shipping, dealer incomes, salaries, and other costs of doing business.

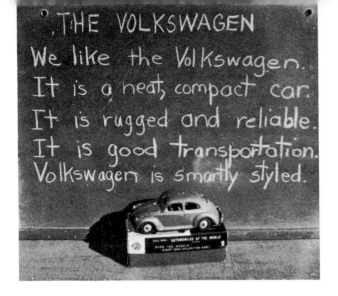

THE VOLKSWAGEN
We like the Volkswagen.
It is a neat, compact car.
It is rugged and reliable.
It is good transportation.
Volkswagen is smartly styled.

MY DADDY BOUGHT A VOLKSWAGEN

"My Daddy bought one too!" comes the rebuttal from a little six-year-old lady who belongs to what one might call the Beet-le Generation. An elementary school teacher, who at her own request remains anonymous, found her transportation study more than once turned into a free-for-all on the Volkswagen. She was interested and made notes on the discussions; after all, she drove a Volkswagen, too.

Unlike the passing fancies of marbles, "Monopoly" and trading cards, the Volkswagen has found a constant following among the grade school crowd. In fact, the first grader who announces to the class: "My daddy bought a Volkswagen," is sure to win the limelight — whether or not he has done his homework.

Primary grade subjects often include units of lessons on transportation — our class recently completed just such a study. Thanks to these discussions, many a youngster has had the chance to demonstrate that, he too, has been "thinking small."

In one such discussion, one little boy used a VW scale model to implement his short talk. "Pretty slick," admired another. They talked with animation about the car's characteristics, and the VW's improvements. They went on at length about the meaning of the word, "Volkswagen," and felt like adult people of the world when they pronounced it properly.

A little boy in short pants piped up that the local druggist uses a VW to deliver prescriptions — another reported that "Dr. Mason came to our house in a Volkswagen when my sister had the measles." What does all this mean?

A teacher has an ideal vantage point from which to view the developing habits of tomorrow's citizens. And from where this observer sits, nothing is more apparent than that tomorrow's drivers will be driving Volkswagens.

—ANONYMOUS FIRST GRADE TEACHER

By the spring of 1963 a staff of 250 at Englewood Cliffs was engaged in Divisions of Sales, Marketing, Administration, Public Relations, Service and Parts, with department heads reporting to Carl H. Hahn, who had been named vice president and general manager of Volkswagen of America, Inc., in 1959. Educated in Germany, Switzerland, France, Italy and England, he received a Ph.D. from the University of Bern in 1952 where he served as an assistant professor of economics. Practical experience began with a Swiss firm importing American automobiles, followed by a brief training period with Fiat. Hahn joined Volkswagenwerk as head of export sales promotion in 1954.

In 1964, Carl H. Hahn was promoted to the board of management and returned to Wolfsburg. Succeeding him as general manager of VW of A was

Stuart Perkins, who had joined Volkswagen of America as one of its first three employees in 1955. Perkins was promoted to sales and organization manager in 1956 and in 1960 was elected a vice president and named general sales manager. In June, 1964, Heinz Nordhoff, as chairman of the board, announced the election of Perkins executive vice president and general manager. Six months later he was named president. The new chief executive at Englewood Cliffs was born in London, in 1928. He was educated in England and Canada.

Independent dealerships in the U.S. increased from 687 at the start of 1963 to 744 by the end of the year. By the close of 1965 the number reached the 909 level. The continued growth of the Volkswagen sales and service network, presently employing about 25,000 Americans, assures more than two million VW owners in the U.S. the best service the automobile industry has ever provided, VW dealers having made the highest investment per one-line dealership in the industry. All told, investment in VW sales, service and parts storage facilities in the U.S. substantially exceeds $260,000,000 or more than $10,000 invested for each person making his living selling or servicing VWs in the United States.

Hanging out the VW shingle is a weighty business in which more than capital and credit and a good reputation are required. VW of A has developed rules for every detail, though the dealer who bears along with such items does not go unrewarded. (For example, a dealer is required to employ one mechanic for every 150 Volkswagens in his area, with fully trained mechanics on the payroll before he can open the doors.) But the VW dealer, on an average sells more

VW of A, official importer of VWs for the USA, recently moved into a specially built $2.5 million headquarters building in New Jersey. While more than 330 personnel are efficiently installed in the functional modern structure at Englewood Cliffs, building plans for horizontal expansion are now under way.

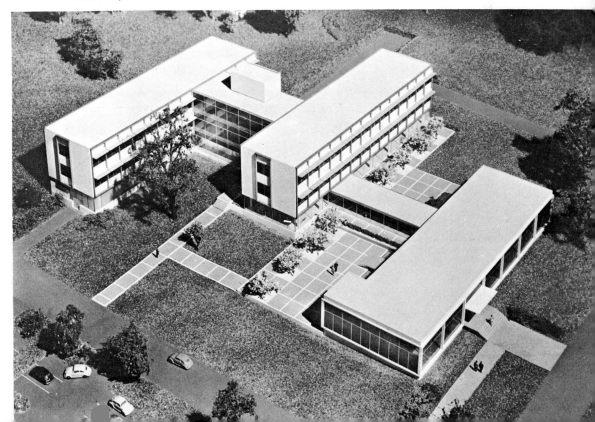

units than any other domestic or foreign dealer in the U.S.   So it seems to be worth all the fuss. And no one shares in the benefits more than the VW owner himself.

REGISTRATIONS OF NEW VOLKSWAGENS IN THE U.S.A.

1949..........2	1955.....30,928	1961....203,863
1950........330	1956.....55,690	1962....222,740
1951........417	1957.....79,524	1963....277,008
1952........980	1958....104,306	1964....322,942
1953......1,214	1959....150,601	1965....371,221
1954......8,895	1960....191,372	

Volkswagen, by a noble cooperative effort among dealers, distributors and VW of A had rolled from obscurity in the U.S. to become the new dimension in efficiency by which *all* cars are judged.

Volkswagen's magazine and newspaper advertisements for its sedans and station wagons were selected by the PRINT-ERS' INK executive panel as "the best print series" in a recent survey. Ad men picked the VW ads for "refreshing off-beat believability and concentration on fact," as well as sales results. ("Look at all the bugs on the road.") VW's winning campaign was prepared by Doyle Dane Bernbach, Inc., under the supervision of Paul Lee and Helmut Schmitz of VW of A.

Think Tall

Our Volkswagen Station Wagon is only nine inches longer than our little VW Sedan. Yet it holds more than the biggest conventional wagon.
How?
Perhaps this picture explains it.
Ideally in a station wagon, you need maximum room and minimum length. We have answered this with a taller car. (The entire top of the VW wagon is level. This gives it the shape of a box. There is not a wasted inch in it.)
This is why things that will not fit in any conventional wagon fit easily inside the VW wagon.
An upright piano standing upright. A standard bridge table opened up. Eight adults with all their luggage.
Or, if you open the sun-roof, a huge old-fashioned wooden wardrobe. Even a horse fifteen hands high.
People are pleased that our VW wagon parks so easily. (If you have ever circled a shopping mart or a commuters' station looking for a big enough space for your big wagon, you can appreciate this.)
When you realize that our VW Station Wagon is a good four feet shorter than conventional wagons you get the picture.

14

THE BOX ON WHEELS

Like its primeval counterpart, the ox, it could carry close to its own weight. The aptness of VW's ultimate design for commercial purpose came to be confirmed and reconfirmed as imitators crowded every market.

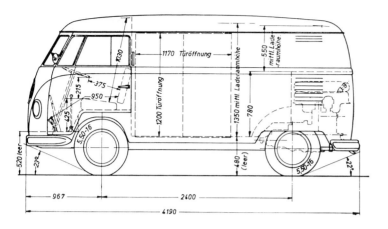

Styling evolved only as a by-product of efficient design layout and provided little latitude for whimsical alterations to outdate for the sake of change. A token resemblance to the sedan was carried over in the V-shaped return molding at the front.

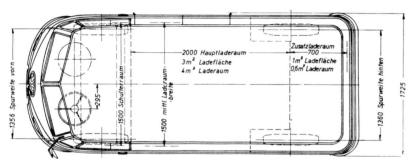

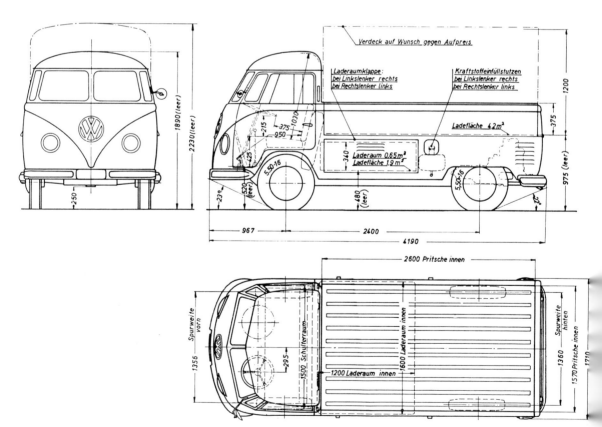

Following chassis convention a prototype panel delivery had been developed back in *KdF* days. Cargo space was so confined by the engine location the car's potential as a commercial transporter seemed obscure.

Once the People's Car became a reality, the *People's Truck* was a natural development to follow. A commercial vehicle was on the VW drawing boards soon after Nordhoff's administration had achieved quantity production of the familiar sedan; Volkswagen management had anticipated the need for such a vehicle long before the public called for it.

After VW tested a series of experimental models, it became clear that the proposed truck might never realize its fullest potential if the body of the standard passenger model were simply adapted to a van or pickup style, following standard practice. While the VW's unusual chassis layout created problems for body designers around the rear engine area, it presented no difficulties in the forward section, which was usually taken up by the engine of conventional commercial cars. By moving the driver's position forward, the VW designers created a miniature chassis layout exactly like that already proven on busses and large commercial vans.

Nordhoff's brainstorming staff kicked around a few challenging questions . . . What would be wrong with building a micro-sized bus or van? Why wouldn't this layout that worked so well on a large chassis offer equal advantages in shorter wheelbase and side-loading access, heretofore not offered in a light transporter? Their answers led to planning what may be considered the ultimate design for the purpose of transporting general light goods — a literal *box on wheels*.

When Nordhoff's staff centered load-space "midships" between engine and driver the payload was solved. Cab-forward layout required an elevated driver position over the front wheels, in turn dictating a taller form than the sedan package.

213

 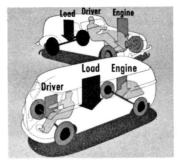 

The center-load transporter provided distinct benefits not alone in carrying capacity—which approached a ratio of 1:1. As shown, the package offered greater square-footage for advertising signs, as well as superior field of view for the driver both by day and by night.

Weight distribution in the VW commercial car design was ideally balanced: the passengers were placed in the front and the engine in the rear. The payload thus was carried in the best sprung part of the vehicle, exactly between the two axles, creating completely even utilization of the weight-carrying properties of the tires and suspension. Independently sprung wheels, a hydraulic steering damper, and minimum front and rear overhang assured outstanding handling characteristics.

As VW's design engineers reflected on the Transporter, they placed greatest emphasis on making the vehicle as versatile as possible for any reasonable — or unreasonable — requirement. They gave first consideration to the loading area, which they brought to 162 cubic feet (and later 170) in a particularly low, easily accessible volume 5½ feet wide, 13½ feet long, and nearly 6½ feet high. They designed the Transporter of all-steel, self-supporting unit body construction. Wide double doors made the vehicle unusually simple to load at curbside with any cargo from eggs to pianos, also created easy entrance and exit for passengers. At the very front of the load area the design staff located an easily accessible heated driver's cab, with excellent visibility and enough room for three passengers.

The sedan instrument cluster, enclosed behind the steering wheel was the extent of forward furnishing, no side-to-side dashboard or shelf being provided in the austere first series.

Though over-all styling continued undisturbed, successive models of the Transporter underwent continuous changes for improvement. Earliest production carried an outside gas filler and an undersized tank. The spare was carried in a vertical position at the right rear. Cargo volume stood originally at 162 square feet.

Transporter performance was more than adequate for practically any job. The Delivery Van was designed with a dead weight of barely a ton; yet it accommodated a payload of 1830 pounds, representing a weight-load ratio of almost 1:1. The Transporter's four-cylinder engine enabled the vehicle to cruise fully loaded all day long at 50 mph, to accelerate to 30 mph in around 9 seconds. Its climbing ability in first gear was pegged at 24%, and it produced 25 honest miles to the gallon of gasoline. Whether designed as a camping wagon, ambulance, or delivery van, the Transporter became renowned for its reasonable and sensible performance coupled with remarkable economy and utility.

An early change embraced enclosing the fuel filler inside the engine compartment and increasing fuel capacity. The spare was then moved to a shelf above the engine. Still, no provision was made for cargo access at the rear and the motor space continued to carry eight cubic feet more than it required.

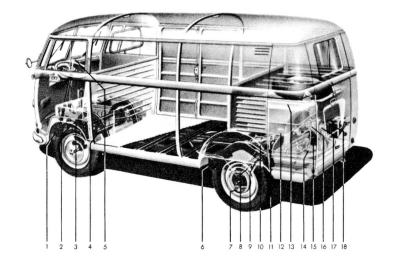

Utility dominated every feature of the Transporter. Two-thirds of the entire volume was load space, affording longer delivery routes per load. Jolting of the load was eliminated by the smooth, cradled ride. Fuel consumption was amazingly low. To light truck users everywhere the Transporter began to make overwhelming sense.

The first Transporter was produced in November, 1949. Truck users immediately discovered that the vehicle had combined the economical performance and reliability already familiar in the VW sedan with transport engineering for maximum load on a minimum wheelbase. It proved itself suitable for an all but unlimited range of commercial uses.

Hundreds of thousands of Transporters have followed for more than a decade, and the only changes in the original design have been improvements to the basic concept in order to better its *function*. Loading access took on new convenience as VW designers opened the hitherto solid back-side with a large upward-opening panel door. Redesign of the forward roof to enclose a fresh-air intake duct above the windshield also created much improved passenger comfort. For 1964 the rear door and window were improved again becoming extra-wide.

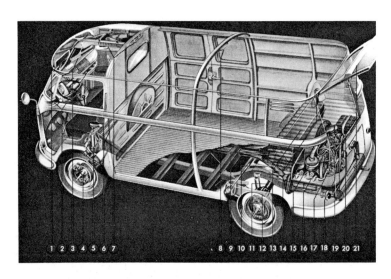

In 1955, an overhead ventilation system was built into the forward roof, ducting from an intake over the windshield. The pick-up model spare tire location (behind the driver's seat) was extended to the full line, allowing a lower shelf over the engine which, in turn, brought the payload volume to 170 cubic feet. A top-hinged door was added at the rear for direct access to the shelf. With these particular refinements what had been very good became even better.

Double doors at the curb side provide ready access to the whole Van area and handling can be saved twice with each load. When required it can be provided at the factory with double doors on the traffic side as well.

Originally the Transporters were manufactured in the main factory at Wolfsburg, where they appeared in the form of Delivery Vans, Pickups, Kombis, Microbusses, and Ambulances. But the VW plant management had long desired to separate the production of the Transporter and the passenger models. In 1956 Transporter body manufacture and assembly was moved, according to plan, to a mammoth plant in Hanover which was expressly designed for this production.

Experts in plant layout conservatively grade the materials handling at the Transporter plant as "ideal". The factory benefits from experience with the original Wolfsburg facility built 18 years before. Here in Hanover 23,000 persons turn out a steady stream of Volkswagen trucks, station wagons and air-cooled engines.

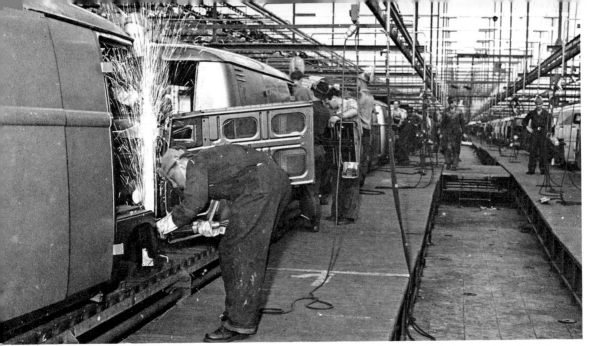

Every bit of unnecessary dead weight has been designed out of the truck. Self-supporting, all-steel unitized construction is so expertly engineered and assembled that even component door panels literally lend their part in total torsional stability. 800 units are produced every working day.

HANOVER FACTORY

A passenger on a barge, floating along the Mitteland Canal westward from Wolfsburg, passes through miles of the pleasant, pastoral countryside of Lower Saxony. But in the *Vorort* (suburb) of Stoecken, just outside Hanover, rises alongside the canal another of the monuments to postwar Germany's industrial growth: the VW Hanover Transporter assembly plant. In order to create more space for further production of VW sedans, Nord-hoff chose to move Transporter production from Wolfsburg to another location. He selected a one million square meter tract of land between the *Autobahn* and the Mitteland Canal; and after the remarkably short construction time of nine months, the Hanover factory began production early in 1956.

Many tasks done by hand in Transporter production at Wolfsburg have become largely automated at Hanover. But while automatic priming and painting equipment now assures speed and quality in these operations, no substitute for wet sanding and rubbing by hand has been found to insure quality in the final finish.

The single wooden body part of a Volkswagen is added by workers at left from stacks nearby. Unfinished hardwood has been found least damaging to any foreseeable cargo and is used for bed runners on the Pick-up truck. By 1961 VW trucks accounted for 42% of the German truck market.

Gute Fahrt, a German motoring magazine, published some interesting figures about the VW Hanover Plant. 2.5 million sacks of cement, 8.5 million concrete blocks, and 400,000 square meters of tarpaper were required in the construction of the plant. The foundations necessitated the removal of 256,000 truckloads of dirt.

All Transporter production facilities are now located in Hanover. Initial schedules called for 5000 workers to build 250 Transporters daily, but these figures have long since been surpassed. 23,000 persons are now employed at Hanover, and they work in one of the most modern and perhaps one of the most beautiful automobile plants in the world. The experience gained in the main factory at Wolfsburg has materially affected the new plant's layout. Volkswagen engineers predesigned all technical equipment, handling, and

As in the sedan plant, each Transporter is built to meet the exact order of a Volkswagen dealer. At left a Kombi rolls off "in the white" (primer finish only) on the order of a particular customer who likely will have the unit specially painted at the point of delivery.

A continuous conveyor system at Hanover begins for the body with sub-assembly of the floor panel; then it snakes its way through the plant with supplies furnished from below till the completed body emerges, ready to join its running gear in final assembly.

operation methods, then built the factory around a largely mechanized assembly line, on which parts for assembly are rotated continuously to be picked up at the right time at the right place. The latest automatic body priming equipment has been installed, and workers now use power tools on many former hand jobs. All parts not moved directly by conveyors or cranes are transported on a floor beneath the assembly shop.

Only the plant's superbly practical product approaches the space utilization and overall efficiency of this factory at Hanover.

Of VW's five plants in Western Germany the installation at Brunswick is the baby, since it employs only about 5,000 workers in its concentrated production of front axle assemblies.

Demand for the VW Transporter has come from every corner of commerce, and half of total production is now exported all over the world. Confirmed long ago was the wisdom of Heinz Nordhoff's original prediction: when a box on wheels is the basic need, then the production of a literal *box on wheels* is the perfect answer.

That the Microbus offered double the capacity of other station wagons seemed apparent, though the absence of a conventional hood left many Americans with the impression that the Microbus was vastly larger than a conventional wagon; one glance down the center inside only seemed to confirm the suspicion. It came as a surprise to some that the VW Wagon rolled on the same wheelbase as the Sedan, was only 9" longer overall, and was about four feet shorter than the usual wagon. But for more people everywhere it came as a pleasant surprise; and every user became a booster.

How would you get at the stuff in front

Does your pick-up keep things from you?

Do you still have to unload the stuff in the rear, and then the stuff in the middle, to get at something in front?

Our Volkswagen would never make you do that. Our sides get out of your way.

All 3 sides drop on the VW. Like tailgates. You load it like a flatbed.

You work with a clear deck, 5 feet wide and 8½ feet long. It's 2½ feet longer than a standard half-ton.

And it's all flat. No wheel well.

You can carry 1,764 lbs. on our deck with no strain. Some owners even carry light tractors on it.

If it rains, you can get hoops and a tarp that turn the VW Pick-Up into a kind of covered wagon. (These are extra.)

if the sides didn't come down?

There's also a weatherproof locker 4 feet long and 5 feet wide under the bed. You can store tools there at night.

The VW Pick-Up is built a little differently from most others. For one thing, its body is welded into practically a solid hunk of steel. No bolts to loosen or rattle.

For another, its engine's in the rear. You get traction in mud, sand and snow. And it won't ever boil over or freeze up. It's air-cooled.

Up on deck and down in the engine room our pick-up has little ideas for helping you that other pick-ups haven't quite caught up with yet.

One of the littlest is the price.

$1,885.†

Volkswagen, the truck that picks up more for less

The VW Pick-up makes friends because it makes sense. Although it's almost three feet shorter than standard half-ton pick-ups, it carries over 75% more (1,764 lbs.) and costs about half as much to operate.

You get 45 square feet of load space, plus 23 cubic feet more in a closed, lockable compartment—a fine place to store tools and other valuables.

Hinged sides and clear platform let you convert to a flat-bed truck. By adding stakes and a fitted tarpaulin (optional at extra cost), you convert it to an all-weather van. The VW Pick-up is really three trucks in one.

Count on about twice the gas mileage of standard half-ton pick-ups, with no oil between changes and no anti-freeze at all. (Its engine is air-cooled.) With half the usual unladen weight, there's half the usual tire wear. You also save on service, depreciation. We have actual cost reports furnished by VW owners. Come in and see them—and take a ride.

Unlike much of American passenger car advertising, truck promotions, traditionally, have had to be based pretty much on facts to be successful. Ad writers had fun telling the truth about the Pick-up; there was so much they could say. One logging company began practicing what the ads preached by trying one. Soon it switched over its whole fleet, including Station Wagons, six-passenger Pick-ups and Panels, because "Volkswagens were the most dependable pieces of equipment" ever purchased.

A nurseryman found that the hinged. drop sides permitted all the convenience of a flatbed for heavier articles with the load security of a regular Pick-up.

One imaginative VW agent engineered a removable rack (on rollaway wheels) to transform the Pick-up into a glass-carrier, and the prospect into the happy user of a two-in-one truck.

A sheet metal fabricator discovered the completely level bed ideal for hauling bulky assemblies which rode best when closely compacted.

Just how "right" the Volkswagen Transporter concept *really was* came to be seconded by imitations all over the globe. European and British makers quickly patterned models after the popular choice. By 1961 even U. S. builders had climbed on the *Wagen* too. A tremendous combined promotion for "Volkswagen-type" trucks followed, opening the market for the late-comers, and serving to expand sales for *the original*.

"Look who's following us!"

THE SINCEREST FORM . . .

The Volkswagen Transporter has created more diverse commercial uses for itself than any other mode of highway transportation now in production. As just one example, the leader of a dixieland band in suburban Los Angeles finds the VW Microbus the ideal vehicle to carry six swinging musicians, a tuba, a set of drums, a washboard, a trombone, a trumpet, a clarinet, the pianist's library of music, and, of course, the piano. All over the world people have discovered that the VW Transporter enables them to do things they never did before — at low cost and with pleasure.

Established makers of conventional trucks discovered that the VW Transporter not only had penetrated their light truck market but that it sold also *beyond* the field of conventional truck offerings. Significantly, the world volume leaders Chevrolet and Ford, in an all-out effort to profit from the market established by the Transporter, followed suit with facsimile "boxes on wheels" of their own in 1961. Though these giant companies have gotten into the act in a manner flatteringly similar to the original VW, the Volkswagen Transporter substantially remains the most economical in operation.

Ford, like several foreign car makers, retained a conventional chassis layout, actually doing little more than relocate the driver to achieve its cab-forward design. The skittering, nose-heavy compromise produced few real characteristics of the VW beyond a token emulation of body silhouette.

Chevrolet came nearer to duplicating the VW Transporter concept in chassis and function. But in translation, the *agile, lightweight, all-business* image of the VW somehow had become blurred. No one came to envy the Transporter's genuine operational economy more than the former owner, who had traded "up" to the Corvair truck only to discover with a shock that *true economy* had become no more than a pleasant memory.

Striking testimony to the merit of the Volkswagen as an investment would seem confirmed by a prominent bank's use of the Deluxe Station wagon to transport customers between parking lot and bank floor. The service was promoted by distributing 1,000 miniature models to customers. The Deluxe (series 241) is distinguished from the regular wagon and trucks (series 221) by having rear quarter windows and a larger rear glass.

COMMUTER CLUBS IN VW'S

The VW Transporter has contributed a happy solution to one of America's most pressing problems. A recent article in *The Wall Street Journal* described the operations of a number of commuting clubs in the San Francisco Bay area. Every weekday around 5 p.m., a dark green VW bus pulls up to a crowded corner in downtown San Francisco and takes on a group of eight typically harried commuters, who have just scurried out of their offices in the downtown area. 50 minutes later the bus deposits the commuters at their front doors across the Bay in Orinda, Calif. Members of the Orinda Commute Club report that their Microbus makes the daily trip 15 minutes faster than available public transportation and that the VW is 25% cheaper than any commercial bus service.

There are nearly a dozen such clubs in the Bay area, and their number is growing daily. They lease VW Busses from San Francisco firms, who have cut their rates to promote this long-term, dependable type of rental contract. The commuting clubs arrange the details of operation in various ways, but they all avoid many of the disadvantages of the conventional car pool. Generally each member takes a turn at the wheel of the Bus every week. He parks it at his own home the night before and the next morning picks up the other riders at their homes. The clubs then lease parking places in the city for daytime use.

Commuting has become an increasingly serious problem in the Bay area, especially after the abandonment of the Key System interurban trains; and every urban area in America has similar problems. In a few years the VW bus could well be the means whereby suburbanites all over America commute.

Anchors aweigh! In at least one city a gob's first sight of the salty sea is from aboard a recruiting VW Station wagon. Some boat! When a vehicle carries up to eleven adults comfortably (it only advertises eight), in a space four feet shorter than an ordinary station wagon, its adaptability reaches wide; the word gets around.

Who dunks trucks? Volkswagen.

Every VW Truck body gets dunked in a vat of special rust resistant primer.

Not sprayed. Not splashed. Submerged. Joints, seams and crevices are all protected. There's no place for rust or corrosion to begin. No missed or "weak" spots.

After the primer come three more coats of paint with two complete hand sandings. Then a final rubdown. (You get 44 pounds of paint altogether.)

You can't tell this by looking at a VW. It shows up in longer body wear.

A dunking in primer is only one of the VW's quality features that don't meet the eye.

Body and frame are a single welded steel unit. No squeaks. No rattles.

All four forward gears are synchro-meshed. You can even downshift into first without stopping.

The engine is bench-run and tuned before installation. There's no breaking-in period. You can run a brand new VW Truck at top speed all day.

Like to know what else the VW has under its paint job?

Come in and find out.

As truck ads began to appear in American periodicals, they were studied by the public as keenly as the already famous Sedan ads. No one read them more carefully than competitive makers. At Hanover every body receives a dunking in corrosion-inhibiting primer because Volkswagen feels this is a superior way to construct a long-life body. Speaking of "dunking," after testing two other makes of panel trucks (they were "too big; they cost too much to run") a midwestern truck franchise operation standardized on VW for outfitting as mobile doughnut shops.

The Fireman may not have much to keep him busy in this piece of rolling stock as he perches up front beside the Engineer. But this workcrew-carrying "engine" has no time for "featherbedding" as it follows a close schedule over the Long Island Rail Road.

A conspicuously painted VW serves one TV station as a traveling billboard as it is moved about to make news films and tapes on location. A platform topside has proven handy for covering parades and field events, and permits the camera crew to be in action while the Microbus follows a parallel course.

You can save enough running a Volkswagen Truck to buy yourself a Volkswagen Sedan

WHAT YOU CAN SAVE AT 20,000 MILES PER YEAR		
Usual Truck	**Volkswagen Truck**	**Savings**
Gallons Gasoline At 8.97 mpg, 2,230 gallons at 27¢ $602.10	At 21.68 mpg, 923 gallons at 27¢—$249.21	$352.89
Tires, 4 at $26.50 each 106.00	none	106.00
Oil, including changes 34.50	none	
Maintenance 188.00	11.50	23.00
License 22.50	133.00	55.00
Anti-freeze 5 gal. at 3.25 16.25	20.00	2.50
Repairs 230.00	none 110.00	16.25 120.00
Totals $1,199.35	$523.71	$675.64

Savings of $675.64 per year would pay for a VW Sedan (East Coast P.O.E. Cost $1,565) in 27 months and 25 days. Based on actual Case History available on request.

Start with gasoline costs. Your VW Truck will generally give you twice the gas mileage of the usual half-ton.

And that's only part of what you save. Volkswagen's air-cooled engine needs no oil between changes, and no anti-freeze at all. With half the usual unladen weight there's half the tire wear.

You also save on depreciation, maintenance and, in some states, insurance and license fees. So in a very short time, depending on how much you drive, you can save enough for a VW Sedan.

We have the figures. Come in and see them soon.

The Transporter turns a trick! Any effort to supplement the ad copy reproduced here would likely detract more than it would add.

Dramatic proof that the Panel is only inches longer than the Sedan was shown by one imaginative dealer who painted a comparison worth a thousand words. Women known to have shied at the apparent "bigness" of the Station Wagon or Kombi have been won over by this promotion, graphic evidence that while VW trucks are roomier than domestic wagons, they are also shorter and easier to handle.

Forward-looking airline companies were among the earliest to recognize the Microbus as particularly apt for their needs. Today the VW Station wagon delivers bonus passenger loads in limousine service at airports all over the world. The Panel and Pick-up also have become familiar favorites for shuttling baggage between terminal and aircraft.

Volkswagen plays the title role in a business using specially-equipped station wagons to transport children and elderly and infirm adults home from confinement. The originator, himself handicapped, put 18 Volkswagens in this service in his own home city. Since then the idea has also been franchised in other locales. Handicab, Inc., not only specially outfits the VW and furnishes it under a long lease, but offers everything from collapsible wheel chairs and local advertising materials, to field representatives skilled in developing business with hospitals and other institutions.

While it needed to replace its whole fleet of panel trucks, one company was reluctant to take on the VW. Almost as a joke it did purchase one VW Panel after a representative had proposed the single unit as a sporting proposition. Operating costs were carefully kept. After 30,000 miles over normal delivery routes little convincing remained to be done. What the firm thought of the Volkswagen's record became clear as the whole fleet was changed over to VW at a single stroke.

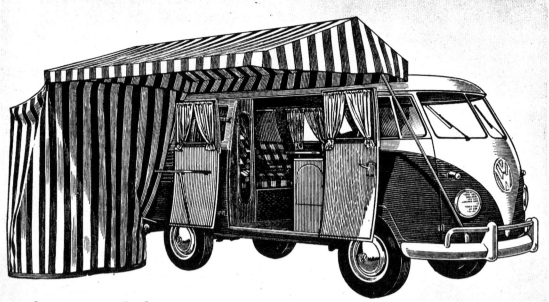

Why spend the money for a vacation place when the Volkswagen Camper takes you any place?

You don't just *move* in a Volkswagen Camper — you move *into* it! The Camper gives you generous room to sleep two adults and two children. Comfortably! (The driver's seat folds into children's bunks; the upholstered seats convert into a double bed.) Plus a spacious wardrobe, two tables for indoor and outdoor serving and a 23-gallon water tank. Even the curtains, lights and the red-and-white striped awning tent are included as standard equipment. The VW Camper Add the optional cupboard (with ice box), portable chemical toilet and 2-burner stove and you're off for a weekend or for months. Before you even think about your vacation plans, come see — and drive — the Volkswagen Camper.

The Camper doubles as a day-to-day station wagon too.

"Home is where the heart is." From the first Spring that VW Station wagons were in use, enamored sportsmen adapted their business vehicles for week-end pleasure. Later a custom-fitted model, the *Westphalia* illustrated in this ad, became a part of the line. Some dedicated enthusiasts, it has been recorded, have literally lived in their Campers.

Taking no chances on the embarrassment of a water problem on its own service vehicles, one progressive automotive radiator repair shop employed *radiatorless* Volkswagens for all mobile service.

So light-footed was the Transporter, compared with the public image of the usual plodding, commercial vehicle, that it inspired comedy like this cartoon: *"Zum Donnerkiel!— due sollst langsmaer fahren!"* Namely, "Damn it, leadfoot —slow down!"

Those at Volkswagenwerk probably imagined some most unusual applications for the Transporter. But who among them would have envisioned it as part of a Cape Cod cottage? Well, sort of, anyway. To one encyclopedia publisher the VW Panel became ideal as a sales presentation booth only after complete outfitting as a cozy fireside setting, complete, that is, except for the hearth.

Who puts raincoats on pick-ups? Volkswagen

This is an optional extra that makes a lot of sense.

It's the tarp and bows you can get with the Volkswagen Pick-Up that converts an open truck to a closed one. In minutes. When you have a load you have to keep protected and dry.

The VW Pick-Up itself needs no coddling. Four coats of paint seal every seam, inside and out.

It goes where others flounder. With its engine in the rear, it has the traction to keep on hauling through mud, sand, ice and snow.

It's air-cooled: no water to boil over or freeze.

It's capacious. The loading floor is 5 feet by 9 feet. Absolutely flat except for the wooden ribs bolted to the frame to keep cargo from shifting. Both sides and back are hinged. Go down for easy loading. Stay down for a flatbed.

An extra you pay no more for is a weathertight compartment under the loadbed. A lockable tool box. 23 cubic feet.

Rain or shine, the VW Pick-Up carries 1,764 pounds, nearly half again the load of a standard half-ton—at half the cost per mile. (That's only 236 pounds less than the maximum load of a one-ton.)

Maybe you don't need the raincoat. But if you ever do, isn't it nice to know that we've got one for you?

You can come in for it anytime, and get out of the rain.

Like the oxen, the Volkswagen transporter can carry close to its own weight. But while the oxen has diminished as the beast of burden, the covered wagon seems to be as popular as ever.

One user with bulky materials to handle built a demountable stake body to the particular dimensions of his special load—in this case, seven by ten feet.

In dead of Winter, when trucking uncertainties increase in every cold clime, VW brought "Christmas" to commerce. Those who have discovered Volkswagen find it just about as likely to freeze up or become snowbound as a jack rabbit. Air-cooling and rear-mounting of the engine, which increases traction in ice and snow, make VW all but blizzard-proof.

Truckers driving the VW Pick-up find the experience almost as embracing as the winter air. The extra maneuverability for tight spaces, allowed by shorter wheelbase and less overhang, like the hinged sides for access at the handiest quarter, have become daily stepsavers. VW truckers have found a sure thing for winter—as well as any other time.

Why deliver 1,600 lbs. nobody ordered?

Frame.
Driveshaft.
Radiator.
Hood.
Why buy gas for this load?
Volkswagen owners don't. We don't make trucks this way.

The Volkswagen engine is in the rear. There's no heavy driveshaft. No $100 replacement in case of repairs. (And no hood or fenders.)

Our engine is air-cooled. No water. No radiator. No anti-freeze. No hose to leak or pump to replace. Nothing to freeze up or boil over or flush out.

Okay, but—no frame?

No frame.

We use a welded, unitized construc- tion. This gives Volkswagens extra strength for heavy loads. Instead of bolting the body together, we weld it into one piece. (13,000 welds per truck.) Result: a solid hunk of steel.

That's one reason we carry 830 lbs. more than a half-ton. On half the gas. For years and years.

Is it true what they say about Volkswagen trucks in the ads? Well, yes, but company claims tend to be rather conservative. They say the Transporter gives twice the tire mileage of domestic panels. Actually, tires are more likely to outlast three or four sets on a conventionally sprung, undertired American light truck. (The author replaced the original tires on his Microbus at 70,000. The best one, still showing 25% or 30% of the original tread, was kept as a spare.)

No other type beats the VW Panel in square feet for promotion space. But not satisfied with this, at least one user has discovered that additional area may be utilized for signs on the inside of the doors, as shown above. Letters on the front of the trucks have been reversed, a clever touch for being read in rear-view mirrors.

One music mart ordered double-doors on the offside of its station wagon on account of the store's captive location on a one-way street. Doors on both sides proved even better than expected for loading pianos, organs and other heavy instruments.

This smiling driver has just walked by a conventional high load truck and reminded himself again how much easier his load is made. He actually reported: "VW enables a driver to make twice as many deliveries per day, due to ease of loading and maneuverability."

How much longer can it stay in business?

The delivery bicycle was a great time and money saver. In its day.

As long as the order wasn't too big for the basket. And other orders weren't piled up waiting. And it wasn't raining too hard.

Anyway, there wasn't much competition in those days.

Today, more and more small businesses are using the Volkswagen Panel Truck.

Almost no order's too big for the VW Panel with its 4 ft. wide side doors.

And no order's too small. With this truck you can deliver one order or one hundred efficiently and economically. (Operating costs average around 2¢ a mile.)

Orders don't pile up. The VW Panel carries over 1,800 pounds. (Nearly twice the load of a standard half-ton truck.)

Weather doesn't matter.

The air-cooled engine in the rear gives you dependable traction in mud, sand, ice and snow. (And because the engine's cooled by air, there's no water to boil over or freeze.)

Besides, where can you find room on a bicycle for your company name and phone number in letters a foot high?

15

A FLAIR FOR FASHION

. . . a daring design from Ghia, a creation of the master Karmann — a remarkable combination by any standard.

The trim, lithe body lines of the Karmann-Ghia were distinctively new. But the tradition behind its body construction was nearly as old as this Bavarian church.

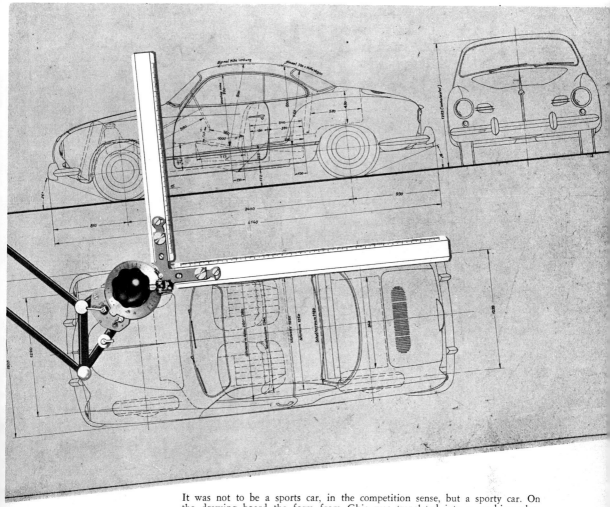

It was not to be a sports car, in the competition sense, but a sporty car. On the drawing board the form from Ghia was translated into a working plan, straining to take on the third dimension at Karmann to become Volkswagen's most beautiful product.

Today's small sport coupé evolved through the years for lovers of a personal automobile who sought a close, sporting relationship with their machines, but still wanted the comfort and convenience of a closed cockpit.

As virtues of the Volkswagen became known the dependable beetle appeared with a more stylish, sporting coupé body. Body manufacturer Wilhelm Karmann, the same body builder who supplied the stock VW cabriolet, accomplished the transformation of the Volkswagen when it went into production in 1955 on an elegant coupé design created by Carozzeria Ghia of Turin, Italy.

The sleek VW Karmann-Ghia benefited from a half century of automotive experience. Karmann had been building bodies in Osnabrueck, Germany, since 1901, when it took over a coachbuilding handicraft shop originally established in 1874. It maintained a reputation for quality while expanding its operations through the years. In recent times the firm Wilhelm Karmann, G.m.b.H., has employed over 3,000 people; it is the biggest enterprise of its kind in Germany.

Karmann operates today primarily in three fields: press tool making, manufacture of pressed sheet metal parts, and production of all-metal automobile bodies. Karmann makes tools and pressings to the specifications of over 15 European auto manufacturers — among them the English Ford, Citroen, Simca, Fiat, Volkswagen and Porsche. A consistently high respect for Karmann products has brought the firm to its present prominence in continental industry.

The Karmann front office for a long time gave thought to building a deluxe body on the VW chassis. Karmann designers could undoubtedly have built a finely styled body, and many of their ideas were incorporated into the final coupé design; but they wanted to create an automobile distinctive among German manufacturers. Recognizing that the imaginative Italians had shown an unusual feeling for elegant lines, not only in high fashion and architecture, but in automobile styling as well, the Karmann management negotiated a contract for the design with the renowned Ghia design studio of Turin. Ghia in turn called upon its designer Luigi Segre to come up with a suitable body to Karmann's specifications. Signore Segre's efforts evolved into a beautiful form which found Karmann's full approval. After receiving assurance from Wolfsburg in 1954 that a steady supply of chassis would be available for Ghia coupé production, Karmann began setting up tools for the coupé assembly lines.

Functional discipline distinguishes Karmann from most other body builders. Where repetitive schedules of body production for many different manufacturers dictate continuous change, the art of tool making meets a daily challenge. Fixtures for each job must be ready to move into position with a minimum of fuss when additional or new production runs are ordered on crash notice.

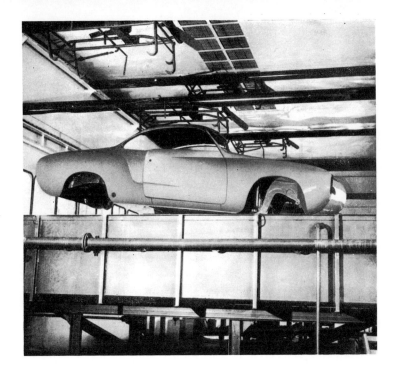

To be officially marked as the special deluxe VW, Karmann-Ghia had to be as good as the regular Volkswagen. This meant being very good. Though only 100 bodies were to be submerged each working day, a full sized vat was installed at Karmann for complete dipping of the Ghia body unit in a bath of rust-proofing primer, duplicating the procedure at Volkswagenwerk. Any substitute method would not have been as good; nothing less would have been *Volkswagen*.

The introduction of "everyman's Porsche," as some have dubbed the Karmann-Ghia coupé, was the culmination of a calendar of faultless timing. A Karmann convertible sedan had been a deluxe offering of the VW line ever since 1945, and its detail quality was widely recognized. The dependability of the VW chassis had been proved beyond question by the 1,000,000 VW's then on the road. The Porsche car demonstrated that a certain segment of the public was willing to pay the price for superb quality, irrespective of a car's size. Karmann's plan to produce a plush coupé using the standard Volkswagen chassis could not have come at a more opportune moment. The car was introduced at major European auto shows in the fall of 1955.

Final assembly finds the VW Cabriolet moving out in the same line with the Ghia. Both Karmann Volkswagen models are par-excellent custom products of Germany's busiest and most able independent body builder. A battery is added to the new car at the station shown, and it becomes a live thing for the first moment—and a true Volkswagen dressed in more stylish sheet metal.

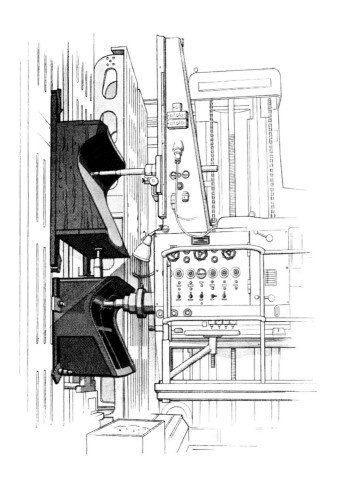

From the drawing board wood
craftsmen route the full dimensions
of a Karmann panel in hardwood
like the motor deck lid shown.
These models then serve as guides
to be carefully traced by copy-
routers in steel, later to be
toughened as a die.

After precision finishing and hard-
ening these dies are set up in
multi-ton stamping presses where
they will draw out actual body
panels for series body production.

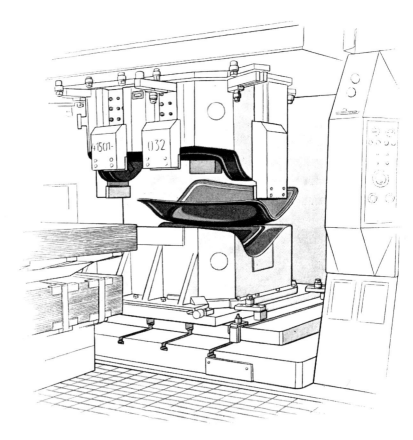

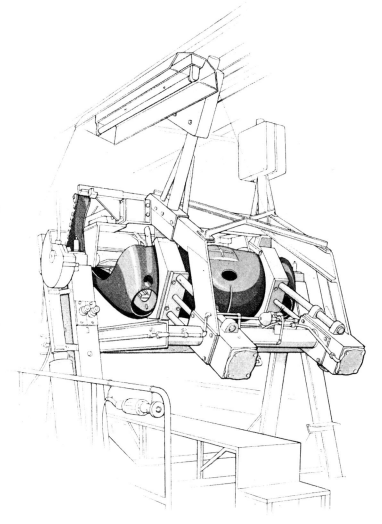

Pressing tools are limited to forming
contours that may be removed by
drawing the shaped panel away
from the die. Reverse details cannot
be produced in a single piece.
When design dictates, as in the
case of the undercut shapes of the
frontal area, precision jigs hold an
assembly of separate sections in
perfect relationship while they are
effectively joined by spot welding.
Later processing will lend the whole
form a one-piece finish and
appearance.

THE CREATION OF THE BODY

Creative automobile body design is the product of long months of development
before it ever reaches the assembly line and series production. Experiments and planning
strive to eliminate difficulties before production, reaching for the optimum of trouble-
free construction. From the drawing board, the way leads through the small wooden
model to the 1:1 model and finally to the handmade steel body. Then production spe-
cialists can attack the details.

Countless hands that never touch the car itself are engaged in its manufacture. Many
make the tough steel dies that will form the body parts from raw steel. Just a few of the
machines needed are the hundreds of stamp presses, the molders, trimmers, benders and
finishers, punches and cutters. And just as many hands labor to create the jigs and
templates that hold the sheet metal in place until it can melt into the single form of
correctness. For a body — both alone and in conjunction with the chassis — must stand
up to the demands of hard driving. Countless checks and inspections monitor the flow
of work, impartially eliminating the faulty and imperfect.

Sketches by Siegfried Werner delineate the creation of the coupe at the Karmann
works with classic simplicity in the following pages, adapted, by arrangement, from a
feature originating in *Motor Revue*.

The drawings show how a beautiful three-dimensional form can grow from the
wilderness and confusion of line that is a single-facet drawing. To the layman it is only
the end result that counts, that miraculous creation — the coupe.

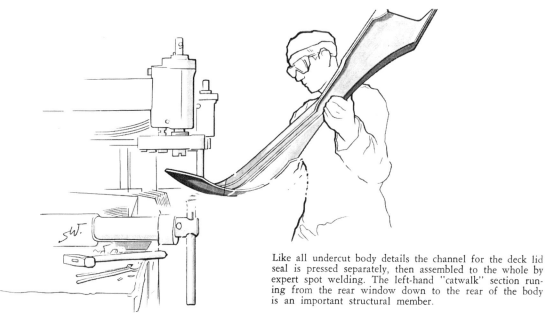

Like all undercut body details the channel for the deck lid seal is pressed separately, then assembled to the whole by expert spot welding. The left-hand "catwalk" section runing from the rear window down to the rear of the body is an important structural member.

Discount all the inner soberness and technique emerges, full of wonder. The transformation of an idea into a detailed shop plan is no smaller wonder than the formation of a construction segment in the machine tool shop or even on the assembly line, working from a drawing. Following the formation of a car body, through all the construction steps, is a pilgrimage of wonder. For a car body must satisfy the demand for interior comfort, functional perfection, aesthetic appeal of line, and simplified construction — all without revealing its inherent complexity.

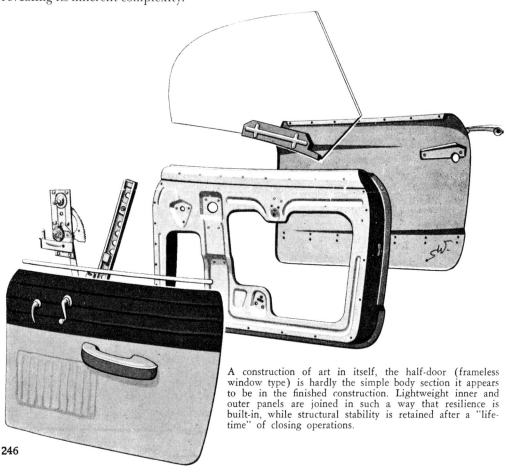

A construction of art in itself, the half-door (frameless window type) is hardly the simple body section it appears to be in the finished construction. Lightweight inner and outer panels are joined in such a way that resilience is built-in, while structural stability is retained after a "lifetime" of closing operations.

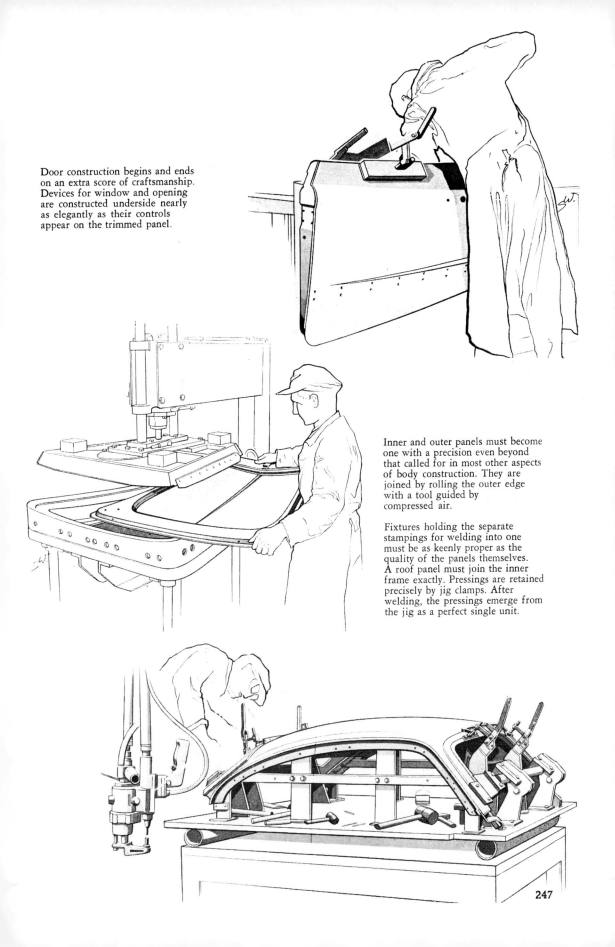

Door construction begins and ends on an extra score of craftsmanship. Devices for window and opening are constructed underside nearly as elegantly as their controls appear on the trimmed panel.

Inner and outer panels must become one with a precision even beyond that called for in most other aspects of body construction. They are joined by rolling the outer edge with a tool guided by compressed air.

Fixtures holding the separate stampings for welding into one must be as keenly proper as the quality of the panels themselves. A roof panel must join the inner frame exactly. Pressings are retained precisely by jig clamps. After welding, the pressings emerge from the jig as a perfect single unit.

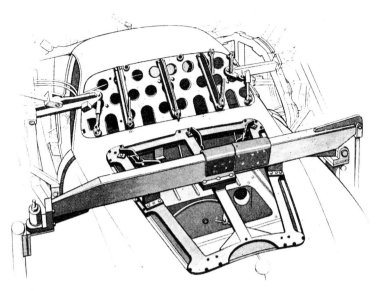

Part is added to part and they gradually grow into the rough body. Coloring follows, more important today than ever. But the sheet metal must be prepared for the priming coat. And then that primer must be carefully polished so that the first and second coats of paint will have a firm base — so that the finished car will have a mirror finish.

Only the final assembly combines the body with the chassis. And there is still much to do. Cables are strung, seats mounted, instruments installed, windows fitted, hardware and chrome attached — the young form of steel and synthetics, leather and light metal, becomes that which is the desire of the century — a car. For somebody beyond the factory door it will be a companion and friend.

When the individual panels are set up together in jigs for joining into one piece, unless relative positions in the fixture are exactly on-the-money, doors or hatches may not fit the aperatures. Each Karmann is locked up just right before welding, and the opening gap between body and opening panel is exactly constant all the way around.

Each stage of construction finds the space that will contain the doors being given special care. When in place the opening must be filled snugly. The "half-door" construction in the Ghia represents the ultimate challenge to precision fitting, as the unframed glass must seat no less than *perfectly* to become wind and water tight, and at the same time prevent breakage when the door is slammed.

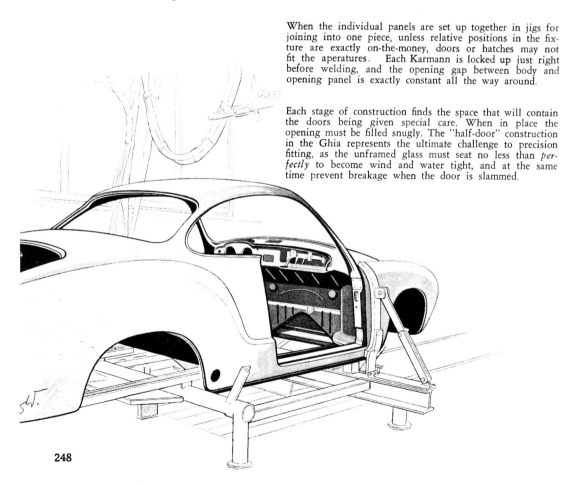

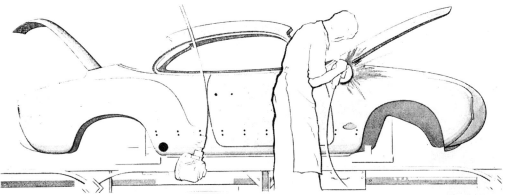

After the body is unlocked from the master fixture the open welding seams between panels are filled over and the irregularities ground to a smooth continuous surface.

Following a complete dipping in rust inhibitive primer craftsmen rub out the pre-coat carefully by hand, then repeat the process after the first coat of color.

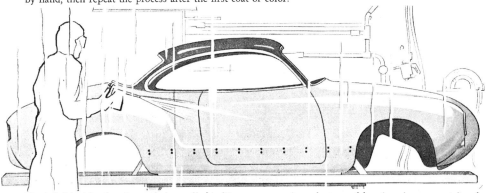

Final finish (the fourth coat) is applied with spray guns in a dust-proof booth, where a curtain of water falling behind the spray draws all excess color particles away leaving the air clean.

Finally the daring design from Ghia, a creation of the master Karmann, is dropped neatly onto the proven Volkswagen chassis in grand style— a remarkable combination in any language.

Ghia's rolling, heavily undercut frontal shapes for the fenders and hood section achieved individual identity for the design, and an all but voluptuous sensitivity in the longer appearance on the standard VW chassis. Here was the most dependable, economical vehicle available for those buyers who wanted something more than transportation.

The Karmann-Ghia's smartness, practical prestige, sound engineering, and quality construction made it an instant success. Production never since has been able to stay abreast of demand. Initially Karmann ran off three to four hundred cars each month, but the figure rose steadily to 1000 per month by the end of 1956. Since then output has doubled, and now exports account for half of all Ghia production.

The smartness of a meter-width door (39+ inches) did not end with half-door (frameless) design. The door windows themselves were vertically curved—the signature of no less than a body-building virtuoso, since the fit never varied from a completely dustproof seal.

Part of the elegantly trimmed luggage deck behind the bucket seats was designed to tilt up for emergencies and provide a foam-padded occasional seat for extra passengers.

Touches of hand-crafted finesse abounded everywhere within and without the Karmann-Ghia, literally a custom-bodied car for which the owner was privileged to pay but a fraction of what comparative body quality in lesser production would have had to bring in the market. The Ghia was bargain-priced in any language.

Not long before, this convertible body consisted only of a stack of small, individual pressings. Each was shaped for a precise position in what could be likened to a three-dimensional jigsaw game. Now they are all in place and the body approaches the primer dipping vat with the appearance of a single stamping. Seams have been covered and filled as few makes bother to do any more at any price.

Karmann plans had from the very beginning included production of a convertible Ghia; but the factory wisely allowed sales of the coupé at VW dealers to level off somewhat before introducing the convertible model in 1957. It, too, was an immediate success, and Karmann presently builds around twenty Ghia convertibles daily.

As wheels are bolted on, the joint concept of Karmann and Ghia becomes identified as a *car*. It will never be known as an *ordinary* car; there is nothing ordinary about the automobile. Inspections *of* inspections have assured and reassured that each Karmann is finished as perfectly as though the entire plant had been occupied with building that single unit alone. And so it had!

Like the Volkswagen convertible, which rolls off the same trim line at Osnabruck, the convertible Ghia is fitted with a fully headlined interior. When viewed from within, the top appears hardly capable of folding, all mechanism being concealed.

One of the hallmarks of the lithe styling, which commanded uncommon respect for the Karmann-Ghia almost overnight among the design-conscious, was the handsome grace of its upperstructure. While the convertible model necessarily substituted a cloth upper for this delicate, spider-light steel and glass top, by the device of an equally fast backline on the convertible roof, the original hardtop character was, in substance, retained.

After seven years Karmann-Ghia underwent its first facelift. The forward surfaces of the front fenders were redeveloped more objectively, and the lamps raised. A slightly bobbed appearance around the headlights in the original treatment (above) was gone. Fresh air intakes in the catwalks were redesigned. Instrumentation and interiors became even more plush. The classic Ghia configuration had not been disturbed, but only *enhanced*. The new model presented owners of the earlier series with the first good reason for trading.

This ad is 6 years late.

In the last 6 years this car has mystified millions.

People have called it everything from an Alfa Romeo to a Ferrari.

We've never advertised it in any national magazine before. You may have seen one on the road and wondered what it was.

Brace yourself.

It's a Volkswagen.

Our Karmann Ghia.

(We didn't mind its being Brand X. But we can't have people calling it by somebody else's name. The time has come to speak up.)

The Ghia is a limited production car. Only around nine thousand are made for this country each year.

It's because of the handwork that goes into the body.

We wouldn't even try to make it in the VW plant.

Most auto bodies are designed for an assembly line. One stamping per part. Thunk, a fender. Thunk, a door. Thunk, a hood.

The Ghia stopped us on the first thunk.

It was designed by Ghia of Turin, Italy, with lines that are too sculptured for mass production methods. The curve in the fender alone has to be made in 2 sections. Then welded together. Then shaped down by hand.

You can't stop and do this in a plant that's turning out 950,000 other cars.

So we turned to one of the most celebrated custom coachworks left in Europe, Karmann of Osnabruck. In the time it takes to mass produce three ordinary cars, Karmann makes one Ghia.

Inefficient? Of course. So was Cellini.

It takes over 185 men to make the Ghia body alone. That will give you an idea of the handwork that goes into it.

(You can't find a seam anywhere. Not even where the fenders join the hood. One lady said it looked as if it had been carved out of soap.)

But under its wanton exterior, the Ghia's all business.

'Its lower center of gravity will hold a bumpy barreltop road at over 70—and take curves with any sports car if you're ever in a squeeze.

Best of all is the Volkswagen engine, transmission, suspension and chassis.

32 miles a gallon, regular gas, regular driving. (Some get a bit more, some a bit less.)

And a Volkswagen by any other name is just as sweet to service.

This is no temperamental prima donna that needs $40 monthly tuneups and $100 carburetors.

VW parts fit it and you can get them anywhere.

You also get VW's rear-engine traction in snow. And our air-cooling. (No water to freeze up or boil over. The Ghia keeps a cool head in the longest traffic jam.)

And VW's 40,000 miles on tires. And they almost never need balancing.

The Ghia also has the VW independent torsion bar suspension for all 4 wheels. When one hits a bump, it keeps it to itself.

(Most Ghia owners had VWs first and knew just what they were getting.)

Inside you'll find all those little things you've told yourself you'd put in a car if you were the factory.

Bucket seats with backs you can adjust. A door with stops to hold it in 3 different positions.

A defroster for the rear window.

Even a soundproofed interior, with an acoustical ceiling like a modern office. If you hear a siren in the distance, pull over. It's right behind you.

Now then, how much?

$2,395* for the coupe, $2,595* for the convertible. Heater, electric clock and all.

Sorry we can't do anything about strangers who think it's a $5,000 car. You may still find bellboys and doormen expecting bigger tips.

But nothing's ever perfect, is it?

"Most Ghia owners had VWs first and knew what they were getting." So it was that the very limited production of this model was absorbed almost casually by established Volkswagen enthusiasts without a stick of advertising promotion. In the USA the Karmann-Ghia story was not told in national ads till 1961. And what a story! Fifty percent of all Ghias are exported; 80% of these go to the United States.

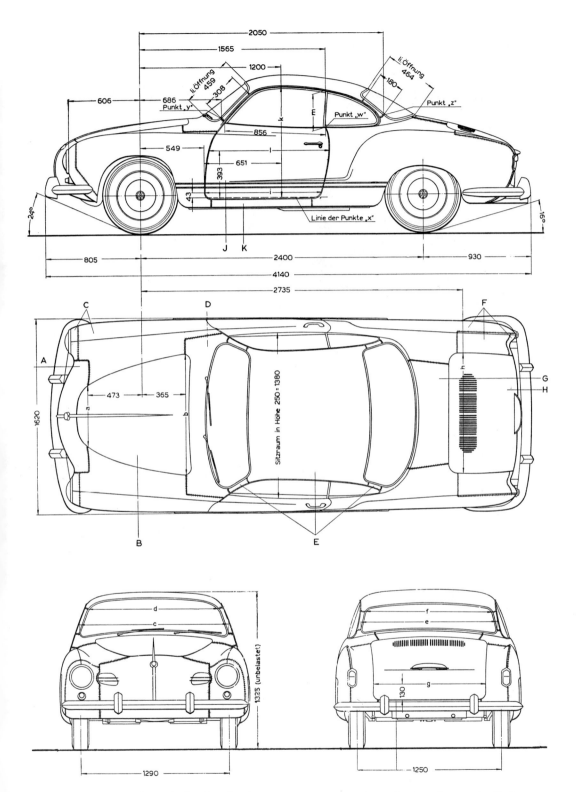

Though these plan and elevation drawings carry measurements in centimeters, they constructively indicate where sheet metal pressings are joined. So expertly are these sections filled and surfaced into one seamless form on the finished body that reference to a chart like this may be necessary to appreciate where the hidden seams lie.

The Ghia flair for design, as executed by Karmann, has delivered in full measure that distinction so important to the driver who looks to his VW not only for excellence of performance, but also for individuality, elegant hand craftsmanship, and rare beauty.

An extra sparkle in appearance and performance made Ghia an early favorite among sports people. As it became the very symbol of freshness, youth was seldom far afield. Like the ancient construction lining the far riverbank, Karmann-Ghia was hand-built as well as the knowledge and skills of its time permitted.

16

CHAMPAGNE(?) IN A STEIN

For those declining a carbon copy of anyone else's VW there is the "special." Sometimes professionally built, but more often home-grown, its quality and effect run the gamut.

A convertible coupe was the earliest custom body built in series for the VW chassis, enjoying a ready market on the Continent in 1948 and 1949. The single-seat model by the little firm of Heb-mueller made the most of stock body panels, not only utilizing the original front end sheet metal, but adapting doors and rear quarter panels, as well. Doors were reworked to half-door style, and a rear deck and cockpit edge were developed to the form of a convertible coupe. Production of this snappy number was unaccountably discontinued after a short run of only 750. A revival of this body style today might wake to a healthy reception among VW enthusiasts.

Ever since those first post-war days when German motor enthusiasts transmuted the *Kuebelwagen* and *Schwimmwagen* models into machines of sport, the VW chassis has challenged countless coachbuilders. Many were backyard, one-off customs; but some larger firms, recognizing the appeal of the rugged, roadable VW chassis, have designed for the world market.

Of the latter group, the Karmann-Ghia high fashion creation was developed to become a part of the authorized VW dealer line. Other self-appointed VW coachbuilders have sunk into oblivion, most often because they did not face the challenge squarely and were trying to peddle an inferior product. In several cases smaller builders managed to offer a highly acceptable product, but most of these lacked the financial backing to publicize their specials sufficiently to achieve the necessary sales volume. For them production ceased when their capital was gone. Other custom body shops offered VW body shells in addition to other established lines or repair business.

By far the most successful of these special body firms is the Karosserie Friedrich Rometsch in Berlin-Halensee. Rometsch produces a completely hand-built sport cabriolet and sport coupé on the VW chassis. The buyer of the Rometsch is the temperamental auto enthusiast who refuses to drive a carbon copy of anyone else's car.

Rometsch-bodied VWs were first imported into the U. S. by a few discerning American travelers who, on discovering the car abroad, had become entranced with its royal nature. Few had warmed to the 1955 model on esthetic grounds, but the elegant hand construction on the familiar VW export chassis had proven an appealing combination anyhow.

The first to appear with a VW offering for the caviar trade, Rometsch has been serving up luxury sport Volkswagens for a number of years in a progression of models. The latest Rometsch, redesigned to keep pace with international taste, features a wrap-around windshield and extra-wide doors that dip forward under the cowl to allow special ease in entering or leaving the two/four passenger cockpit. The foot and knee room inside the Rometsch is particularly accommodating, befitting a luxury car. Interior trim and exterior treatment are at the option of the individual purchaser. Unusual among German convertibles is Rometsch's completely disappearing top, which folds away into the body, covered by a metal boot that becomes a continuation of the body form.

Design advice was sought from fresh quarters, and by 1958 the Rometsch line was somewhat more acceptable on a styling basis. Much of the earlier lack of design continuity was gone. Lines of the new series carried a theme.

Methods at Karrosserie Friedrich Rometsch in West Berlin are of the old school in which the time to do a job right is the equivalent of the time it takes to do that job by hand. Nothing is stamped with steel dies. There are no dies. Bodies are completely hand-formed of aluminum by master metal craftsmen who reputedly devote around 2,000 man-hours to the process of producing each single body.

The present Rometsch, completely hand-formed of aluminum over a heavy superstructure, weighs a scant 35 pounds more than the stock sedan. Rometsch German craftsmanship has turned this creation into a jewel of quality detailing. The Rometsch firm has been recognized repeatedly by national awards for beauty and comfort in the 1300cc class.

The Rometsch shop has grown from a one-man body building firm some thirty years ago to its present facility, which is one of the most prominent body shops in Germany. But Rometsch craftsmen still practice their trade of coach-building in the long-established hand manner for that mink and diamond strata of owners who demand something different, something nicer, something that outstrips all other VW's in passenger comfort.

One can little appreciate the quality of the interior from a photograph. He must pick up the scent of the top-grain cowhide while he sinks several inches heaven sent into the plush region of the driver's seat to discover for himself why Rometsch has secured its reputation for creature comforts.

The Sedan was never a bus; that's why the Microbus was created. It was *almost* never a bus, that is. The car's infinite versatility inspired many a jest.

Volkswagen's reputation for stout heart inevitably brought the Sedan into favor wherever its reliable character and operating economy could be capitalized. A lengthened, four-door model (with sufficient stretch for straight-opening rear doors), built by Rometsch for several years, became a common sight among taxicabs in Berlin. Later the stretched sedan saw duty at resorts high in the Alps, where its excellent capacity for cold-weather starting enjoyed special favor.

The coachbuilder's work was up to its famous name. The finished Rometsch, following the design of the stock sedan exactly, appeared to the uninitiated more as an addition to the line than a special custom-built body.

As the VW running gear became well known for its longevity and trouble-free performance, several Continental coachbuilders took the VW as a challenge for special body making. Beutler of Switzerland, the fine body firm that had built the first series of Porsche cars in 1949, came up with this handsome coupe in 1954. Stock hubcaps, bumpers, and horn vents were carried over from the Wolfsburg model; but there the similarity ceased.

Crowds of auto enthusiasts admired another beautiful, luxuriously fitted Volkswagen special body at the Geneva Auto Salon in 1954. A Swiss VW representative had ordered and arranged for the display of a small series of coupés and cabriolets from the Beutler Body Shop in Thun, Switzerland, near Bern. Beauty and individuality in cars cost money, particularly when they are found in the same package; still a number of fine car lovers with well-padded pocketbooks became captivated enough with the long, sleek special to lay down the $4000 purchase price at the show.

As years passed, Beutler designs, which generally were offered both as hardtop and convertible models, took on refinements of the original theme. The hood line was lengthened by moving the grille forward at the center. Stock body components were used no more; there was little externally to identify the low, handcrafted specials as VWs. Magnificent surface development particularly characterized the products of Beutler.

Only the familiar pedals, shift and parking brake reveal the hearty heart under the skin of this Beutler special, superb specimen of the coachbuilder's craft.

Beutler and VW grew together. As VW refined its chassis Beutler carried a distinct original VW style theme through a progression of refinements. By 1960 the Swiss special had reached maturity of line bringing world acclaim. The investor in a 1960 Beutler hardly could have done better to put the car's cost into stocks and bonds. His car was destined to become a prized collector's item.

Geared exclusively to custom production, the Beutler shop encourages its clients to order the car "in the white": that is, with the job ticket blank concerning details of design, features, colors, and interior trim, so that the customer may express himself fully in his special order. About twelve weeks later the patron completes his transaction with Beutler, as he takes delivery of a Swiss coachbuilder's masterpiece.

Beutler's way added overhang front and rear, and certainly a fraction of the famous VW maneuverability was sacrificed in the name of style. But well so. It was the only VW custom special bearing such a mastery of proportion in its body design that it appeared larger than it was, when viewed without familiar objects nearby to form a measuring point of reference.

Passionate interest among owners led to customizing. Back in 1948 one Swiss enthusiast, following the American production design practice at the time, reformed his VW front fenders into the doors. Most other efforts to alter the original generally detracted more than they added.

Most restyling efforts brought side glances from other owners less in envy than in pity. While crowds gathered wherever one Hamburg owner parked, talk about the panoramic windshield he had managed to graft into his sedan generally resolved o n l y into spirited debate whether the body should be modified at all.

A Canadian company offered several glass fiber replacement hoods for a time, each intended to alter the entire styling theme in a different direction. Most owners felt they were shameful miscegenations, and their interest span was only the time it took to cast a vote for the ugliest. The line design shown balloted high.

Dummy grilles were offered to a few takers. What began as a diecast accessory later degraded into a pair of do-it-yourself decals. Home custom crews all seemed to confirm the same point: *Volkswagen's classically simple body styling is best if it is left alone.*

A hand-rubbed acrylic finish, as well as wiring and the fitting of upholstery, hardwood, and even a laminated safety windshield, were included in the $1,295 factory price of the complete kit.

As the Volkswagen's popularity in the United States mushroomed, the crowd which had been driving MG-TDs transferred its allegiance to the beetle-like sedan, almost to a man. Enterprising American owners began to envision the VW more in the configuration of a sports car. The fruits of their labor, generally translated through the medium of glass fiber, were brought to market, adding further to the world list of VW Specials.

One West Coast glass fiber firm came up with a unique do-it-yourself kit. The Devin furnished a complete steel frame with a glass fiber body shell to which major VW components were to be bolted into place. Makers claimed the process of mounting the engine, transmission, front axle, and other VW parts could be performed in less than a day.

Under the Devin skin, lightweight steel box section side rails, with tubular cross members for rigidity, were designed to permit bolting on the VW components to the otherwise complete sports car.

The builders had designed the body to bolt on the VW chassis in place of the Sedan body in a matter of hours, with alteration principally confined to the suspension (to compensate for 200 pounds less weight). Stock VW units were used whenever possible to retain Volkswagen identity. Where use of these parts might have limited the design, stock units from other makes—notably in hinges, latches and glass—also were accommodated in the basic construction to reduce the changeover cost.

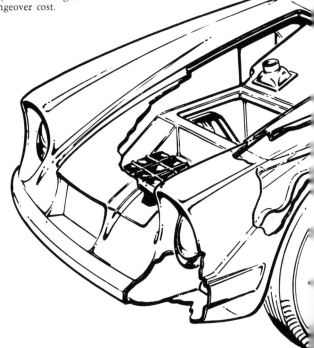

Cross and transverse integral bulkheads gave the body exceptional rigidity, and prevented the cracking and racking often associated with glass fiber body construction.

The Alken Corporation of Venice, California, under the management of Dr. Allan White and John McNamara, was an American body firm which produced an excellent special — with striking styling and thoroughly adequate body engineering. The Alken fiberglas body briefly achieved a measure of renown in auto circles, though fewer than fifty bodies were made. Company capital proved insufficient to sustain production until sales could be promoted to a profitable level.

Alken offered perhaps the simplest and most durable replacement ever designed for an imported chassis. The principal changeover from a factory sedan body to the Alken special could be accomplished in a matter of hours. The conversion was a simple, positive operation that could be performed at home, and the Alken body required only minor modifications to the stock VW chassis and suspension.

Alken designers, working with consulting plastics engineer John A. Wills, overcame the flexing and drumming rattles of inadequate fiberglas body construction by using a series of 16 aircraft-type bulkheads designed integrally within the body. These stations welded the entire structure into one rigid member.

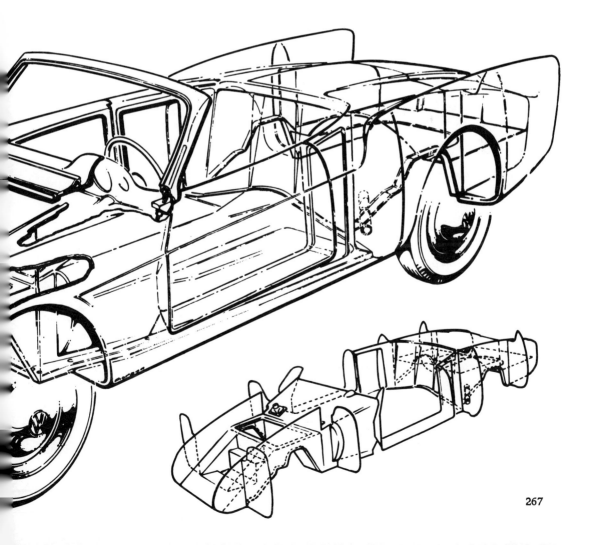

Experienced body engineering, by the plastics engineer who pioneered the glass fiber body process, assured the Alken a forthright character that might well have provided something special for a growing number of VW sports enthusiasts. Every element to do with the Alken reflected a basic honesty, even to the time reported for making the body changeover. Removal of the Sedan body and complete Alken installation and modification ready for painting was stated as a job from 16 to 19 hours for a novice crew, whereas it had been accomplished by experts in a specially timed performance in just four hours. The product reflected best intentions, the sincere effort of a small, independent band of qualified men dedicated to a common goal. Considering an observation in *Road & Track* magazine at the time, "As for technicalities, the Alken body is without a doubt the best-engineered piece of fiberglas we have ever seen," that goal was achieved.

The Volkswagen character was strikingly retained in the Alken conversion, which used stock headlights, tail lights, instruments, controls, and even provided a spot on the hood where the Wolfsburg insignia was to be transplanted. The extensive use of factory parts assured quality, simple replacement, and a relatively lower conversion cost.

The Venice firm also developed a number of good accessories, including a removable hard-top; and the Alken was perhaps the only fiberglas model ever offered with perfectly functioning optional roll-up windows.

Dramatically designed by Bill Pierson to stay in international style, the Alken body allowed "the car that is built like a sports car" to look and handle like one. The Alken fiberglas body weighed 200 pounds *less than stock*. The Alken's passing can only be regarded with regret.

17

SPUR TRACK TO SPORT

Design thinking in the Porsche concept so overlapped that of the Volkswagen that interchangeability in the original series evolved naturally.

Man's inhumanity to man set the stage for the development of a car that one day would bear the name of the Volkswagen's creator — by providing time to Professor Ferdinand Porsche to develop his plans.

A few days after war's end Dr. Porsche received an invitation, ostensibly from representatives of the French Government, to Baden-Baden in the French Zone of Germany, to "discuss plans for a French version of the People's Car." Dr. Porsche and his son Ferry were met there by representatives of the French Department of Industry, and a week of seemingly fruitful talks followed. But on a Sunday evening late in November, 1945, members of the French *Sureté* appeared in Baden-Baden and presented Porsche with a warrant for his arrest, charging collaboration with the Gestapo — a charge later proved entirely without foundation. It appears now that Porsche was the victim of a group of hot-headed Communist officials in the French Government; they had jumped to conclusions about Porsche's associations in some industrial engineering work done in Paris during 1942 and 1943.

PORSCHE IN FRANCE DURING WAR

Porsche, at the special direction of the Nazi War Department, had designed several tanks for the German government; and the Nazis had decided to produce the Porsche tanks at the famous Peugeot works at Montbeliard, France, during 1942 and 1943. Porsche spent some time in Paris during these two years, setting up and supervising production in the huge factory.

The French underground successfully carried out two acts of sabotage on the German-operated factory, bringing production to a temporary halt in 1942. The Nazi Gestapo retaliated by arresting three of the French directors of the company, shipping them to a concentration camp, and later executing them. As the war tide began to turn, cases of sabotage became even bolder. Retaliation began to reflect desperation. Finally Stormtroopers moved in, occupied the factory, and demolished the entire plant. They were determined to leave nothing of further use to the French after the Nazis had been forced by sabotage to abandon the production of tanks.

When the group of Communist officers heading the *Sureté*, France's swift-acting police organization, heard after the war of Porsche's association with the Germans at Montbeliard, they incarcerated him immediately without investigating his personal attitudes and actions at the time.

The French did not learn until much later that Porsche had himself saved the life of Jean-Pierre Peugeot during the war by intervening in Peugeot's behalf with Gestapo chief Heinrich Himmler. Monsieur Peugeot thanked Porsche for his help on several occasions — once, so the story goes, with a present of a dozen new English golf balls, an extremely rare commodity in France in 1943!

But the revenge-bound French in 1946 perhaps understandably lost their heads; they branded Porsche as a war criminal. And besides, the proud Communist officers of the *Sureté* did not want any German, no matter how famous an engineer he might be, working on *their* People's Car. Porsche's imprisonment was quick to follow.

PORSCHE IN PARIS AT THE RENAULTS'

The well-known Porsche factory racing driver and German automotive journalist, Richard von Frankenberg, in his book *Porsche — the Man and His Cars,* relates an interesting anecdote about Porsche's French imprisonment.

"... [Porsche had just been put into the local temporary prison in Baden-Baden.] A few weeks later he was taken to Paris and there given quarters in the porter's lodge of Renault's villa. The first experimental cars of the '4CV' had just been finished, but did not satisfy their engineers. Porsche's opinion was sought and he made a number of suggestions for improvement which were gratefully accepted by Renault."

Ironically, despite the *Sureté*, at least one French People's Car bore the mark of a German engineer.

Dr. Ing. Ferdinand Porsche's own experiences translated literally the axiom, "Wisdom comes not to him who moves down a tranquil path, but to him who goes through Hell." His long-nurtured wisdom would forge into reality a sports car concept that would abound with details of perfection.

So disorganized and chaotic were the conditions in immediately post-war Europe that it was nearly two health-breaking years later before Dr. Porsche was allowed to return to his home in the Austrian countryside. His mind had never wandered, however, from the projects of his fertile imagination; and in August, 1947, he rejoined his son Ferry at the revived engineering office which had been his idea development headquarters.

"I was so hungry in those French prisons that I got over my gallstone trouble," he reflected. By nature, Porsche was quick to "write off" his time of imprisonment, for he was too much a technician to allow his disdain for the political developments that had used him as a helpless pawn to burden him for long.

The then aging father of the Volkswagen turned to more happy thoughts of what might lie ahead. "Project 12," first set down in 1931 as a series of small car designs, and since then a many-lived progression of developments, once again was revived anew. Though formed from scraps and pieces of the military VW, the then current homebuilt German racing cars were surprisingly efficient. They created a general enthusiasm for improving performance in light cars which spawned a new tradition within the motor sport. Refinement of engineering and body design were natural and continuous in both amateur and professional circles. Porsche thought, "Why can't we build a practical sports car which could double at the tracks on Sundays?"

Soon after the first hand-built Volkswagen came off the line, Dr. Porsche adapted one chassis for the distance run from Berlin to Rome, scheduled for September, 1939. While the streamlined, one-man racer carried an 1131 cc VW motor, a top speed of 86 mph was attained in tests, though the race was never run. Experience with this experimental enclosed sports creation, though it provided no comforts for touring use, unmistakably influenced Porsche's post-war thinking. It was to foreshadow a most unusual future.

Aware of a greater horsepower potential in the VW engine than had been extracted for the production model, Dr. Porsche and his son adapted a special head to the 1131 cc VW block and fitted a single downdraft carburetor. The changes rendered 40 hp. They knew the body could be made substantially lighter. But there was to be no more compromise with comfort for touring and luggage. Their first prototype, constructed in Gmuend, Austria, in the early Summer of 1948, allowed Ferry not only to retire a *Wehrmacht* VW he had been using for sport, but proved so well thought out that many details were carried over directly into initial production design.

Applying his experience with the Auto Union racing cars and the Volkswagen, Porsche began development in 1947 of what he and Ferry considered to be a "week-end sports car." Planning for mass production appeared all but out of the question, and so Porsche found no reason to design short cuts in materials or construction to achieve low production costs. The result was a private open car for Ferry of uncompromising comforts and quality in detail.

Ferry's roadster, agile in competition and uncompromising in construction, attained a speed of 135 km, which advanced to 140 km when windshield and extra seat were removed. It became a sensation among sports car enthusiasts wherever it appeared. No other German manufacturer was offering a car for competition driving, and Germany was not importing cars to fill this need. A series production of this Project Number 356 might be saleable . . .

Tubular bridge-girder side rails gave the first Porsche maximum rigidity with minimum weight; production design switched to a box section chassis-frame.

The modified Volkswagen engine was relocated forward of the rear axle close behind the driver's seat, as it had appeared on the Auto Union racing car 15 years before (and would later reappear on the Type 550 racing Porsche).

Dr. Porsche had moved in the same direction as the crowd that was souping up the Volkswagen for racing.. He had based his speed machine heavily on the use of Volkswagen parts. His intention in allowing use of many stock components — then becoming available again from the reactivated Wolfsburg factory, with which he now had no connection — was not to achieve economy production, but because his design thinking in the Porsche concept so overlapped that of the Volkswagen that interchangeability came naturally.

Many years later, the first Porsche still collected crowds of admirers among owners wherever it was seen. The close adherence to original wheelbase and body form, even to the shape of the wheel cutouts, may be seen in this comparison with a later model. The original car went into private Swiss hands in exchange for 7,000 Swiss francs (about $1,700) in September 1948, in order to acquire capital toward initial production as a coupe.

At the International Motor Show in Geneva the production
Porsche appeared publicly for the first time, in March, 1949.
By this time the configuration of the prototype had been
refined through a series of tests and the car emerged as a
coupe for an initial production run of fifty units in the
little Austrian engineering plant at Gmuend. It was an
international car, bodies being made by the Swiss builder
Beutler of Thun.

The open Porsche prototype was followed by an enclosed two-seater, which
was refined subsequently as the first production model Porsche coupé. Designated as the 356, it had a top speed of 86.8 mph, all on a displacement of little
more than one liter — 1089 cc. Porsche used high performance cylinder heads
along with a more efficient type of combustion chamber, membrane pump gas
feed, and twin down-draft carburetors. The engine developed 40 bhp, 15 more
than the stock Volkswagen, at 4000 rpm.

Part of the first series was exported
all over the world. One of the first
Type 356 cars sent to Switzerland is
shown here in the Fall of 1949, in
Lausanne. The initial series was visibly distinguished from succeeding
models by the divided door window.

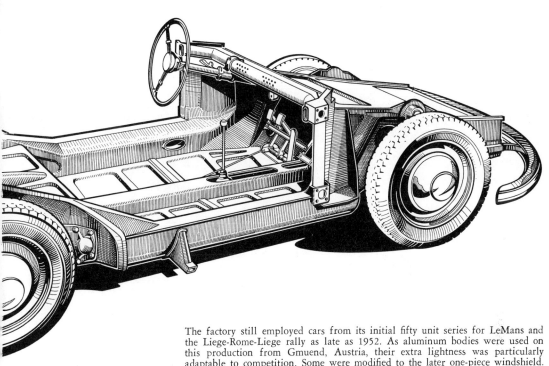

The factory still employed cars from its initial fifty unit series for LeMans and the Liege-Rome-Liege rally as late as 1952. As aluminum bodies were used on this production from Gmuend, Austria, their extra lightness was particularly adaptable to competition. Some were modified to the later one-piece windshield. A car kept by the factory for competition could be recognized by an outside fuel filler cap near the cowl.

While the Porsche 356 engine appeared familiarly like the Volkswagen engine, closer examination revealed special V-value, high-performance cylinder heads with changes in the combustion chamber design making the Porsche engine substantially different. A few years later Porsche was to change every part, reducing inter-changeability with VW to zero.

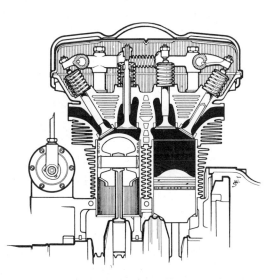

Still regarded as a modern race car, the 1.5 liter, supercharged 450 hp. Cistalia of 1946-47 was the only 12-cylinder opposed, rear engine racing car in the world that provided the driver an option of two-wheel or four-wheel-drive while under way.

Porsche suggested a sloping front hood theory being that the front would be pushed downward to enhance road-holding, as the car moved forward through the air.

Porsche's famous servo-synchro ring transmission, later to become an important feature of the Porsche, as well as the Volkswagen, under license, was first used on his Cistalia.

Opposed, or "boxer" cylinder layout first appeared in Porsche's aircraft engine designs in 1912.

This engine plan, along with other basic chassis characteristics, appeared together in an automobile as early as 1931-33 in the forerunning models of the Volkswagen.

The aircooled boxer motor design for the Porsche stemmed directly from the torture-proven Volkswagen.

Testing was extensive and relentless. Prototypes of the VW, built by hand in private garages for Prof. Porsche, were tested for a 100,000 km. stretch. Next a series of 30 prototypes was tested for 2 million km. By 1938 series production was planned. The war was to bring on the hardest test of all.

The aerodynamic body was confirmed Project 356 by tes form in a windtu strings attached to the pattern of air

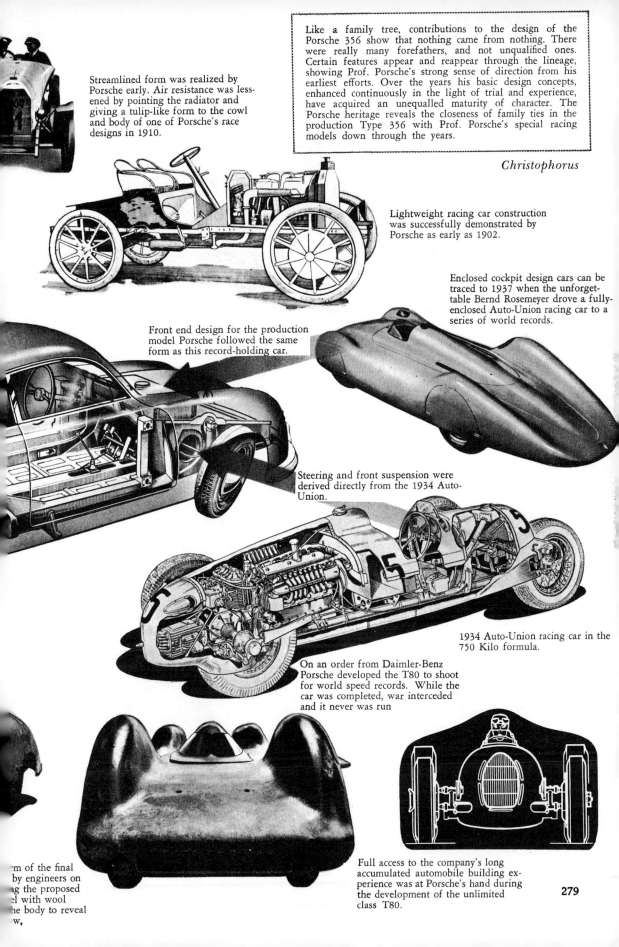

Streamlined form was realized by Porsche early. Air resistance was lessened by pointing the radiator and giving a tulip-like form to the cowl and body of one of Porsche's race designs in 1910.

Like a family tree, contributions to the design of the Porsche 356 show that nothing came from nothing. There were really many forefathers, and not unqualified ones. Certain features appear and reappear through the lineage, showing Prof. Porsche's strong sense of direction from his earliest efforts. Over the years his basic design concepts, enhanced continuously in the light of trial and experience, have acquired an unequalled maturity of character. The Porsche heritage reveals the closeness of family ties in the production Type 356 with Prof. Porsche's special racing models down through the years.

Christophorus

Lightweight racing car construction was successfully demonstrated by Porsche as early as 1902.

Enclosed cockpit design cars can be traced to 1937 when the unforgettable Bernd Rosemeyer drove a fully-enclosed Auto-Union racing car to a series of world records.

Front end design for the production model Porsche followed the same form as this record-holding car.

Steering and front suspension were derived directly from the 1934 Auto-Union.

1934 Auto-Union racing car in the 750 Kilo formula.

On an order from Daimler-Benz Porsche developed the T80 to shoot for world speed records. While the car was completed, war interceded and it never was run

...m of the final ...by engineers on ...g the proposed ...el with wool ...he body to reveal ...w.

Full access to the company's long accumulated automobile building experience was at Porsche's hand during the development of the unlimited class T80.

Though the Porsche factory began in the smallest way, its reputation was built from the beginning out of the crucible of racing. It was the first German company to participate in a big international race after World War II, and the only German *marque* represented in 1950 at *Le Mans,* where two Frenchmen brought in the single entry—an aluminum coupe—at the top in the 1100 cc. class.

Where Porsche factory participation was absent, enthusiastic private owners pushed their own cars to glory in sporting events all around the world. Hans Stanek, driving a Gloeckler-Porsche special (patterned after the original Porsche by Walter Gloeckler.

Even the original 1948 roadster continued to pile up honors. Here it is seen as car 106 piloted by Marco Engler, who had replaced the original modified VW engine with a Porsche motor.

The earliest series cabriolet, in aluminum, a product of Beutler in Switzerland, carried a quality of detail that established the superb standard of excellence for other Porsche coachbuilders to follow.

While the quarters proved only temporary, this building housed the engineering and administrative staffs of the house of Porsche in the early summer of 1950.

The automobile world was captivated by the first series of Porsche's slipper-like personal sports car. The response to the first models was so overwhelming that the firm elected to set up permanent production facilities; and after obtaining the necessary governmental permission, Porsche moved his facilities from the country to a small shop in Stuttgart-Zuffenhausen, rented from the Reutter body firm.

If one were to slip in behind this wheel he would be sitting in one of the original Beutler cabriolets.

Excitement of the traditional *Le Mans* Start was heightened in the early 1950's by the startling performance of the cars from Stuttgart. Ever since, Porsche cars have entered the classic 24-hour race against all comers each year, and have won in their class almost continuously ⟶

Always at hand for consultation, Dr. Porsche has been called here to confer with a testing crew at the dynometer.

Early cars could be readily distinguished from later production by the fully wrapping bumpers that formed the bottom edge of the front and rear fenders.

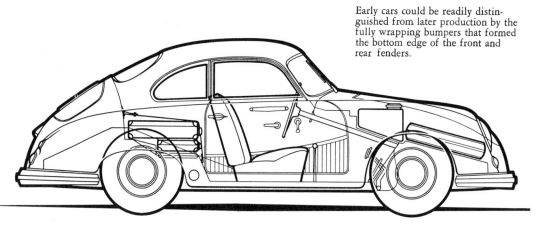

Early quarters at Reutter were limited to a room of 500 square meters and every corner had to be put to use. Engines were individually identified by hand lettering the mufflers with a brush.

Since body construction and trim are a most readily tangible measure of detail quality in the Porsche—even to the casual viewer knowing little of mechanics who may never hear the car run or be aware of its capabilities on the road—the body builders have attained new esteem as the Porsche became a synonym for excellence all over the western world. While the roadster bodies were produced by Drauz and brought to Stuttgart from Heilbrun, the more familiar coupe and cabriolet have been proud products of the firm of Reutter, from the day in 1950 when the house of Porsche moved from its Austrian barracks to establish production quarters in Stuttgart in a corner of the Reutter shops . . . When the clamps are snapped away from this mass of light stampings, which the craftsmen have introduced to the jig and artfully hand-wedded, one by one, another ambassador of Reutter quality will emerge in the familiar form of a new coupe body.

Front axle and steering design of the Porsche 356 derive from a concept first used by Dr. Porsche as early as 1931, and later proved on various models from his office from the world record Auto-Union racing cars to the ubiquitous Volkswagen. This typifies the development of most engineering details of the Porsche, which have evolved to a state of perfection from initially sound conception, in turn strenuously tested, proven, and bettered by meticulous refinement.

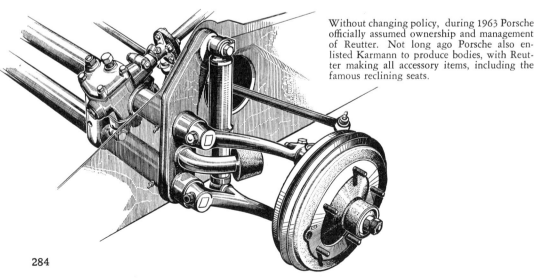

Without changing policy, during 1963 Porsche officially assumed ownership and management of Reutter. Not long ago Porsche also enlisted Karmann to produce bodies, with Reutter making all accessory items, including the famous reclining seats.

While present models vary only slightly in appearance from the original coupés, mechanically the Porsche has been improved and refined continuously until it has become one of the most successful and desirable sports cars ever produced. Interchangeable parts with Volkswagen became fewer and fewer and are now all but non-existent. The Porsche 356 later appeared with 1300, 1500, and 1600 cc engines; and since 1948 the uncompromised quality of every car to bear the *marque* causes the Porsche owner to feel he almost cheated the factory in not paying more, even though the price of a Porsche has always been in the luxury car range.

The *marque* Porsche became indelibly prominent on the sporting scene abroad. Here a pack of Porsches, led by GT champion Hammarlund, drift through a right curve in a tight field in Sweden, with MG, Morgan and Triumph tilting in from behind.

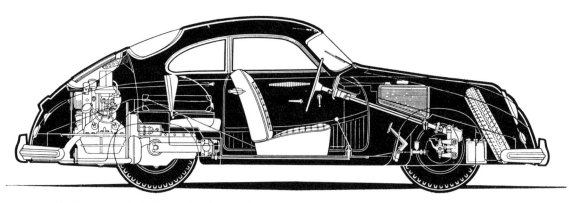

By late 1952 the full-wrapping integral bumpers gave way to bumpers set away from the body, the windshield was reduced to a single piece radiused at the center, and storage space was increased by relocating the spare wheel and tire.

Special light roadsters, following the concept laid down by Ferry's original roadster (tubular frame and engine mounted forward of the rear axle), were built by racing enthusiast Walter Gloeckler in the early period before Porsche produced its own race-bred Type 550. One Gloeckler-Porsche competed successfully in the many racing events in the United States when Max Hoffman was the general importer. Another went to Switzerland where it was driven to a string of successes by Hans Stanek, shown here leading two coupes driven by top Swiss drivers Walter Ringgenberg and Arthur Heuberger.

The Porsche was race-bred in a very literal sense; and the factory racing program, which was initiated to prove innovations for production models, has been a continuous ordeal of testing. The cars are all but unbeaten in their appearances in competition all over the world.

What would evolve into series production as the Type 550 began with the enclosed *Le Mans* car of 1953 which carried the standard 1500 Super engine. Later this car took the crown in its class in the Pan-Americana in Mexico. The racing car differed from the familiar 356 series in two distinct features. It used a tubular frame, and the engine was mounted forward of the rear axle just behind the driver. These features both appeared in the original 1947 Porsche roadster prototype configuration.

The racing model had taken new form as an open car when it debuted at the Paris Automobile Show in the Autumn of 1953 with a four-camshaft engine and further modified underframe.

At the Brussels Motor Show the "hunchback" Type 550 first appeared. In the Fall of 1954 this model also was included at the Geneva Automobile Show in the Volkswagen factory exhibit under a Riviera motif. This "touring edition" carried a full windshield and offered special comfort and built-in roll-bar protection.

Finalized design of the 550 for racing eliminated the headrest hump, substituted a small windshield for the driver and carried a cover over the empty side of the cockpit. Its full-breakaway rear body section allowed maintenance crews full access during harried pit stops. 100 cars were built late in 1954.

Before each year's 24-hour race the factory crew moves into the same secluded shop in a nearby village in France where the *Le Mans* cars can be prepared.

The clean, tubular frame of the Type 550 reflects a directness in design and finish which keynote much of Porsche engineering.

Journalists confer with Ferry Porsche at a showing of the model line for the press at picturesque Solitude Castle not far from Stuttgart. The modern-day *Wehrmacht* model in the rear was tested in a quantity of 60 by the West German army.

Practice for the Nürburgring 500 km. event ended for one Spyder after slight damage which ripped off the rear body shell. Porsche's sports director Huschke von Hanstein appears to voice "It could have been worse!" while a race steward and Porsche team driver Richard von Frankenberg survey the damage.

Ken Miles, taking a corner hard at Torrey Pines in California, first won prominence as an MG driver in his native England. After moving to the U. S. he continued with MG, then advanced to fame as a Spyder driver in the von Neumann stable, winning among others the 1500 class at this annual event near La Jolla. Front wheel brake cooling was increased by enlarging the brake air scoops on his early (vertical headlamps) Type 550.

The late French champion Jean Behra leads the field out of a tight S-bend in an airfield circuit in Austria in 1958, with Edgar Barth, Count von Trips and Huschke von Hanstein also in Spyder RSK or RS models pressing him on. Falling back are a big Maserati and a 3-liter Ferrari.

The Spyder engine for Type 550, recognized by its specially effective double blower and dual overhead camshafts, proved the basis for a succession of hotter versions at the hands of Porsche's race department. As shown in original form it was used in 1954 by factory cars at Reims, the Nürburgring and at Avus.

Edgar Barth goes into a curve on the Nurburgring during his record lap of 10:02.2 qualifying for the German Grand Prix in 1957. This almost legendary performance was nearly equaled in the race at 10:04.9. Comparatively, Sterling Moss reached only 10:13.3 the year before in his Maserati. Barth's achievements were the most important driving events of the 1957 1500 cc. class.

Jack McAfee, an American sportsman who ventured to the great courses of the world to compete, drives a tight race in his Porsche 550 Spyder "at home" in California at a Torrey Pines event.

By early Summer 1959 Porsche appeared at the racing cir-
cuits with a test car which departed from the sports car
concept. It was an out-and-out Formula II 1500 cc. racing
car. Like the Spyder its construction principles were related
closely to the production model Porsche cars. After testing
at the *Nuerburgring* it was entered in the Gran Prix of
Monaco, and later appeared at Reims driven by Joakim
Bonnier and Hans Hermann.

For the 1960-61 racing season Porsche's racing endeavors were with the RS-60 roadster
and with the limited production Abarth coupe using the Carrera four camshaft, twin
dual Weber carburetor setup. It placed first in its class at the 24-hour race at *Le Mans*.
A body by the well-known Italian body builder was one effort toward cracking the body
bottleneck in Porsche car production. But quality from Abarth did not immediately come
up to Porsche standards.

As an elderly man paused at the summit to look back over the road he had traveled, behind him lay a lifetime spent pursuing firm convictions against often relentless odds. Soon the sun would lengthen the shadows of this beautiful day, just as the sun was already setting on his life. But the sun was not to set on the ideas Dr. Porsche had nurtured to perfection. On his account a new unburdened day lay ahead for all the continent, and for countries over the free world, where the Volkswagen and Porsche cars would bring owners more than they had been promised.

The car that is "almost human" has attracted a sensitively human group of owners. On September 3, 1950, some forty sports drivers from West Germany and Switzerland "crashed" a party being given in honor of Dr. Porsche's 75th birthday at the Solitude Palace near Stuttgart, each arriving in a Porsche 356. The old man was visibly moved by the assemblage as he personally inspected each car, met and talked with each driver. The day was a pleasantly emotional one in the life of the man who had contributed so much.

An early event to gain a place on the annual calendar of the Porsche club in Germany, and one of the best attended of the season, is the trek to the Solitude Castle outside Stuttgart where cars park next to the historic Schwaebish Hall while members tour the grounds.

The little Austrian who had given his touch of genius to nearly every mode of transportation — trains, tractors, tanks, boats, airplanes, automobiles, and even an amphibious vehicle — had lived each day only to design, create, improve, and produce. But much of his life had depended on politics alien to his soul. Porsche's health had been destroyed by his time in the French prison, and he lived little more than four months after this commemorative birthday celebration. His resting place is the 300-year-old chapel near his estate in Zell am See in Austria — in accord with his wish to be "away from the big cities."

Porsches both, so to speak, when one considers that the supercharged Mercedes-Benz Model S was designed by Ferdinand Porsche while at Daimler-Benz shortly before he was to start his own engineering office, which eventually would lead to the production of the design at the right.

The weatherman was kind to Porsche enthusiasts for this fine Spring day when the cars journeyed to Langenburg castle in Schwaben for coffee and cake. (As royalty goes, the princess of Hohenlohe-Langenburg may be recorded as the sister of Queen Elizabeth's consort, Philip.)

Porsche clubs grew almost spontaneously in major cities all over Germany as enthusiasts met, compared interests, and consolidated their travels for all to enjoy. Tiny Belgium became one of the first foreign countries where a group was formed.

With 50% of present Porsche production being exported, and the lion's share of this going to the USA, the role of the car among American sportsmen has increased more rapidly than anywhere else. Many owners have united under the banner of the Porsche Club of America. Some cars from an outing of the Potomac Regional line up here before the Jefferson Memorial in Washington, D. C.

Owners everywhere have shown a camaraderie reflected by certain events common to every country. No club's season schedule would be complete without a gymkhana of timed trials through traps, the standard icebreaker for getting acquainted fun wherever a Porsche club has been formed.

Probably the quickest police in all Europe patrol the *Autobahn* in North Rhine Westphalia where specially trained crews have been equipped with Porsche 1600 cabriolets for several years. Traffic congestion and chain reaction accidents were reported on the decrease soon after 10 Porsches were put into two-shift use.

With no basic change in principle or policy at the family-controlled house of Porsche, since the days when the elder Dr. Ferdinand personally supervised all phases of the operation, Dr. Ferry will probably continue to stand in the shadow of his legendary father, even though he is an outstanding engineer in his own right. With his father from the firm's beginning, the younger Porsche was a participant from the earliest days of the *Volksauto*; he conducted the testing program during VW prototype development. The Old Man would hardly recognize Porsche, A. G. today, after a decade under his son's direction. Under Ferry's hand the company has expanded a little each year, by making the most of increased technical experience among members of an ever-growing engineering staff, to attain a world prominence for its all but unique services.

Today the Porsche engineering office continues as a great force in the hands of Dr. Ferdinand's able son Ferry at Stuttgart-Zuffenhausen, where Porsche cars are bred in increasing number; but each Porsche still adheres to the original formula of quality first.

Each Porsche is subjected to most exacting inspection before final release for delivery. A road test takes the car over the *Autobahn* and over stretches of bad road selected for their terrors. Then the car is returned to the factory to be examined and worked on again. Only after an inspection *of the inspections* does a master inspector, acting independently of manufacturing, stake his very reputation by signing a small windshield sticker: "Microscopically examined and released for delivery."

Today in Stuttgart . . . Karl Rabe, Ferry's senior engineer, has been associated with the Porsches, father and son, almost continuously for fifty years (beginning the association in 1913) and Erwin Komenda (standing), with the firm since its early months. "We get a great deal of experience from our racing activity," Ferry Porsche has explained. "We pick up information and put this into our production cars. Racing is a good way to experiment with production cars, we think . . . Americans get the same kind of experience on their proving grounds as we do racing, except that when my engineers go to a race they have more enthusiasm."

FASHIONS AND THE PORSCHE

Ferry Porsche gave a concise presentation of the Porsche philosophy upon introduction of the latest Porsche.

"Ladies and Gentlemen . . .

"Everything connected with fashion is continually changing. In the new year last year's dress is very often completely out of fashion. One is always searching for something new, and fashion even affects automobile construction. There are firms who change the looks of their cars every year. Always new lines, new faces, new bodywork, can be found. The public wants it that way. We construct cars on a different principle. No, we aren't so conceited as to say: we never found it necessary to make any changes; what we once designed will, without alteration, still be good for decades. But when we do change something, we don't just make small alterations, following the dictates of fashion. We are, and I openly admit the fact, proud that we don't follow the current fashions in automobile construction — in spite of the fact that we have more than once influenced them: our refinements — and sometimes these are very numerous — are very often invisible ones. For we change little on the outside. The engine, the road-holding, the safety and the driving comfort: these things above all are the goals towards which we strive with regards to improvements.

In the first place we are technicians. We want to produce an automobile which stands up to the most critical technical tests. A well thought out automobile.

We have our own ideas about cars. The internal safety, for example, doesn't, as far as we are concerned, begin with the padded instrument panel, with the soft sun-shield or the safety steering wheel: this we have as well, as a matter of course. We start with the brakes, the road-holding, the exact steering. We don't even want to have accidents happen in the first place . . .

Our cars are driven all over the world. Every year more Porsche cars are produced than in the preceding one, but even so the total is still a very small one. That which is called mass-production does not exist for us. Neither do we have any conveyor belts, and we are proud of this fact, too. Our car is a hand-made article, which has as background an engineering department which has existed since 1931. We make an individual car.

Visitors at the Stuttgart factory have shown particular affection for Plant #3, where the adjacent yard fills with completed Porsches waiting for inspection and dispatch—each car an individual, destined for an appreciative individualist. Car in lower left, for example, specially ordered without a hood handle, will be forwarded to its waiting owner exactly as requested.   Of the 230 Porsche dealers in the United States, Volkswagen dealers and distributors predominate as representatives. These Porsche dealers in the U. S., who may expect about 5,000 cars from Stuttgart each year, traditionally order so far in advance that the factory is literally "sold out" before production begins.

We are, and I really don't need to emphasize this fact, very closely connected with motor sport. Fashionable details, to be forgotten next year, don't count for anything in sport. There only performance counts. Sports successes don't pale and fade away. The sports car and the car for the customer — these two are very closely connected. In our case it is very clearly to be seen that sport serves series production manufacture. Take any one of our cars. The new car which I here present to you, and which came out for the Frankfurt Automobile Show in the fall, also shows very many more internal than external improvements. The basic lines of the body have hardly been changed at all, simply because these basic lines are still ahead of the modern tendencies. We have touched up odd things here and there, made little improvements. Yes: detail, hand-made accuracy and feeling for ultimate refinements — that is the main thing, in our cars, in the men who design and make them."

While refinement is continuous, external changes at Porsche are so rare they remind one of the schedule at Volkswagen, where an enlarged rear window made big news for the 1958 model. Occasionally changes are visible, as between the 356 and the 356 B. Taking into account the fact Porsche must share the road with other makes and models, the "B" bumpers were redesigned and elevated to improve function, with a pair of vertical overriders being added as inconspicuously as good design would permit.

Performance can never be higher than braking is adequate. Porsche's superior reputation in this department is carred on in the 911 with disc brakes at all four wheels.

While the 356B gave way to production of a 356C, the nature of accumulated experience and discoveries at Porsche, during the course of refining the 356 since its introduction in 1949, now pressed in favor of issuing a sister model in which the basic specifications of the 356 were not imposed.

By 1964 this all-different model was ready to bow. Porsche proudly announced a 150 HP, single-overhead camshaft, six-cylinder, five-speed luxury sportster — the first wholly new chassis and body in fifteen years. Soon established as the model 911, the car appeared in testing to be all that its designers had intended. It was all Porsche, only *more*. As suspension of the 911 quickly proved outstanding its handling characteristics became legend overnight.

Porsche had not turned its head on the original 356 series; both models were produced side-by-side to order. But the call for the "natural" companion model among enthusiasts in the new form became clear, and by the spring of 1965 Porsche had it ready. Externally the new 912 was a carbon copy of the 911. But it featured the seasoned 90 HP four-cylinder, pushrod 356-C Super engine, and except on special option carried a four-speed box. Predictably the 912 will eclipse production of the original 356-C in all markets.

Entrance is easier on the 911/12. Visibility has been substantially improved. With the wheelbase extended four inches (to 87.1") there is space to squeeze in 2+2 seating. Without question the new Nine-hundred line (which includes competition models), through a subtle progression that only the team at Porsche can create, will be current for at least a decade to come.

A two-liter, four-cylinder, 180 HP racing version applies proven competition features like box-section frame and engine placement forward of the rear axle, but initiates glass fiber for the body.

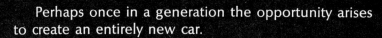

Perhaps once in a generation the opportunity arises to create an entirely new car.

To start with a dream and a clean sheet of paper.

To apply insights gained in seventeen years of testing, racing and refining what was already the most advanced car of its time.

To design and build—almost without compromise—the ultimate car for getting from here to there in the quickest, safest, most enjoyable manner possible.

Result: The new Porsche.

New in every detail, yet unmistakably a Porsche.

Go ahead. Drive it. You'll never forget it.

The high-performance, unusually well-instrumented Porsche 911 has new 6-cylinder, air-cooled, 148-hp rear engine, new 5-speed gearbox. Top speed 130 mph. The lower-priced Porsche 912, sister to the 911, has famous SC, 4-cylinder engine, new 4 or 5-speed gearbox. Top speed 115 mph. New Porsche fastback design offers 75% more field of vision, even better suspension, far more elbow room and under-the-hood luggage space. Superb 4-wheel disc brakes, precise handling, welded body make Porsche one of world's safest cars. Complete interior safety package is standard. For domestic or overseas delivery, see dealer or write Porsche of America Corp., 107 Tryon Avenue West, Teaneck, New Jersey 07666.

18

NINE LIVES LATER

More reasonable fuel consumption is only the beginning. First cost is more nearly the only cost.

In the early Twenties at Austro-Daimler Porsche was assisted by a brilliant young mechanic named Alfred Neubauer, here seated in a Mercedes prepared for racing. For these men racing afforded a workshop in which sum totals in trial and error could be computed, analyzed and acted upon. More recently Neubauer achieved greatness at Daimler-Benz as manager of their racing team.

The legend of the Volkswagen's nine lives concludes with an international triumph. Nine times its development was stopped dead; nine times it lived anew. Nine lives later the VW attained a universality beyond the fondest hopes of its persevering designer. Today *Volkswagen* has become a synonym for *transportation* in the daily life of 130 countries around the world — a far cry from the People's Car's first existence.

The Volkswagen was first born as a small car image in the mind of Ferdinand Porsche during the 1920's — when he was internationally best known for his big luxury and racing cars. The VW then was no more than the desire to develop a light vehicle that would be compatible with the economics of the average family. The idea took form in some measure during Porsche's work on the small A-D "Sascha" sports car in 1922, the Mercedes "200 Stuttgart" in 1926, the "Steyr 30" in 1929, and the Wanderer cars of 1930 and 1931.

But each of these models was developed under the critical eye of a conservative, profit-minded sponsor who saw no commercial potential in offering a practical transportation vehicle for the great mass of people — especially in an era when credit buying was virtually unknown. Porsche was repeatedly restrained from completing any design that might be interpreted as today's Volkswagen, and the small car died the first of many deaths.

The *Volksauto* image in Porsche's mind might never have materialized at all had he not taken the bold venture of forming his own engineering office in 1931. There, free for the first time to do as he chose, Porsche himself gave the light car idea new life, developing it on paper for the first time, designating it "Project 12."

The Volkswagen drawings were interred in the Stuttgart office files while Porsche and his staff completed the many other projects which brought in the bread and butter. Project 12 could have been obliterated by time, had not Porsche's initiative persuaded the Zundapp Motorcycle people to support the small car. With Zundapp's backing, Porsche's ruggedly unorthodox concept took its first physical form, only to be killed once again when Zundapp officials suddenly withdrew their backing.

But Ferdinand Porsche and his *Volksauto* would not give up, and soon the VW lived anew. Porsche was successful in finding another backer to build prototypes of his little automobile — this time Zundapp's rival, NSU. But this project, together with much of the world's creative thought, was killed by the Great Depression sweeping Germany in 1933.

Smashing successes with the Auto-Union brought Professor Porsche social notoriety. This sunny afternoon in 1933 he discusses a record run with prominent racing enthusiasts. It might have been as much on the strength of his personal fame, as for an interest in the outcome of his persistent small car project, that financial backers were attracted to Porsche during this period.

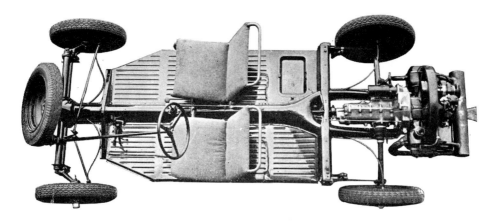

While some details of this polished 30 (sometimes called "60") series display chassis foreshadowed production design almost exactly, other features were to undergo gross improvement before freezing on the Type 38. Outfitted with battery and fuel tank, a similar bare chassis was driven about in the neighborhood of Porsche's garage during this development period, affording clinical testing of fine points in the torsion bars and trailing arms of the suspension. Use of the same system on Porsche's famous Auto-Union racing cars already had proven this type of suspension as desirable for the People's Car.

The VW's next incarnation came as Hitler's pet political project, the best financed attempt up to that time. Receiving the financial blessings of the Nazi Party, first in a limited way and then later without reservation, the VW appeared destined at last to become the car of the People. Three prototypes, anticipating closely the ultimate VW, were first built in Porsche's garage. Then the impressive Series 30 test cars which followed duplicated the VW image in quantity for the first time.

Hitler's harangues and wild promises alone proved insubstantial, however; the small car idea needed a cohesive driving force that would combine plans for practical production and promotion before the VW could become a finished, mass-produced automobile. Without this vital support the Volkswagen could have withered on the Nazi propaganda vine. But Robert Ley, the Nazi Party Labor boss, supplied the necessary push, as he organized the VW project under the *KdF* program, setting his five-mark subscription plan into motion. For the first time in several lives up to this moment, the Volkswagen was actually offered to the People — although more figuratively than literally. The Nazis killed civilian sedan production after only a few pilot models had been delivered.

On the very brink of success, the Volkswagen was struck down as a People's Car by what seemed the final, lethal blow — World War II. Hurriedly camouflaged in its forced incarnation as the *Kuebelwagen* and *Schwimmwagen*, the VW thrived on battle, endearing itself to German troops during the trying and bitter conflict — only to capitulate at war's end.

The VW was lifted up out of the rubble of its mortally wounded factory by British Occupation, who restored the car to a literal phoenix-like life in what was probably the car's most critical period. But this time the English auto industry acted as executioner as it proclaimed the German People's Car "commercially unfit for quantity production."

The VW rose once again, however, in the guise of makeshift sports cars and scavenger-built passenger models. It could not have survived long under these conditions of diminishing supply; and according to superstition and all good sense the VW was through. Its ninth life expired with Petermax Mueller's retirement from sandlot racing competition.

Then Heinz Nordhoff performed his Wolfsburg version of the German Miracle, and the Volkswagen was given its tenth and current chance at life.

That this was the beginning of the Volkswagen's true maturity is history.

A CHARACTER APART

Why has this insignificantly-sized, beetle-shaped car met with surging success in every country in which it has been introduced? The answer is as simple as it is impressive—

Primarily Volkswagen offers *true economy*. Relatively more reasonable fuel consumption is only the beginning. It is distinguished from other so-called economy cars by an uncommon durability, almost limitless adaptability to extremes of climate and terrain, and dogged dependability. It is easy and inexpensive to repair, its first cost being more nearly its only cost. No power assists or optional equipment at extra cost are required to make VW manageable and comfortable.

Volkswagen standards of workmanship set it apart from most other automobiles. Years of continuous refinement centered on a single design have freed the car from detail faults in design, engineering, and assembly — so characteristically annoying among cars built under the pressures of the customary 12 or 24 months design change cycle. It effects its owner like a good pair of shoes; it is a warm and personal relationship. VW presents welcome contrast in a commercially "dishonest" age in which planned obsolescence has obscured quality — except as a minimum standard.

Volkswagen changes are made only for improvement. The legend of the "unchanging" Volkswagen is really a story salted with continuous change in the finer details. While the configuration is that laid down in 1938, *every part* has been altered since, some many times over. While a group of changes are incorporated at new model time (after the annual company-wide summer vacation), less physically apparent improvements are adopted successively all through the days of production.

The Volkswagen owner often drives with an air of new confidence, since buying the little car may well have been the first financially smart automobile purchase of his car-buying lifetime. Resale value has proven unique in an industry where heavy depreciation has been taken for granted and calculated owner discontent has been built into many models. Timeless styling has paid off. The total cost of a new VW amounts to no more than the first year's depreciation on a bigger Buick. Later the VW can be resold, much hard use logged, for relatively more of its original cost than any other make.

AUTOS
A Greenbacked Year
On the Dusty Lots

While the car has quite literally become a "foreign object" in the very "eye" of the American motor car industry, what makes news today is not that VW is *foreign*—it isn't even mentioned—but that Volkswagen has challenged leading U.S. makes, on *their* terms, and has been doing all right, *in any language.*

While all eyes are on the pace of car sales in the nation's auto showrooms (April set another monthly record), 1963 is also proving a greenbacked year for the men who preside over the dusty, sun-baked used-car lots.....Because of the bigger demand for used cars, there are fewer bargains to be had. Prices are up slightly from a year ago even though there are more cars for sale, and the hottest used seller is the car that also leads the new-auto field: Chevrolet. Volkswagen also ranks high as a used car; last week at a wholesale auto auction, the place where the trade sets its prices, a 1960 VW carried a wholesale price of $1,080 v. $1,000 for a 1960 Ford Galaxie that when new cost $1,000 more than the VW.

TIME, MAY 17, 1963

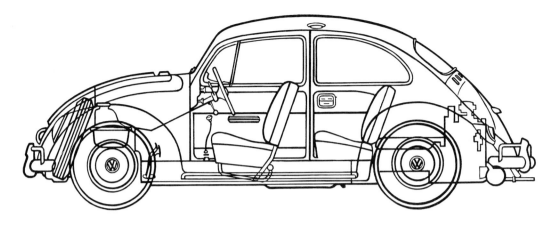

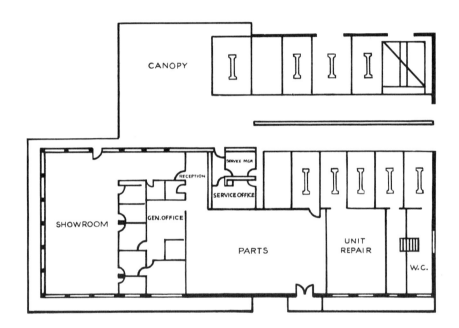

CANOPY

SERVICE MGR

RECEPTION

SERVICE OFFICE

SHOWROOM

GEN. OFFICE

PARTS

UNIT REPAIR

W.C.

Why is a Volkswagen dealership like a Volkswagen?

Because the same people who design the car, design the dealerships.

Volkswagens are designed to last, and Volkswagen dealerships are designed to make them last.

So, like the car, the thing that makes them work is in the back.

(In fact, dealership plans provide for parts-and-service areas between five and nine times the size of the showroom.)

And, like the car, Volkswagen dealerships shun the unessential.

Anything that doesn't serve to make the Volkswagen function efficiently and economically, simply isn't there.

The same holds true for our dealerships.

There are no strings of lights, no gay profusion of flapping flags, no wall-sized signs proclaiming big sales.

What there is, is simply the space and equipment, the parts and personnel, to service VWs efficiently and economically.

And, like the Volkswagen, year after year, it's always the same.

© VOLKSWAGEN OF AMERICA, I

19

BYE, BYE, BEETLE?

**Logical evolution of principles proven in the Volkswagen, after lifting
traditional interchangeability requirements with the original, have led
to a big brother — rather than a successor.**

Suspicions of a "new" Volkswagen had long been beer talk in motor circles throughout the Continent, though there was nothing to tie the rumor on, except for a healthy, if not hallowed, respect for the capability of VW management. When official announcement was made, the company already was advanced in the project practically to the point of production. At the Frankfurt Automobile Show in September, 1961, other makers, as well as the public, got to see and touch the all-new VW-1500.

THE PASSWORD: "FOR A NEW EUROPE"

In the beginning of 1500 development the project was not even known at Wolfsburg — except among a core of directly involved top engineers who paid regular visits to a burned-out engine plant, ostensibly on business related to redevelopment of the facility. The early lead-time was so neatly obscured by Volkswagen management that it makes conversation even today among other motor makers on the Continent. Even so, competitors, respecting only Dr. Nordhoff's astute feeling for product as a lead, treated the assumption that VW would supplement its line as an immutable fact in their planning, literally years before VW confirmed the 1500 early in 1961.

The car reflected logical evolution of principles proven in the Volkswagen after traditional interchangeability requirements with the original had been lifted.

As smartly economical in use of space as in use of fuel, the tightly arranged new engine now fitted neatly under the rug of the rear trunk. Luggage could be stowed in the rear, as well as the front, with outside access. Wheelbase was the same, but horsepower had been jumped from 40 to 53. Only six inches longer, and less than three inches wider than the original Volkswagen — which then became known as the 1200 — the new car offered substantially more conventional features, while remaining historically practical and efficient. But it no longer looked like a beetle.

Though built for several years before scheduled for distribution in the U.S. market, Volkswagen early spotted key locales throughout the USA with emergency 1500 warehouses from which authorized dealers could draw parts, a policy insuring against possible "erosion" among 1500 sedans finding their way into the States by "grey" market channels.

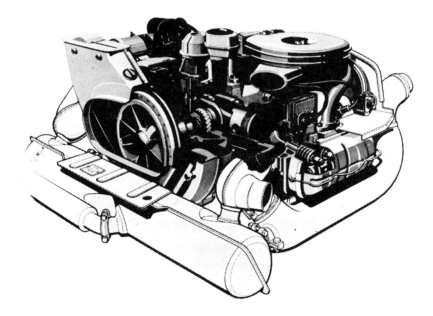

Performance is sprightly. Like its classic brother, the Type 3 squareback sedan (previously the Variant) cruises all day at close to its limit. In August, 1963, a Super 1500 was introduced in Europe, distinguished by greater horsepower and trim. Two years later, again improved, it would become the 1600.

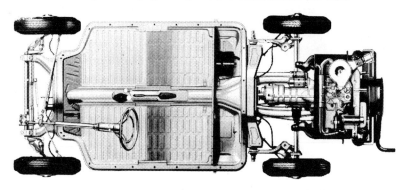

WHY CHANGE... ISN'T THE ORIGINAL A CLASSIC?

Ah, yes, the original is classic. The 1500 was not designed to replace it, but to become a companion model. One must know how it has been going in Europe to understand the 1500. The standard of living in much of Europe, starting at a debased level after the war, has risen more rapidly than that in the United States. Recent times have brought cars of various characters spewing from factories all across Britain, France, Sweden and Italy, as well as Germany. As the Continent shaped toward a Common Market, with prospects of an end to tariffs, it could be seen that the regular VW would fall into direct competition with other makes offering more luxury, power, and, well, trunk space. Even at home, some prospering Germans, it could be predicted, might want to "trade up". The 1500 would allow them to do so with familiar VW quality.

Behind each showroom where the 1500 has been introduced alongside the 1200, a servicing staff and a complete parts stock stand ready for the new model, just as with the original car. At first, sales were confined to certain limited European markets with which pilot production facilities for the VW-1500 at Wolfsburg could keep pace. By summer, 1963, about 800 of the new all-different models were being produced each day, compared with over 3600 of the 1200 series, along with 800 trucks.

AN OLD EUROPEAN CUSTOM

Unlike Americans, who have grown accustomed to seeing a different line of cars every Fall, the European public never has raced the clock in accepting new models. As a consequence, the industry abroad has been able to enjoy a make-ready period free from the anxieties inherent in hell-bent tooling up of a new production line, knocking out a backlog, then gambling all on an unpredictable public at Introduction. In producing the 1500 alongside the 1200 VW follows an easy custom in Europe.

After four years of testing and refinement in other countries, the Type 3 became official at United States dealers in October, 1965, when the proven squareback shared introduction with a brand new fastback sedan. The designation 1500 no longer was appropos: Both Type 3 models (the bug is properly Type 1; the transporter Type 2) turned into American Avenue with 65 h.p. and 1600 cc. and were so named. The 1200 had also been upped in cc., transforming it into a super beetle known as the 1300.

Following the factory vacation in August, 1962, labor unions at Volkswagen agreed to work Saturdays, not then a general working day in Europe. With this advance in capacity larger markets could be opened to the 1500. In the U.S.A., where 20% of VW production goes, and the car presently ranks way up in sales among all makes, a stupendous build-up of parts and service training was necessary before the VW 1500 could be introduced, along with a production volume capable of absorbing an almost overnight "land-office" increase in demand. While its vast northern neighbor, Canada, in population a far more nominal market, had issued the 1500 for several years, scheduling for the United States could be realized only after completion of a great additional plant for concentrated export production at Emden.

Output of the basic Volkswagen continues alongside the supplementary big brother series with ever-boosted volume. As long as this traditional, and presently unflagging, demand for the endearing beetle persists future manufacture is certain; factory production closely meshes with the worldwide fabric of its dealer orders... Even as the call for this 1200 continues beyond production in every arena where the model is known, the manufacturer has acted in cadence with a universal trend toward greater power and luxury: For 1966 a 1300 c.c. engine of 50 HP gives the original car greater handling ease than before and the larger companion series has a 1600 c.c. engine.

Though designations may change to reflect increased displacements, and the VW buyer may select as never before, the bug, mettle-proven through nine "mortal" lives, now appears more firmly on its way to Immortality than ever.

As volume production of the 1500 engine was attained it was first feasible for the Company to offer 1500-powered station wagons for distribution in the U.S. market, providing authorized dealers with the opportunity to become formally acquainted with mechanical details of the larger companion series power plant. An improvement change for 1964 was the substantial widening of the rear door and window on this model, a boon both for wide load handling and aft visibility.

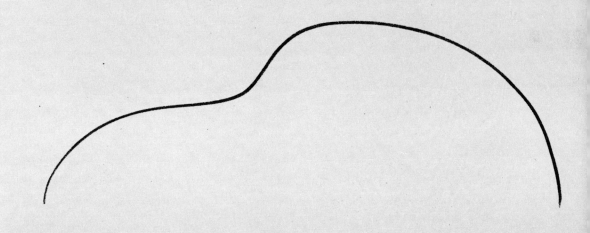

How much longer can we hand you this line?

Forever, we hope.

Because we don't ever intend to change the Volkswagen's shape.

We play by our own set of rules.

The only reason we change the VW is to make it work even better.

The money we don't spend on outside changes we do spend inside the car.

This system gives us an immense advantage: Time.

We have time to improve parts and still keep most of them interchangeable.

(Which is why it's so easy to get VW parts, and why VW mechanics don't wake up screaming.)

We have time to put an immense amount of hand work into each VW, and to finish each one like a $6,000 machine.

And this system has also kept the price almost the same over the years.

 Some cars keep changing and stay the same.

Volkswagens stay the same and keep changing.

BIBLIOGRAPHY

Automotive News: the newspaper of the Industry. Pete Wemhoff, Editor. Detroit: Slocum Publishing Co., Inc.

Christophorus: Zeitschrift fuer die Freunde des Hauses Porsche. Richard von Frankenberg, Editor. Stuttgart: Dr. Ing. h.c. F. Porsche KG.

Clay, Lucius D. *Decision in Germany.* Garden City: Doubleday, 1950.

Foreign Car Guide: featuring Volkswagen. Frank W. Coggins, Editor. New York: Rajo Publications.

Fortune. Chicago: Time, Inc., August, 1963.

German Volkswagen, The (United States Army Technical Manual / TM E 9-803). Washington, D.C.: U.S. Government Printing Office, 1944.

Gute Fahrt: Die Zeitschrift für den Volkswagenfahrer. Arthur Westrup, Editor and Publisher. Bielefeld, Germany: Verlag Klasing & Co.

Hoffmann, Heinrich, Prof. *Hitler, Wie ihn Keiner Kennt. NSDAP (National Sozialistische Deutsche Arbeiter Partei)* Berlin: Zeitgeschichte Verlag, 1940.

Hopfinger, K. B. *Beyond Expectation: the Volkswagen story.* London: G. T. Foulis & Co. Ltd., 1954.

Horne, Alistair. *Return to Power:* a report on the new Germany. New York: Frederick A. Praeger, 1956.

Investigation of the Developments in the German Automobile Industry During the War Period (Great Britain, Board of Trade, British Intelligence Objectives Subcommittee Final Report No. 300, Item No. 19) London: Her Majesty's Stationery Office, 1945.

Investigation into the Design and Performance of the Volkswagen or German People's Car (Great Britain, Board of Trade, British Intelligence Objectives Subcommittee Overall Reports, Number 998, Item No. 19) London: Her Majesty's Stationery Office, 1946.

Los Angeles Times. Norman Chandler, Chairman & President. Los Angeles: Times Mirror Company.

Motor Car Industry in Germany During the Period 1939-1945, The (Great Britain, Board of Trade, British Intelligence Objectives Subcommittee Overall Report No. 21) London: Her Majesty's Stationery Office, 1949.

Motor Revue. Heinz Ulrich Wieselmann, Editor. Stuttgart, Germany: Paul Pietsch, Publisher, Winter, 1956.

Popular Science Monthly. New York: John R. Whiting, Publisher, May, 1944.

Road & Track: the motor enthusiasts' magazine. Dean Batchelor, Editor. Newport Beach, California: John R. Bond, Inc., Publisher.

Safer Motoring: the independent international magazine for VW owners. Robert F. W. Wyse, Editor and Publisher. London: Bon Accord Bureau.

Small World: for Volkswagen owners in the United States. Herbert W. Williamson, Editor. Englewood Cliffs, New Jersey: Volkswagen of America, Inc.

Time: the weekly newsmagazine. Chicago: Time, Inc.

Volkswagen, Type 11: instruction book. Wolfsburg: Volkswagenwerk, March, 1948.

Volkswagen, Type 82, Schwimmwagen: instruction book. Wolfsburg: Volkswagenwerk, 1943.

Volkswagen Weathervane, The: dedicated to the men who sell and service VW in the U.S. Englewood Cliffs, New Jersey: Volkswagen of America, Inc.

von Frankenberg, Richard. *Die ungewöhnliche Geschichte des Hauses Porsche.* Stuttgart: Motor Presse Verlag, 1960.

von Frankenberg, Richard. *Porsche — the Man and His Cars.* (English version by Charles Meisl) London: G. T. Foulis & Co. Ltd., 1961.

VW Autoist, The: official publication of the VW C of A. George McAleer, Editor. Plainfield, New Jersey: Volkswagen Club of America, Inc.

Wall Street Journal, The. Bernard Kilgore, President. New York: Dow Jones & Co., Inc.

Westrup, Arthur and Klaus Peter Heim. *Besser fahren mit dem Volkswagen: Ein Handbuch.* Bielefeld, Germany: Verlag Klasing & Co., 1957.

We can all do something for peace in this world in the scope of our personal activity. It isn't immaterial how you operate your business or how you treat your workers! It is no more immaterial how the worker and employee treats his colleagues on the job! Every person in a high position, every educator and teacher, and every mother can accomplish a great deal for peace, or else can fail to carry out irreplaceable work, for which we can never make up.

— Dr. Heinz Nordhoff, Christmas, 1953

ANNUAL STATEMENT FOR 1965 / FROM THE
PRESIDENT OF VOLKSWAGEN OF AMERICA, INC.

We expect the sales of imported cars to climb above 600,000 vehicles during 1966, challenging the all-time high of 614,131 in 1959. We estimate that Volkswagen will account for about 400,000 of the 1966 total.

While our sales volume never has, and never will, represent more than a small fraction of the total car market in the U.S., it has steadily increased since 1949. I believe our sales increases are due to the fact that our vehicles fill a special need not filled by other vehicles.

Our owners are as diverse as the general population, ranging from young college students to retired grandparents. There seems to be no typical Volkswagen buyer, either in age or income, in occupation or family status. The addition to our line of the VW Squareback and Fastback sedans provides an ever wider choice and, we feel, will disperse our ownership even more.

Our dealer network continued its steady growth during 1965 and passed the 900-mark during November. We expect to exceed 1,025 authorized dealers by the end of 1966, bringing greater convenience to the growing number of Volkswagen owners in the U.S. That total reached the 2,000,000-mark in December as VW registrations climbed toward a record 375,000 units for 1965, about 10 percent ahead of 1964.

The Volkswagen organization in the U.S. currently represents an investment of $260,000,000 by independent businessmen. The average dealership investment is about $250,000 and $3,000,000 or more is invested at each of the 14 independent distributorships which supply dealers with vehicles, parts and other services. Total American employment at the dealerships and distributorships is now over 25,000 persons.

During the year, VW distributorships enlarged or built new administrative headquarters and warehouse facilities in New York, Maryland, Ohio, Florida and California. Work currently is in progress on a major addition to Volkswagen of America's headquarters in Englewood Cliffs, N. J. Occupancy is expected by the middle of 1966.

Nationwide, about 80 percent of the Volkswagen dealerships are in buildings no more than four years old. This helps provide better service for VW owners as the new dealerships are built to national standards which virtually guarantee efficiency.

There has been a continued growth in production rates at the Volkswagen factories in Germany, Brazil and Australia. Daily output increased from 5,742 vehicles during January, 1965, to more than 6,800 during December and total production during 1966 is expected to exceed the 1,600,000 Volkswagens built this year. The bulk of the total is produced in Germany which accounts for about 6,300 units a day in our plants there.

J. Stuart Perkins
President, V of A, Inc.

Englewood Cliffs, New Jersey
December 22, 1965